Chance, Character
and
Change

John
Mattausch

Chance,
Character
and
Change

Transaction Publishers
New Brunswick (U.S.A.) and London (U.K.)

Library of Congress Catalog Number: 2008021825
ISBN: 978-1-4128-0763-0
Printed in the United States of America

Library of Congress Cataloging-in-Publication Data

Mattausch, John.
    Chance, character, and change / John Mattausch.
        p. cm.
    Includes bibliographical references and index.
    ISBN 978-1-4128-0763-0 (alk. paper)
    1. Social change. 2. Social history. 3. Sociology—Philosophy.
    I. Title.

HM831.M393 2008
303.409—dc22   2008021825

Contents

Preface

When George Eliot set out to illustrate "the remedial influences of pure, natural human relations"[1] in her novel *Silas Marner* she happily allowed a chance event to start the redemption of the Weaver of Raveloe (the accidental death of Eppie's mother in the snow nearby Silas's cottage coinciding with an onset of Silas's catalepsy). The remedial power of "natural human relations" was a common theme in nineteenth-century progressive thinking, the substitute for divine redemption championed at a time when religion was adjusting to the rise of industrialism and falling under increasing critical scrutiny, a critical assault with which Eliot was sympathetic, engaged, and instrumental having translated into English both Strauss's *The Life of Jesus* and Feuerbach's *The Essence of Christianity*. Just as characters in novels, including Eliot's, never seem to need to visit the toilet, so too the subjects of social science are never affected, nor troubled, by chance and so when Elliot's intellectual contemporaries set out to explain this process of secular redemption in rational, factual terms they did not assign chance a role any more than had the Church. Both clergy and progressive secular philosophers shunned chance.

Across the Channel, the French Positivists Auguste Comte and Emile Durkheim, and back in England Eliot's one-time suitor Herbert Spencer, vigorously argued that religion belonged to an earlier stage of societal evolution, an evolutionary development following a law-like pattern with religion, tradition, and superstition about, or so they claimed, to be superseded by a new, Positivist age of progressive scientific certainty. This prophecy of monumental societal change, wholesale change to an entirely new kind of society, was and is a commonplace in sociology: I will argue that this picture of societal change is wrong, that there are no laws of society, that society cannot evolve and that chance is an unignorable, real cause of societal change. Intellectuals such as Comte, Durkheim, and Spencer were building upon and responding to the accumulated arguments of earlier Enlightenment thinkers and so I begin by sketching some reasons why critical Enlightenment works came to be written, how international merchant trade had brought to Europe not only increasing profit but also an increasing awareness of the variety of the natural and social world, a challenge to eighteenth-century Europeans which they tackled by means of law-like explanations. This recourse to reductionist, law-like explanation proved a quixotic failure when it came to explaining the social world but for the natural world Darwin's theory of evolution celebrated variety as the essential diet upon which natural selection fed. Unlike social theory, Darwin's theory went from strength to strength, its progress graced by moments of good fortune, complemented in the twentieth century by genetic science.

The evident success of Darwin's explanatory mechanism when coupled to genetics proved an irresistible lure to those who, like their nineteenth-century forerunners, preferred reductionism and laws over variety and chance. I trace the rise of sociobiology, evolutionary psychology and behavioral genetics and I show that these modern reincarnations of pseudo-evolutionary social science have been little more successful than their nineteenth-century predecessors in explaining what I call the "artificial world," the world of our own making, the world in which we increasingly live, a world of social customs, social practices, sultana scones, technology, creeds, and much else besides. Nowadays, thanks to the spread of capitalism, nothing is for free in the artificial world, everything comes with a price tag and so in order to understand how chance plays out in the world in which we live we need to turn to political economy, to Marx's writings.

Like Eliot, Marx too was familiar with Feuerbach's arguments, arguments that he developed in order to explain how redemption from capitalism was possible. Marx had reasoned that chance was only significant at the birth of capitalism but I argue that it remains vibrant and that we need to rethink his revolutionary theory in the light of ever-present chance influences and interventions, an argument I make with the help of Mr. and Mrs. Mandela attempting to buy a retirement home in the south of England.

I suggest that chance has three expressions as contingency, coincidence and as character and that its effects are found not only in individual biographies but also in the history of nations. This latter point about the wider, sometimes large and decisive effects of chance I illustrate with the history of the British in Gujarat (a state in western India), and now Gujaratis living in contemporary Britain. Having arrived, by the end of chapter 5, at a workable theory of chance I then apply this theory to the topics of first higher education, looking at the chancy world of undergraduates, and then ethnic relations, introducing two fictional students, an English girl called Alison and a British Gujarati boy named Kalam, fiction now being one of the few sanctuaries left for characters following their exile from would-be factual writing.

It is not the argument of this book that everything happens by chance; I show that this would be just as impossible as societal evolution. Rather, I argue that chance, though episodic—for Silas Marner, Eppiesodic—is real, that it is a cause of change, that it is quite compatible with conventional determinism and that to neglect chance, to presume it is just trivial or residual, is unwise at a time when the world around us is, quite literally, rapidly growing more chancy. Lastly, and perhaps more controversially, I further argue that not only are we buffeted by chance but also that *we are chance* and so to neglect chance is not only to misunderstand the world, it is also to be neglectful of ourselves.

Note

1. This quote is from Q.D. Leavis's instructive Introduction to the 1967 Penguin edition of *Silas Marner*. Leavis discusses the part played by chance in this episode, judging that for Elliot Silas's redemptive good fortune was deserved, in her footnote to chapter 12.

Acknowledgements

My thanks to all those who either manfully hid their boredom, or were actually interested, when I spoke to them about the arguments that found their way into this book. From these many conversations I benefited far more than they and my special thanks are due first to those students who over the years took part in seminar discussions as part of their second-year theory course; second to my colleagues in my current department; third, to my good friends Professor John Macnicol for rejuvenating evenings, and to Dr. Richard Smith and Dr. David Smith for their help with sourcing references. Soon after starting to write I landed up in hospital owing to a car accident: though not the genesis of this book, the patients with whom I shared a ward needed, unlike most academics, no convincing that chance and character were of great importance, which along with their company was comforting and I would like to thank Brian, Tel, and Spike and all the other patients who were in Leigh Ward, East Surrey Hospital, during September 2002.

By tragic misfortune, shortly after completing the manuscript my elder son, Ravi, was diagnosed with a malignant brain tumour. His bravery and the strength of his character in the face of this vicious chance disease have, once again, reinforced my belief in the arguments set out in this book – and, and more importantly, made me love Ravi with admiration. All the author royalties resulting from the sale of this book will be given to the Royal Marsden Cancer Campaign (registered charity, no.1095197) in small appreciation of the wonderful care that the Royal Marsden Hospital have and are giving us.

Lastly, I would like to thank my family: my mother, Nancy Mattausch and my brother-in-law John Passmore read drafts of each chapter and their comments and suggestions improved this book greatly; my other brother-in-law, Manesh Pandya, read a draft of chapter 7 and corrected my cultural stupidities; my wife, Dipti, and my two sons Ravi and Kaveet had to put up with the many failings of my character, especially in the final stages of writing, which they did with good grace and bad jokes.

This book is dedicated to my two sons, Ravi and Kaveet, in the hope that they will, one day, read it.

1

New Cargoes and Blind Absurdities

This chapter sketches the broad currents of European social philosophy that swept chance and character away from respectable academic company. Not a bad place to begin charting these currents of thought is in the early seventeenth century, with the early voyages of the English East India Company, the world's first joint-stock company whose investors had been lured by the strategy of directly exchanging pig iron, woollens, tin, and other European goods for spices from India and other distant countries, so avoiding the exorbitant charges of the Middle Eastern middlemen who infested the terrestrial trade. Once safely unloaded and stored in the Company's London warehouses, the precious spices, medicines, and cloths should realise a fabulous profit for the investors. The latter part of this strategy succeeded famously, large profits were made, but as experience quickly showed, pig iron and other English products such as heavy woollens had limited appeal to Indians obliging the Company to relinquish their plan of just trading with India in favor of also paying for pepper, cotton goods, opium, jewellery, saltpetre, indigo and the other desirable cargoes available from Surat, the premier port of Gujarat in northwest India, and for most of the seventeenth century the premier Indian entrepot.[1]

The sixteenth-century voyages of discovery, and the seventeenth-century voyages of the European trading companies, brought more than mere profit to London and other European capitals. They also revealed the unexpected *variety* of the natural and human world. The exotic cargoes demanded further examination, better understanding, for reasons both of simple curiosity as well as commercial gain. So for illustration the production of indigo, then one of the most sought-after of cargoes and the source of blue dye prized at a time when English woollens needed coloring and all dyes came from natural sources, was monopolized by a federation of castes in Sarkhej in central Gujarat. Indeed, in the first half of the century, India was the only known source of indigo and Sarkheji indigo was particularly fine. At Sarkhej the indigo plant was processed in pits and then rolled in to the distinctive small patties, called "flats" by the English, in which it was sold. Eager to break the lucrative Sarkhej monopoly, and to avoid being palmed off with inferior adulterated supplies, the English traders tried to establish their own processing site, an ambition that demanded they became familiar with the nature of indigo (they had not, however, reckoned with the guild strengths nor the craft skills of the traditional suppliers and so were forced to abandon their plans for independent production as too were the Mughal Emperor's agents who had also tried unsuccessfully to wrest control away from the Sarkhej producers).[2] Similarly, the medicinal merits and recreational pleasures of opium stimulated curiosity: how did the stuff actually work?, was it safe? how much should you take?—questions worth answering as the unsuspected addictive quality of opium snared those who became overfond of the sticky resin.

What leant mystique plus profit to the sticky resin, to the berries buds and nuts, was the fact that they only grew in far-distant, remote, and fabled places. And not just pepper, nutmeg, and opium; new sorts of animals as well as spices and medicines were appearing in the returning ships' cargo holds. In 1699, a sickly young chimpanzee disembarked and following its death, soon after, its corpse was sent to Edward Tyson, a physician who carried out a post-mortem revealing the close similarities between chimp and human morphologies. If chimps were notable for their obvious similarities with humans then some of the new species, for instance the kangaroos encountered when the British arrived on Australia, were remarkable for their oddity. So odd did kangaroos appear at first meeting that English artists travelling with Cooke's crew struggled to draw them, struggled to draw a mammal that stood upright on two legs, carried their offspring in a pouch, and hopped. Familiar or odd, it was clear that these newly discovered animals were well suited to the particular environments they inhabited. This sympathy between environment and appearance also seemed to hold for very small animals, for the tiny lice, flies, and other insects whose extraordinary miniature structures Robert Hooke observed under his newfangled microscope and drew for his best-selling *Micrographia* that was published in 1655.

Accompanying the arkfuls of new species, joining the ranks of beautifully distinguished insects, came knowledge of new kinds of societies, new religions, and new social customs. These cultures may have been news for Europeans, but it was clear they were of long standing, some clearly ancient, rivalling the antiquity of the Classical Mediterranean models. Like the newly discovered, rapidly expanding range of creatures and plants filling the European catalogues these new cultures demanded further investigation because they illustrated unexpected variety, the various forms that human society could assume. Fuelling further investigation, these new cultures challenged Europeans to scrutinize and then justify their own religions, customs, and morals: were the new gods more divine?, the new customs preferable?, European morality questionable? And, as with the new animals, were the new cultures somehow appropriate to the places they were found?

The Baron de Montesquieu met this cultural challenge sitting reading in the impressive family library of his large chateau near Montpellier, southern France. The affairs of the Bordeaux high parliament, for whom he served as a President a la Mortier,[3] could temporarily be forgotten as Montesquieu lost himself in the pages of the travel writing that had become the favorite genre of privileged early eighteenth-century European readers. Part of the appeal of these travellers' tales lay in their eroticism, in their tales of foreign marital arrangements, of foreign sexual mores, of polygamy, harems, temple prostitutes and the like. Montesquieu, in his own first book, shrewdly exploited this erotic appeal. In his *Lettres persanes* he has two fictitious characters, Usbek and Rica, seek sanctuary from persecution in their native Persia by touring Europe, and France in particular. In exile, the fictitious Usbek and Rica write equally fictitious letters to those they've left behind in Persia, including letters written by Usbek to his many wives he left behind in his seraglio (harem). In an age when authors, printers, and booksellers were liable to torture, exile, or execution if their books were judged blasphemous by the Catholic Church or offensive by the powerful, Montesquieu and his fellow writers practised circumspection. Books, including both of Montesquieu's, were published in Protestant countries beyond the reach of the Vatican censor; fictitious foreign characters could voice criticisms of French society whilst shielding the critic himself.

Predictably, Montesquieu's saucy, gently critical, allegedly witty first book proved a great success with the French book-buying public. On the strength of this success Montesquieu sold his judicial position as President a la Mortier and spent the rest of his life travelling, meeting other men of letters, and in writing his massive master work, *The Spirit of the Laws*. Published in 1748, this rambling, incoherent tome included a template for the American constitution along with the first new comparative political analysis written in two millennia and the book could lay claim to be the first true work of Enlightenment social theory. In *The Spirit of the Laws* Montesquieu develops themes and ideas he had sketched in his earlier *Lettres Persanes*, themes and ideas reflecting the challenges posed by the ever-expanding diversity revealed in all arenas. This time round, themes such as polygamy are served with a helping of rational analysis, minus the titillating relish. What distinguishes the *Spirit of the Laws* was not the actual content of these analyses but, rather, Montesquieu's explanatory intention and the architecture of his explanations: Montesquieu tries to account for the variety of human social customs by appeal to law-like explanation. It is this explanatory innovation that lifts Montesquieu up on to the pedestal reserved for genuine pioneers of modern social theory.

Amongst the subjects first sketched in his *Lettres Persanes*, and then analytically fleshed out in the *Spirit of the Laws*, was polygamy. In Book XIV Montesquieu addresses himself to the problem of why polygamy is found in some societies rather than others and his explanation was that in hot countries women mature physically faster than they do mentally, only to find their beauty and charms fade commensurably quickly. In hot countries where it was easier, opined Montesquieu, to provide for dependants it made sense for men to marry early and then take another wife as her predecessor began to wilt at an early age; whereas in colder climates women's mental powers had time to mature as their beauty slowly blossomed, making them more attractive long-term wives, and hence encouraging monogamy. Montesquieu seems not have held any definite personal view about the comparative merits of the two marital systems, unlike his strong condemnation of slavery. Slavery might be "in its own nature bad," nonetheless it was a feature found in some societies and not others and, in common with polygamy, it was this uneven patterning of the vile institution that required explanation. Once again Montesquieu in Book XV of the *Spirit of the Laws* explains this patterning in terms of countries' different climates. In hot countries, men are so "slothful," "dispirited" and enervated that they can only be motivated to work by the "fear of chastisement" and so slavery was more in "accord with reason."

Montesquieu's "Theory of the Climates" was designed to explain all manner of national variations, (for instance, the liveliness of warm-blooded Italians versus the restraint of frigid English opera audiences, the prohibition on alcohol in hot countries versus its acceptance for those living in colder nations – "Drunkenness predominates throughout the world in proportion to the coldness and humidity of the climate"). In support of his explanatory model, Montesquieu cited the evidence of papillae on the tongue which he had observed under a microscope shrinking when cold, expanding when heated, a reaction that he believed affected the whole of a person's body. And it was not just this evidence of papillae that nurtured Montesquieu; he also drew sustenance from the method, as he saw it, of natural science. Laws, for Montesquieu and many of his contemporaries, were the hallmark of scientific rationalism: in Letter 97 of his *Lettres Persanes* Usbek writes to Hosain, "a dervish of the mountain of Jahrum," telling the wise dervish of the scientists whom he has met on his travels whose discovery of "general laws, immutable and eternal" has led them far along the "path of human reason." Summarizing Newton's law of motion, Usbek writes that "There, sublime dervish you have the key to nature; and from these fertile principles consequences without limit can be drawn." True to its title, the *Spirit of the Laws* begins with a statement of faith in laws, a faith prompted by the startling success of contemporaneous natural science:

> Laws, in their most general signification, are the necessary relations arising from the nature of things. In this sense all beings have their laws: the Deity His laws, the material world its laws, the intelligences superior to man their laws, the beasts their laws, man his laws.

They who assert that a blind fatality produced the various effects we behold in this world talk very absurdly; for can any thing be more unreasonable than to pretend that a blind fatality could be productive of intelligent beings?[4]

This opening declaration captures perfectly the methodological cast from which the social sciences that appeared two centuries later would be moulded. The new faith in science, and the characterisation of science as the business of discerning laws, implied a radical change in the believers' view of the world and of God. God became a new sort of law-giver, in Montesquieu's words: "God is related to the universe, as Creator and Preserver; the laws by which He created all things are those by which he preserves them."[5] Faith could be sustained, but now it became faith in a deity who had designed and set in motion a mechanical universe. Variety in human customs was to be explained by unvarying laws governing human behaviour: the same laws operated and produced uniform effects but, as in Montesquieu's Theory of the Climates, the circumstances in which these laws operated were varied. In this theoretical model there was no room for differences between individuals or for chance to play a role in shaping outcomes. In addition, even if his explanations for the variety of human customs had been correct, then it would imply that what was naturally suitable in one place was unsuitable elsewhere and that no neutral yardstick existed for comparing and judging their respective merits.

The new naturalism, the faith in explaining human behaviour by the same means that science explained the natural world, was driven by noble hopes and aspirations. It seemed as though the successes of natural science could be mirrored in social life, and for the first time, as the historian of the Enlightenment Peter Gay tellingly observes,[6] the European conception of time altered fundamentally: whereas earlier men had looked to the past, to the Garden of Eden or the Classical world, for their ideals of a better life and saw history as a process of degeneracy, now they could look hopefully to a better future, betterment made possible by applying the new scientific methodology to society. Clearly, this change of historical sensibility required a new picture of how societies had changed in the past, a picture to show how instead of degenerating, society (or at least European society), was improving. Sure enough, in the eighteenth century these new histories of societal development began to be published.

The most influential of these histories were written by men from what became known as the "Scottish School."[7] The histories written by this School were notable for the analytical device of dividing societal history into developmental stages. Free from the artificial disciplinary divisions that would later segregate topics and methods, 18th century men of letters happily stepped over academic boundaries that tripped up their 19th century successors. Adam Smith for example drew inspiration from Lord Kames, inspiration bordering upon plagiarism from David Hume, and he happily mixed ethics, politics, sociology and historical speculation in his recipe for political economy. In common with Montesquieu, the key methodological ingredient in Smith's recipe was his identification of the "laws" of the market place, the "laws" of supply and demand. The focus of Smith's analysis was upon what he saw as a new societal variety that he called "commercial society" and which we now know as capitalism.

Smith's analysis had two facets; first, his explanation for the rise of commercial society; second, his explanation for how commercial society operated. The latter explanation sought the reasons for commercial society's historical superiority, how it permitted the greatest wealth to be produced while at the same time also permitting its citizens to enjoy unparalleled freedom. Smith thought that it was the growth of the division of labor that led to an increase in industrial production, how by dividing factory work up in to specific tasks instead of individuals undertaking all tasks, productivity rocketed. In his example of the pin factory, a factory making metal nails, one man doing all the jobs himself could scarce produce one pin a day, similarly ten men could only make ten pins, but if they each stuck to just one part of the process, for instance sharpening, then they could each day produce upward of 48,000 pins. There was, however, a price to be paid for this boost to material production; Smith reasoned that the increase in the division of labor led inexorably to the mental and moral impoverishment of the workers.[8]

Even by the time Smith published this argument, in 1776, it was challenged by the introduction of factory machinery powered by water mills and soon the productive power of divided labor was dwarfed by the adoption of the steam engine. Just as Smith proved to be wrong about the force that bolstered material production, so too he wrongly identified the reasons why individuals engage in capitalistic behavior. Having read David Hume's *Treatise on Human Nature* as a student at Oxford, Smith became wedded to Humean empiricism. Empiricists held the conviction that all knowledge came from experience, opposing the belief that we have any innate mental capital, a view captured earlier by John Locke's depiction of the mind as a *tabula rasa*, a blank sheet inscribed upon by life's experiences. Refined by David Hume and then adopted by Smith, empiricism underpinned his analysis of commercial society. Ironically, empiricism as a philosophy emerged just at that time when, as in the example of Montesquieu in his library, actual first-hand experience was diminishing in importance. One concealed implication of the philosophy was its privileging of personal experience; nobody else could know with the same vivacity what you yourself experienced. As a corollary, it followed that the individual experienced his own self-interest with more intensity than anyone else's. If this were true, then the best way to grasp other people's thoughts and feelings was to imagine yourself in their position, to imagine you had their experiences which in turn depended upon the presumption that we are all of a kind and so will respond in like fashion. This empiricist stance had been explored by Hume in his *Treatise*, and in his disciple Adam Smith's first published book, *The Theory of Moral Sentiments*, it was largely copied and presented as an explanation for how ethical behavior is possible given that we are all chiefly motivated by our own self-interest. In

Smith's second book, *The Wealth of Nations*, self-interest had become the chief motive driving capitalist behavior.

It is easy to see why Smith was wrong: quite simply, there is no reason to think our behavior rests on just one common motive, and all our experience shows us that different individuals in similar circumstances respond differently. And anyway if we substitute an alternative motive, for example, curiosity, then the rest of Smith's analysis is undisturbed – if, as Smith himself had previously thought, we are motivated by insatiable curiosity then his analysis of the outcomes of capitalism would be unaffected. In these failings, Smith echoed the faults of Montesquieu, faults both men reached because of their obsession with single, mono-explanations; both theorists, crucially, presented humans as uniform, homogenous creatures who only became varied by different climates or different experiences.

Empiricism appealed to theorists of all political and moral persuasions, it appealed to those who like Adam Smith sang the praises of early capitalism and to those who sang from a more radical hymn sheet. For empiricism, by emphasizing the common state of ignorance shared by us all at birth, an equality of uniform ignorance, implied that adult inequalities and differences of status and fortune resulted not from innate individual qualities but from circumstantial variety. "Human nature" became displaced by the formative influences of varying circumstances. Whereas Smith had presented capitalist entrepreneurs as "greedy," "rapacious" individuals whose self-interested actions led to a materially beneficial public outcome because of the unintended consequences of their actions within capitalism, over the channel Jean-Jacques Rousseau also drew upon the prevailing uniformitarian view in support of his radical educational program based upon his assumption of natural human goodness, goodness only spoilt by man's mistreatment of nature: "God makes all things good; man meddles with them and they become evil."[9] Having abandoned his own progeny in a home for foundlings, Rousseau argued that children could be molded in any way we choose, the proper education would produce proper adults. As for proper educators well, in *Emile* Rousseau resolved this problem by assuming for himself the role of a fictitious guardian-educator. Sure enough, under their wise guardian's tutelage Emile and his companion Sophie grow to be model citizens. Rousseau's arguments captivated the imagination of the rising generation of enlightened Europeans, especially the imaginations of young bachelors like Thomas Day who, after the Bible, held *Emile* in the highest esteem. In an ironic twist, Day enacted the story of Rousseau's *Emile*, attempting to bring to life Sophie as his future wife. Unable to find his ideal female companion, Davy visited two orphanages, one at Shrewsbury and one in the Foundling Hospital in Coram Fields, London; from each orphanage he selected a young girl, gave assurances to the orphanages for their future well-being, renamed the girls Sabrina and Lucretia, and took them away to begin a Rousseauesque education that he believed would mold them into the kind of ideal women he sought. As any parent could have foreseen, this experiment in social engineering ended dismally; the two girls did not ape their fictitious inspiration, Davy was forced to abandon his dreams of creating the ideal wife, Lucretia was apprenticed to a milliner, Sabrina packed off to boarding school, and both girls later married men of their own choosing. Contrary to Rousseau's beliefs, it proved easier to change the girls' names than to change their characters.[10]

Of course, empiricists didn't rule the Enlightenment roost unopposed. Awoken from his "dogmatic slumbers" by Hume's empiricism, Immanuel Kant accepted Hume's belief that "... all our knowledge begins with experience," but, he reasoned, even "... though all our knowledge begins with experience, it by no means follows, that all arises out of experience."[11] Rather than a simple *tabula rasa*, rather than a simple blank sheet awaiting the inscriptions of experience, the human mind in fact more closely resembled a blank book. This metaphorical mental book had a number of pre-given features, and just as the physical make-up of pages direct and organize the business of writing (for example, pages with pre-ruled lines and margins), so too our mental architecture organizes and directs our thinking (for example, leading us to think in causal ways about our experiences). Although sharply distinguished from Humean empiricism, Kantian philosophy likewise stressed the essential uniformity of our mental architecture and so theory inspired by Kant also came to assume a uniformity of individuals who, just as in the empiricists' model, then became differentiated by different experiences.

If it was varying experiences that led to varying individuals, then an explanation of variation required a theory of how our environment changed through time. For social theorists, this required a history of societal development. These new histories of societal development, informed by the key Enlightenment tenets of naturalism, secularism, and progress, became a speciality of the Scottish School. Having witnessed his *Treatise* fall "still-born from the press," and barred from academia in part due to his atheism, David Hume found that switching from writing philosophy to writing history brought the public acclaim he expected. Keen to defend the superiority of commercial society against the claims of those who, like his contemporary Adam Ferguson, championed the martial virtues of classical societies, Hume counter-claimed that modern commerce had permitted the "arts of luxury" to flourish, how in modern society civilized pleasures could be enjoyed by the greatest number, a claim he placed in a developmental historical framework. This framework comprised stages of societal development, starting with the "savage state" of hunters and fishermen, moving through the agricultural stage before arriving at commercial society wherein the "arts of luxury" could be enjoyed by the greatest number of people. As with most of his other chief ideas, this notion of distinguishing historical stages of societal development was later purloined by Adam Smith from David Hume, first for his lectures on jurisprudence when Smith was lecturing at Glasgow University and then to underpin his books on ethics and political economy.[12] Like Hume, Smith painted a progressive societal history; each of his four stages (hunter-gatherers, agricultural nomads, pastoralists, commercial) leading to the acme of liberty and material wealth enjoyed in capitalism. In this progressive sequence the focus was upon the changing ways in which men produced food and material goods; ideas and social institutions such as government reflected this unfolding sequence, a sequence, a history, that ended with capitalism as its full stop.

Smith's new societal history was not original and nor was it the only version; Smith had been preceded by his mentor Lord Kame, Sir John Dalrymple and John Millar had written in a similar vein. These Enlightenment histories were becoming commonplace and they nourished the explanations for human variety: variety was to be explained by uniform law-like responses to differing circumstances and now circumstances, or at least societal circumstances, themselves developed in uniform, law-like ways. All societies travelled along the same developmental path.[13]

Just as varying social customs could be explained by their emergence in differing historical stages of societal development, so too the burgeoning variety of species could be understood as expressions of adaptation to differing natural environments. However, this approach threw up its own puzzles: in addition to observing microscopic animals and identifying the cells in cork, Robert Hooke had taken an interest in fossils, some of which appeared to rest in inappropriate places. Ammonites, and other marine fossils, were found far from the sea, inland, or even up mountainsides, leading Hooke to speculate that in the past the earth must have been different and had later come to settle in its contemporary form. Such speculations called into question the Christian reckoning of terrestrial chronology and implied a challenge to the Christian outlook in which European science was developing. The comparatively short time span permitted to Christians, for example the dating of creation at 4004 BC by Archbishop James Usher in his *Sacred Chronology* of 1620, strained credibility in the light of the immense changes implied by species variety.[14]

If the dating of creation was in need of revision, then Christians could at least take comfort from the belief that the evidence of adaptation to varying environments required species to be appropriately, divinely designed to fit their natural niches (the view of God enthusiastically proclaimed by Montesquieu in the opening to his *Spirit of the Laws* quoted earlier). This comforting belief in a divine designer of species became unsettled when, in the mid-eighteenth century Carl Linnaeus, best remembered for his pioneering system of genus and species classification, included humans in the same Homo genus classificatory family as other apes and monkeys. When this classification was disputed, Linnaeus responded by challenging his critics to identify any structural differences between humans and their Homo relatives. Worse still for the orthodox Christian view of humans, Linnaeus had not placed man atop of his classificatory system, all of which sat uncomfortably with the Christian picture of man as a special, vaunted species created in God's own image. As the century progressed, Linnaeus' unsettling ideas were joined by further challenges to the Christian picture of man and His divine creation of the universe. In his *Natural History of Creation*, the first volume of which was published in 1749, Comte de Buffon reasoned that all animals had "one common origin" and that "their present differences have proceeded only from the long influence of their new situation." And in his *Epochs of Nature* Buffon, basing his calculation upon the time necessary for a molten sphere ejected from the sun to cool, arrived at the figure of 75,000 years for Earth's birthday. Inspired by Buffon, Thomas Davy's friend Erasmus Darwin wrote his two-volume *Zoonomia: or the laws of organic life* (1794-96) one chapter of which included the theory of evolution for which his grandson would become eponymous.

Erasmus Darwin did not elaborate upon his explanation for evolution and intervening between grandfather and grandson Darwins were fifty years of competing theories, disputes, mistakes, and muddles. Perhaps the most significant of the explanatory difficulties impeding theoretical progress was the crucial question of how precisely generational evolution was accomplished, how offspring came to differ from their parents. One influential, widely read answer to this question was given by Chevalier de la Marck, remembered bereft of his pre-Revolutionary knightly title as plain "Lamarck," a professor at the Museum d'Historie Naturelle in Paris. Lamarck's reputation rose high upon the publication of his *Zoological Philosophy* in 1809 but he died in poverty and alone, his reputation having fallen after assaults from powerful opponents discredited some of his fundamental arguments. Rather unfairly,[15] following a posthumous critical mauling by his colleague Professor Cuvier, he was cast by historians into the role of the man whose mistaken ideas Charles Darwin eventually corrected and he is now popularly remembered for just his errors: in particular, the mistaken idea that there is an evolutionary tendency for all organisms to become more complex; and the relatedly mistaken idea that characteristics acquired in an organism's lifetime can be inherited by its offspring. The latter idea, commonly known as the "doctrine of acquired characteristics," was not Lamarck's own invention and did not startle his contemporaries. Surely, the sons of blacksmiths inherited their father's muscular arms, muscles strengthened by a lifetime of hard physical work in the smithy? Nor was the idea that evolution equated with progress, in Lamarck's version progressive complexity, an affront to nineteenth-century sensibilities. Styling himself as a "naturalist philosopher," Lamarck amongst his other achievements was responsible for coining "biology" as the title of the discipline that studied living things. By an unfortunate turn of history it was errors of evolutionary theory, Lamarck's and others, that fed the startling ambitions of his fellow Frenchman Auguste Comte, the man who set his sights on establishing a new science of society, a science that he christened "sociology."

Born in the midst of the French Revolution, as a young man Auguste Comte was expelled along with some of his classmates from the École Polytechnique for refusing to apologize for taking part in a student strike against the antiquated examination system. From a modest family, Comte was obliged to find employment and having undertaken some translation and teaching work, and having been disappointed not to be appointed to oversee the establishment of a new French-styled American polytechnic, Comte took a job as secretary to Henri de Saint-Simon. Living through a time of radical upheaval, Saint-Simon and his collaborators sought to establish social and political stability, a stable form of society befitting the new era of French industrial capitalism. Impatient to secure the new order, Saint-Simon advocated and agitated for a society run and administered by industrialists and scientists, a project aided by Comte during the seven years he remained as Saint-Simon's secretary. In 1824, Comte quarrelled irrevocably with Saint-Simon, a trivial quarrel prompted by Saint-Simon's shabby deceit over the publication of an essay written by Comte in a volume Saint-Simon had edited. Underlying this quarrel lay a deeper disagreement for unlike the impatient Saint-Simon, Comte thought political action should be guided by a fully worked-out philosophy. Having left Saint-Simon's employment, Comte set out to write this philosophy needed to secure social order and harmony. On the periphery of the academic world, Comte decided to offer a series of public lectures, lectures setting out his new philosophy. Only the first three lectures were delivered for on the day of the fourth lecture the audience arrived to find the door of the lecture theatre locked, Comte having suffered a mental collapse requiring hospitalization. Discharging himself against doctors' advice, with the assistance of his wife Caroline Massin, a former prostitute, Comte returned home to convalesce. In 1829 he resumed lecturing but the audiences lacked many of his earlier eminent supporters who were becoming critical of and alarmed by Comte's grandiose vision. Comte retreated, became more and more eccentric in his behavior, he stopped reading the "contaminating" work of other authors, concentrated obsessively upon his philosophical system that, in 1830 began to be published as the six-volume *Cours de Philosophique Positive*.

Comte, in the company of Romantics and other dissenters, believed that the Enlightenment emphasis upon the individual and the uncompromising rationalist critique of customs and tradition had bequeathed a destructive "negative" legacy that threatened societal order. His solution was the promotion of "positivism," the philosophy that would secure social harmony and progress. Positivism was conceived as a science, comparable to natural sciences, sharing the scientific method. This method was defined by Comte as the discovery of societal laws. In his uncharacteristically brief history of notable social philosophers Comte identified just four worthy predecessors—Aristotle, Montesquieu, Condorcet, and Adam Smith—an illustrious quartet whose achievements Comte proposed to crown, a quartet sharing his obsession with law-like explanation. The subject matter of the new supreme Positivist science was to be societal change, "social dynamics," change that he would reveal as governed by laws. The subject of these laws, men and women, he held to be naturally sociable, drawn to each other by the need for mutual protection and by their sex drive. Men and women were, he argued, naturally unequal:

> Biological philosophy teaches us that, through the whole animal scale, and while the specific type is preserved, radical differences, physical and moral, distinguish the sexes. Comparing sex with age, biological analysis presents the female sex, in the human species especially, as constitutionally in a state of perpetual infancy, in comparison with the other; and therefore more remote, in all important respects, from the ideal type of the race.[16]

It was accordingly pointless for women to expect or struggle for equality with men; their proper place was in the home nurturing children. The family was the basic social unit and one to be cherished and protected against the attacks of misguided radicals. The family was the font of children's socialisation, so by nurturing them and caring for their husbands, women and the institution of the family were benefiting the whole of society. If women were the lesser gender, perpetual infants, then most men were not up to much either being intellectually mediocre, intellectually lazy and inclined to "consign the burdensome responsibility of self-conduct to wise and trusty guidance." In a chilling passage, Comte notes that "there is a much stronger inclination to obedience" than is commonly supposed: "how sweet it is to obey." But why should we need trusty guidance, and who should we sweetly obey?

Driving societal change according to Comte is the growing division of labour. Unlike Smith, Comte argued that the division of labour is found throughout society, in the family as much as in the workplace. As it grows we become dependent upon people unknown to us, a new ethic of mutual cooperation arises that cements the social order. However, left unchecked the growth of the division of labour would lead to rampant specialisation and echoing Smith, to the lopsided, restricted mental development of workers confined to narrowing occupations. More worryingly, an uncontrolled division of labour would threaten the precious social order and so:

> It appears to me that the social destination of government is to guard against and restrain the fundamental dispersion of ideas, sentiments, and interests, which is the inevitable result of the very principle of human development and which, if left to itself, would put a stop to social progression in all important respects.[17]

It will come as no surprise to find that Comte identifies sociologists as the men (and, yes, only men), who will assume the role of trusty guardians, guardians of the social order. Their qualifications for this role rests with their superior scientific knowledge; once sociologists had explained the true nature of men and women, once they had specified the laws governing society, the masses would be obliged to accept, to acquiesce to their inevitable social fate as mapped by their trusty guides.

This disturbing Positivist vision of societal change, natural human qualities and sociological philosopher-kings was expressed within and dependent
upon an evolutionary framework. Sociology didn't simply copy a generic
scientific methodology, it itself evolved from the science of biology. Comte
held that there was a hierarchy of science with each discipline conditioned
by and indebted to its predecessor. Sociology, at the top of the hierarchy because of the complexity of its subject matter, was fathered by biology from
which it took the principle of analysing component parts of an organism in
terms of how the parts related to and functioned for the benefit of the whole
organism. For instance, just as biologists could explain the human heart by
examining how its structure permitted blood to be pumped around the body
thus ensuring the individual's well being, so too sociologists could explain
the institution of the family by examining how its structure permitted children to be socialised for the benefit of the whole of society. Society too, in a
further exploitation of biology's methodology, was held by Comte to progress
through three evolutionary stages, stages corresponding to the evolutionary
development of the human mind. The Positivist laws of societal change were
evolutionary laws, not simply successive historical stages of the kind discerned
by Smith and others from the Scottish School. Comte held the society of
his day, emerging industrialising capitalist 19th century France, to be on the
cusp of the final Positive stage. The future would be peaceful, harmonious,
positive in all respects.

Not known for his modesty, Comte sat back awaiting the plaudits and com-
memorative statues he felt to be his due. He waited, literally, in vain. Local
Positivist societies were started in several countries, the philosophy attracted
public attention, but no statues were erected and most of his erstwhile illustrious supporters deserted him. In an odd turn of events, usually thought of a
chance turn, in 1845 aged 47 Comte fell hopelessly in love with one Clotilde
de Vaux, a young woman recently deserted by her caddish husband. This brief
love affair, it ended after just one year when Clotilde died of consumption, tu-
berculosis, wrought profound changes to Comte's thinking. Now women were
elevated from perpetual infancy to a position of precious artistic supremacy
and Positivism transformed from a science into a new Religion of Humanity
with Comte as the High Priest. Little wonder, then, that on the only occasion
they met Comte advised his British counterpart Herbert Spencer to marry, as
the "sympathetic companionship of a wife would have a curative influence."[18]
While the company of a good woman may have helped him recover from his
depression and insomnia it is unlikely to have cured Spencer, who probably
died a virgin, from his incorrigible evolutionary theorising.

Enjoying a large readership for his many books and the friendship of lumi-
naries such as John Stuart Mill, Thomas Huxley and George Elliot (whom he
courted, unfruitfully), Spencer did not share Comte's hunger for public acclaim,
nor for acceptance by academia. He did, however, share Comte's belief that the

development of sociology depended upon the prior establishment of biology and he too firmly believed in societal laws:

> Either society has laws, or it has not. If it has not, there can be no order, no certainty, no system in its phenomena. If it has, then they are like the laws of the universe – sure, inflexible, ever active, and having no exception.[19]

Happy to praise Comte for determining the relationship between "the Science of Life and the Science of Society," and respecting "the greatness of the step made by M. Comte," Comte's notion that societal evolution progresses through growing societal complexity, Spencer criticised his French rival for making several serious analytical blunders. His Lamarckian belief in the fixity of species, the mistaken idea that species are discrete and do not change into other species, had led Comte to misconceive the relationship between "different forms of society" as "… different stages in the evolution of one form: the truth being, rather, that social types, like types of individual organisms, do not form a series, but are classifiable only in divergent and re-divergent groups."[20] Further, Spencer rejected Comte's central tenet that it was ideas that motivated action and were the means for changing society: for Spencer, it was "conditions and not intentions," that were fundamental and these conditions reflected the merciless "survival of the fittest" – Spencer's own phrase, invented along with his theory of evolution independently, a phrase later adopted by Charles Darwin, and intended by Spencer to convey the natural struggle between competing individuals and also the nature of Victorian capitalism. These natural struggles led to a raising of the general quality of society and thus the losers should not be given any assistance to overcome their natural weaknesses:

> Besides a habitual neglect of the fact that the quality of society is physically lowered by the artificial preservation of its feeblest members, there is a habitual neglect of the fact that the quality of a society is lowered morally and intellectually, by the artificial preservation of those who are least able to take care of themselves.[21]

This was just the sort of message Victorian entrepreneurs welcomed as a balm, especially when Spencer joined it with a Lamarckian claim that desirable traits deservedly acquired by superior individuals in their lifetime could, along with the family silver, be inherited by their children:

> That faculties and powers of all orders, while they grow by exercise, dwindle when not used; and that alterations of nature descend to prosperity; are facts continually thrust on man's attention, and more or less admitted by each.[22]

Left to itself the survival of the fittest would ensure that superior individuals would parent superior children, if only well-meaning busybodies wouldn't interfere; indeed, Spencer thought that charity was actually injurious, unkind to both the recipient and to the giver:

> But an unquestionable injury is done by agencies which undertake in a wholesale way to foster good-for-nothings: putting a stop to that natural process of elimination by which society purifies itself.[23]

By the last quarter of the nineteenth century the East India Company along with India itself had been subjected to the Crown, armies of civil servants were joining the ranks of Her Majesty's other battalions, Britain's European rivals were raising their economic profiles and the worst hardships and horrors of industrial life were being softened by Government intervention, a challenge to Spencer's ideal of individuals pursuing their self-interest through naked contractual arrangements. In this maturing phase of 19th century capitalism Spencer's Social Darwinism seemed less relevant, out of step with the times and whilst his books continued to sell well his praise for unfettered brutal competitive capitalism was no longer sung so loudly and his idea of societies "purifying" themselves by "eliminating" their inferior "good-for-nothings" was left to gather dust until the 1930s when two million Germans were sterilised in the name of the same evil theoretical error. One man deeply influenced by Spencer's arguments was the remarkably dull French scholar Emile Durkheim.

It is unlikely that the spectre of Comte would have been impressed by the posthumous statue erected in his honour by public subscription at the Place de la Sorbonne in 1902, in the year when Emile Durkheim transferred from Bordeaux University to become Professor of Sociology at the New Sorbonne. Students attending Durkheim's lectures could, as they walked over to the University's entry court, doff their caps to the statue of the man who had christened their discipline, the man whose deranged megalomania had almost killed the new discipline before it had had a chance to grow.[24] Durkheim's mission was to rescue sociology from French ridicule and academic opprobrium, to realise Comte's dream of a positive science of society. Like Comte, Durkheim equated science with scientific laws, and like Comte he believed that society progressively evolves from simple to increasingly complex forms. The greatest formative influence upon Durkheim's thinking was Herbert Spencer[25] from whom he borrowed the argument against Comte's Lamarckian view of linear fixed-species societal evolution and also Spencer's two-stage model of evolutionary progress. Both Comte and Spencer had argued that societal evolution was driven by the increasing division of labour, but unlike Comte's Law of the Three Stages, the three stages culminating in the supreme Positivist society, Spencer's model recognised only two evolutionary phases, militant and industrial societies, with the compulsion characterising the earlier militant stage becoming replaced in industrial societies by voluntary cooperation of the kind also specified by Comte. In Durkheim's version, Spencer's two evolutionary steps became recarpeted as "mechanical" and "organic" societies, with the evolutionary engine once again being that popular theoretical candidate, the division of labour (on the Positive side, the Lamarckian notion of acquired characteristics was quietly abandoned by Durkheim).

Those dons at the New Sorbonne who had done their best to block Durkheim's appointment could now only shrug resignedly at the fashionable popularity of sociology and the success of the sociology department under Durkheim's suzerainty. The shelves of the University's library began to fill with sociological studies, studies based on the presumptions that societal change was evolutionary and that social behaviour could be objectively explained by scientific laws. By the time of Durkheim's death, soon after the First World War had mocked his optimistic predictions for the future, these presumptions with their integral picture of uniform individuals had been used to explain rates of suicide, the rise of European industrial capitalism, the nature of religion, how the law changes, and much else besides. These studies, along with those studies similarly informed by these Positivistic presumptions issuing from the growing number of university social science departments, were peppered with the errors of pre-Darwinian evolutionary hypotheses. Lamarckian, Spencerian acquired characteristics, the Comtean belief that societal evolution equated with greater complexity, the common belief that evolution was progressive, were all to be exposed as false by the endless process of accumulative refinement in evolutionary thinking. That sociology was christened and established before Darwin's seminal contribution, before Mendel's experiments, and a century before Crick and Watson revealed the secret of genes, was simply a matter of chance, of bad luck. In this unfortunate disciplinary sequence, as in so many other cases, chance was a question of timing; in this case, the sequence of first sociology's, then Darwinian biology's disciplinary appearances.

In contrast, the refining of natural evolutionary thinking, equally peppered by chance timings, sparkles with happy coincidences, fortuitous accidents, with episodic good luck. Charles Darwin, now lionised by evolutionary philosophers and historians of ideas, is lucky to be remembered with such distinction. He won the race for posthumous fame by a nose; or more precisely he was lucky that his nose did not disqualify him from joining the crew of the Beagle. The Captain of the Beagle was a believer in phrenology, in the supposed science of discerning a person's character from the shape of their skull, and only a last minute intervention by Darwin's uncle prevented this pseudo-scientific prejudice disqualifying Darwin from joining the ships' crew on their voyage of exploration. A small chance intervention, but nonetheless a timely one.

Time was not only necessary for constituting chance, it was also vital for developing evolutionary arguments and in this matter both Darwin and Wallace benefited from the new estimates of the earth's birthday, estimates suggesting that many more candles would be needed for the terrestrial birthday cake. The accumulation of fossil discoveries revealed not just, as Hooke's ammonite sitings had shown, that fossils were found in improbable places where the organisms could not possibly have lived, but that fossils were arranged sequentially, sequences corresponding to the strata of the earth. The discovery of "stratigraphy" as it was named, along with the unearthing of fossils of extinct species, helped establish the discipline of geology and encouraged a lengthening in the reckoning of the Earth's history.[26] Stimulated by these new geological studies, and fascinated by volcanoes, Charles Lyell took himself off to Sicily where he could witness for himself the process by which Mount Etna had been built up over time by periodic eruptions and lava flows. There was no evidence that any one eruption had been singularly violent, no evidence for any sudden revolutionary change of the kind spoken of in the Biblical story of the flood escaped by Noah, and moreover the fossils from the Mountain's lowest stratum were of the same species as those currently found to be living in the Mediterranean. These observations suggested to Lyell that Mount Etna was of comparatively recent geological origin and that the Earth's history was immensely long. On returning to England Lyell published his three-volume *Principles of Geology* (1830-1833), the key argument of which was that in the staggeringly long history of the Earth, as the environment changed species became extinct, only to be replaced by new species. How this business of species transformation was achieved, Lyell was at a loss to explain.

Lyell's reasoning, an inspiration for Herbert Spencer, caught the attention of Alfred Wallace, a schoolmaster living in Leicester who had also read other evolutionary tracts, such as Robert Chamber's popular, but unsound, *Vestiges*. Wallace noted the inconsistencies and unresolved questions that these evolutionary accounts contained and determined to sort them out. He travelled to South America where his painstaking studies of plants, insects and other animals led him to reason that every species has another similar species living close by, temporally and spatially, and that the modern world featured species that were the successors to past extinct forerunners. However, like Lyell, Wallace could not explain how new species emerged. Wallace's ideas were published in 1855 in an essay that contained references to Charles Darwin's popular account of the voyage of the *Beagle*: on the 16th of April 1856 Lyell made an appointment to meet with Darwin to warn him that Wallace might well stumble upon the solution to the outstanding problem of species transformation and beat Darwin in the publication stakes. Wallace's detailed studies, especially his collection of thousands of insect species, had acquainted him with the ceaseless variety of life and he had come to the realisation that variety had to be correlated with a species' adaptation to its environment. In 1858, laid up with a bout of malaria, Wallace mused over the arguments of the Reverend Thomas Malthus and was rewarded with the insight that Malthus' explanatory logic was a key to the outstanding problem of species transformation.

Respectful of his wife's religious sensibilities, mindful of the uproar that his theory would provoke, Darwin had only broadcast his ideas to a select, but still largish, network of sympathetic, often eminent, correspondents. Twenty years after he had disembarked from the *Beagle*, Darwin was now occupied with writing his massive *Natural History* when, having reached chapter eleven, he received a short note from Wallace in which Wallace had outlined his hypothesis for species transformation. Wallace's conjecture matched the argument long held in private by Darwin and Lyell arranged for Wallace's paper alongside extracts from Darwin's studies to be presented at a special meeting of the Linnaean Society in London. (Wallace creditably acknowledged Darwin's pre-eminence and gave him valuable support in defending and developing his theory.) Concerned to secure his place in posterity, Darwin abandoned work on his magnum opus in favour of a brief abstract, a synopsis to be entitled *The Origin of Species by Means of Natural Selection, Or the Preservation of Favoured Species in the Struggle for Life.*

That the *Origins*, sold out its first print run on the day of publication measures the appetite of the Victorian reading public for evolutionary tracts, an appetite that Darwin could feed with carefully presented evidence from his Beagle voyage, by his measured arguments, and by his careful avoidance of the question of human evolution. What made Darwin's theory more compelling than those offered by rival authors was his use of Malthus' explanatory logic. Malthus had argued that rampant population growth was naturally kept in check, and stabilised, by the limited supply of food and resources for which individual animals had to compete in order to survive. As populations increased, so too did competition, a competition that only some could win and hence survive. Wallace and Darwin both realised that the Malthus' argument could be seen as a universal principle of evolution: in the third chapter of the *Origins*, Darwin outlines the Malthusian principle, to which there "is no exception," to explain how profligate variety and adaptation to environments is achieved:

> A struggle for existence inevitably follows from the high rate at which all organic beings tend to increase. Every being, which during its natural lifetime produces several eggs or seeds, must suffer destruction during some point of its life, otherwise, on the principle of geometric increase, its numbers would quickly become so inordinately great that no country could support the product. Hence, as more individuals are produced than can possibly survive, there must in every case be a struggle for existence, either one individual with another of the same species, or with the individuals of distinct species, or with the physical condition of life. It is the doctrines of Malthus applied to the whole animal and vegetable kingdoms. Although some species may be now increasing in numbers, all cannot do so, for the world would not hold them.[27]

The strength of this argument, the hawser holding Darwin's theory together, is its essential simplicity, a simplicity that famously led Darwin's champion Thomas Huxley to remark, "How very stupid not to have thought of that for oneself." Malthus' "doctrines" showed how variation between individual organisms, perhaps just a slight variation in say height, would advantage some individuals who would escape predators, win out in the competition for resources long enough to breed, whereas the less favoured, say the slightly shorter individual, would be gobbled up by a predator, or be unable to pick the fruit from the tall trees and so would perish prematurely and childless. In this way, advantageous physical features would be passed on to the next generation, the process Darwin named "natural selection." Darwin in the *Origins* did not attempt to explain precisely how such features are inherited but, in chapter 5, and drawing upon his own experiments with pigeon breeding, he joined with Spencer and others in wrongly arguing that sometimes the physical features of organisms are lost because they are not sufficiently developed through usage:

> I think there can be no doubt that use in our domestic animals has strengthened and enlarged certain parts, and disuse diminished them; and that such modifications are inherited. Under free nature many animals possess structures which can best be explained by the effects of disuse. It is probable that the nearly wingless condition of several birds which inhabit oceanic islands tenanted by no beasts of prey, has been caused by disuse, as the larger ground-feeding birds seldom take flight except to escape danger.[28]

Use-and-disuse heredity was, reasoned Darwin, only partly responsible for modifications, and he cautioned that "… in some cases we might easily put down to disuse modifications which are wholly or mainly due to natural selection."[29]

Darwin's attempt to explain his belief that features strengthened by use could be passed on to the next generation was published in 1868 and this explanation, along with the general notion of acquired characteristics, was incoherent and proved wrong by studies that came to comprise the science of genetics (a topic of the next chapter). This explanatory failure did not however gainsay the general arguments of the *Origins* with its disturbing implications for human mammals. In contrast to the views of social evolutionists, Darwin's theory suggested that evolution was not only a godless automatic process not needing any guidance from a divine designer, it was also purposeless, without direction, lacking any hierarchical ladder. The only evaluation of organisms was in respect to the Malthusian mechanism of natural selection: if the organism survived long enough to breed then it was "successful." There were no "higher" or "lower" species, there was no progress, extinction was as possible for humans as for any other species. Concerned to pre-empt any misunderstanding about the all-important Malthusian mechanism, Wallace urged Darwin to drop the label "natural selection" and adopt instead Spencer's "survival of the fittest": it was, he suggested, possible to misinfer from the term "natural selection" that there was something called "nature" doing the selecting, whereas the Malthusian mechanism incorporated by Darwin was merely a mindless hereditary process.

Accepting Wallace's guidance, Darwin adopted Spencer's nomenclature and in addition to sharing the same phrase, both men also shared a belief in use-and-disuse heredity, their common belief in acquired characteristics. There, however, the similarities ended. Spencer's rabid doctrine of justifications for successful capitalists and his condemnation of congenital "good-for-nothings" became known inaccurately as "social Darwinism" but the doctrine owed nothing to Darwin, the evolutionary ideas having been independently reached before Darwin, a pedigree Spencer was keen to emphasise. "Social Spenceriarism"[30] would have been preferable but this title would not now carry the same ready meaning for today's reader: nowadays few read or remember Spencer, but his work lived on through its Positivist progeny, analytical offspring that grew to smother the very inter-species variety Spencer and his ilk had been unable to explain.

By the end of the nineteenth century the currents of theory that had begun as a slow trickle in response to a growing awareness of natural and societal variety had swollen to a flood tide that engulfed older, alternative theoretical approaches. These currents now ran along well-defined channels, straight-sided channels with no concession to natural bends in the theoretical river, to eddies of eccentricity, or to the channels' obvious shallowness. In danger of drowning, character sought dry refuge in the pages of fiction; a new home for character where the concept could thrive and illuminate aspects of individuals obscured by the broad tide of personality. In contrast to social theory, the methodology of natural evolutionary theory respected and preserved variety, cherishing it as a vital concept, a concept essential to the working of natural selection. Evolutionary theory established and partly defined biology, becoming prominent as genetic science matured and as usual, chance acted as this new science's godparent. We will return to the theories, theorists and key ideas sketched in this chapter but before that we need to continue with the impact of natural evolutionary theory whose successful twentieth-century development proved an irresistible lure for those who, like their nineteenth-century French forerunners, preferred uniformity to variety, homogeneity to individuality, their laws unbroken by chance events.

Notes

1.   This, and the subsequent discussions of British-Gujarati history, draw upon my previously published studies of Gujarat which I footnote as appropriate: additional, cited and prominent sources are also footnoted.
2.   M.S. Commissariat 1957 *A History of Gujarat, Vol. 1 The Mughal period from 1573 to 1758* Bombay, Orient Longmans Chp. XXVII.
3.   A sort of regional high court judge, their title derived from the distinctive hat these judges wore.
4.   Montesquieu 1949 [1748] *The Spirit of the Laws* London, Collier Macmillan, p1.
5.   Ibid.
6.   Peter Gay 1969 *The Enlightenment: An Interpretation Vol. 2* London, Wiedenfield & Nicholson, p319.
7.   This national title is misleading: in fact the Scottish School, in common with other Enlightenment persuasions, was pan-European, in the Scottish School's case enjoying particularly strong links with France.

8. Propagandists for capitalism neglect this part of Smith's analysis which is to be found in *The Wealth of Nations*, Book 5 Article 2.

9. J-J. Rousseau 1974 [1762] *Emile* London, Dent, p1.

10. This example of Davy's ill-fated experiment is taken from Jenny Uglow 2002 *The Lunar Men* London, Faber & Faber, Chp. 16.

11. I. Kant 1934 [1781] *Critique of Pure Reason* London, Dent & Sons, p25.

12. R.L. Heilbroner (Ed.) 1986 *The Essential Adam Smith* Oxford, Oxford University Press, p17.

13. The writing of these histories, and the singular contribution of the Scottish School, are the subjects of Chapter 10 in Roy Porter's highly readable study, 2000, *Enlightenment: Britain and the Creation of the Modern World* London, Penguin.

14. This outline of key developments in pre-Darwinian evolutionary theory is informed by David Young 1992 *The Discovery of Evolution* London, Cambridge University Press in association with Natural History Museum Publications. This is also my source for the anecdote about the arrival of a sickly chimp at the port of London given on page two.

15. For a defence of Lamarck against the popular derogatory reading, see S.J. Gould 1999 'A Division of Worms (Jean-Baptiste Lamarck's contributions to evolutionary theory Part 1)' *Natural History* Vol.108, pp76-81.

16. A. Comte [transl. Harriet Martineau] 1853 *The Positive Philosophy Vol.1* London, John Chapman, p135.

17. Ibid., p144.

18. Quoted in L. Coser 1977 *Masters of Sociological Thought* 2nd Edition New York, Harcourt Brace Jovanovich, p109.

19. Ibid., p99.

20. H. Spencer 1876 *The Study of Sociology* [5th Edition, The International Scientific Series Vol.V] London, Henry S. King & Co., p329.

21. Ibid., p343.

22. Ibid., p337

23. Ibid., p346.

24. W. Lepenies [trns. R.J. Hollingdale] 1988 *Between Literature and Science: the Rise of Sociology* Cambridge, Cambridge University Press, p47.

25. Spencer was the most frequently cited author in the bibliography for Durkheim's (major) PhD thesis, the thesis that he then had published as his first book, *The Division of Labour in Society*.

26. Young, *The Discovery of Evolution*, pp93-94. Young is also my chief source for the subsequent discussion of Lyell and Wallace.

27. C. Darwin 1979 [1859] *On the Origin of Species by Means of Natural Selection, Or the preservation of Favoured Species in the Struggle for Life* London, Faber & Faber, p67.

28. Ibid., p95.

29. Ibid., p96.

30. I owe this observation to Coser, *Masters of Sociological Thought*, p110.

2

Genetic Destiny?

The ambition of sociologists to discover societal laws, laws informed by evolutionary theory, came to nought: no laws were discovered. Neither general sociological patterns nor differences in people's behavior could be explained in law-like terms. Thirteen years after his professorial appointment, toward the end of 1915, Durkheim's beloved son André was killed in the French retreat from Serbia. Durkheim himself retreated into "an almost ferocious silence," suffered a stroke and later died.[1] He lived just long enough to welcome the entrée of the Americans into the war, but not long enough to witness the armistice. The muddy slaughter, the trenches, the mustard gas, had not been on the Positivists' calendar of evolutionary progress and nor were the other key events of the twentieth century. And it wasn't just big events that eluded sociological prediction, for as the century unfolded it became apparent that the Queen of the Social Sciences was unable to make accurate predictions regarding her social subjects' behavior. Sociological laws proved treasonably elusive. The reasons for their elusiveness was hotly debated by methodologists but one embarrassing fact remained undeniable, not a single sociological law had been discovered; promising candidates turned out to be capricious trends that ebbed and flowed but didn't promise a predictable future. Faced with this disciplinary failure, sociologists quietly abandoned the search for laws, consigned Positivism to a disciplinary history of ideas and turned instead to description rather than explanation. Strictly evolutionary pictures of societal change were no longer painted, but the old idea that societal change conformed to some sort of evolutionary logic was tacitly up kept, as was the old picture of congenitally uniform, homogenous individuals becoming differentiated by varying circumstances. Whilst sociology floundered in the intellectual currents of misconceived evolutionary theory in which it had been accidentally launched, biology was favored by serendipity. Several of the key discoveries and developments that led to the completion of Darwinian theory were helped along by chance.

The chief lacuna in evolutionary theory was the missing explanation for inheritance, the explanation for how features advantageous to survival and reproduction were passed on from parent to offspring. Darwin's own tentative explanation proved wrong. Darwin suggested that every part of our bodies produced "gemmules" that incorporated both our inherited and acquired characteristics, that these gemmules congregated around the genitals and blended with those of our sexual partners when a baby was conceived. This theory of "pangenesis" proved useless, for even if gemmules had existed then blending parental features would, as Darwin came to acknowledge, lessen variety in each generation—and of course variety was the essential food on which Malthusian natural selection fed. Besides, Darwin's cousin Francis Galton devised an experiment to test the argument: rabbits having differing colored coats were given blood transfusions; contrary to the implications of the blending-gemmules pangenesis argument, these rabbits gave birth to babies with the same coloring as themselves.

The Austrian monk Gregor Mendel independently discovered an underlying logic of inheritance. His statistical analysis of the data from meticulous cross-pollinating experiments with pea plants revealed unswerving patterns now known as Mendel's Laws of Inheritance. These laws showed that parental features were not blended, instead one type of feature dominated, and that the business of inheritance occurred discretely, one feature's inheritance was unaffected by the inheritance of other features. Features were either dominant or recessive, recessive features having only a one-in-four probability of appearing when both parents passed on recessive genes. So for illustration albinism results from a lack of melanin thanks to a recessive gene: hence, an albino child will be born to two normally colored parents if both are carrying the recessive gene; chances are that an albino and a normally colored parent will not have an albino baby. In 1865 Mendel presented his findings in two papers given to the obscure Brunn Natural History Society, the papers were published, circulated to 120 scholarly societies, and like Hume's *Treatise* fell stillborn from the press. By an astonishingly improbable coincidence, thirty six years after Mendel's death his Laws were rediscovered by three independently working botanists, the Dutchman Hugo de Vries, the German Carl Correns and the Austrian Erich Tschermark.

Mendel's research had been graced by outstanding good luck, by his choice of pea plants for testing inheritance. Frustratingly, when he tried to replicate his experiments using different sorts of flowers the laws didn't hold good. The reason for this, the reason for snapdragons and pea plants exhibiting differing patterns of generational inheritances, was because the features Mendel had chosen to study were all either fortuitously dominant or recessive whereas, as subsequent studies would show, the features, or "traits," passed on to offspring may also be a consequence of codominance or incomplete dominance, and may, as in the case of types of color blindness, be linked to gender. Soon after Mendel's serendipitous laws had been rediscovered, a young graduate student at Columbia University named Walter Sutton published a paper proposing that chromosomes, rod-shaped bodies formed from the nucleus of a cell prior to cell division, were carriers of inheritable information. Each species produces a distinctive number of chromosomes from their nuclei, humans produce 46, goldfish 94, but there were obviously far, far more inheritable characteristics than chromosomes and so, he reasoned, chromosomes comprised smaller genetic particles, each of which was linked to an inheritable trait. Unlike Darwin's fictitious gemmules, genes and chromosomes gained in explanatory credibility as research progressed and assumed the starring roles in answer to the vexed question of how inheritance, how generational variation, was achieved.

On the 28 February 1953 Crick and Watson walked into their local Cambridge pub The Eagle announcing they had discovered the secret of life, which unlike most bar boasts was a claim they made good in their famous paper describing the double helical structure of DNA, the stuff of genes, and the code for all living things. In an enviably modest aside, Crick and Watson casually remarked that "It has not escaped our notice that the specific pairing we have postulated immediately suggests a possible copying mechanism for the genetic material."[2] In other words, the four chemical bases comprising each of the twin strands in the double helix (chemical bases identifiable by their initial letters A, T, G & C) could only pair with its twin in specific ways (A with T, C with G), and thus each strand formed a template from which a new strand could be replicated. Just as the workings of natural selection could be explained by the simple logic of the Malthusian mechanism, so too genetic copying could be explained by the simple mechanism suggested by the structure of DNA. In addition to DNA, all animal and plant cells contain RNA that was found to be of two types, transfer and messenger RNAs that accomplished the transcription of the genetic code, the code for building life. Each individual human adult comprises some 10 trillion cells, 10 trillion fabulously small chemical factories constantly making proteins, some of which are enzymes that act to control our cells' chemical reactions.

From the marriage of Darwinian evolutionary theory and genetic science a new more profound offspring, the Synthetic Theory, was born. This theoretical offspring benefited from the joining of the two explanatory mechanisms, the Darwinian-Malthusian and the DNA copying mechanisms, an accumulation of parental explanatory traits. Children, however, are not simply the sum of parental features, if they were then siblings would be identical in appearance and you are not a replica of your brother or sister. Human reproduction continually delivers inherited variation by "mistakes" occurring when genes are copied, through recombination when cells divide to form new pairs of chromosomes, and through other avenues such as non-disjunction when chromosome pairs fail to separate. Inherited human features are of two types, either discontinuous, you either have the trait or you don't, or polygenic which, as the name suggests, is the result of several genes working together to produce traits, features, which vary to a degree in a range of expressions. So for instance I have four fingers and a thumb on each of my hands which is the result of handy discontinuous variation, and I'm six feet tall which, as in all other cases, is the result of my polygenic inheritance coming of age in the environment in which I grew up. Variations of inherited physical traits are, unlike the purposeful theoretical wedding of Darwin to genetics, often chance outcomes.

In the same way Darwin believed that Malthusian logic could explain all natural evolution, and nineteenth-century social philosophers had been drawn to natural evolutionary theory believing it could answer all societal questions, so too many late-twentieth-century academics thought that the answer to all manner of outstanding questions lay in their disciplinary adoption of the logic of the new Synthetic Theory. The Synthetic Theory glistened like the philosopher's stone, a methodological alchemy that would answer our questions over our behavior and would define our human nature. The wonderful microscopic world of cells, the boggling findings of genetics, the healthy new theoretical infant Synthetic Theory were sure to draw attention, to lure and feed academic ambition. As is so often the case, the renaissance of evolutionary social theory was prompted by chance: bad personal luck led E.O. Wilson down the path that ended with sociobiology:

> Chance led E.O. Wilson to the studies that made him one of the greatest scientific thinkers of our age. Born in 1929, he grew up in comfortable circumstances, his mother having divorced his father (who was an alcoholic) and remarried a successful businessman. He developed an interest in the natural world as a young boy when he spent the summers exploring Paradise Beach in Florida, but lost the sight of his right eye in a fishing accident. Later, in his teens, a hereditary defect caused him to lose some of his hearing. [....] Given his disabilities, Wilson chose to pursue a life as a naturalist by studying creatures that could easily be picked up and inspected using his remaining good eye. He became an entomologist and spent his career at Harvard, where he was curator in entomology at the Museum of Comparative Zoology for nearly a quarter of a century. It was through studying the behaviour of ants that Wilson developed the intensely controversial discipline of sociobiology for which he is chiefly known.[3]

In the 1970s, Wilson published a trilogy of books, the last chapter of the first of which (*The Insect Societies*, 1971) was entitled "The Prospect for a Unified Sociobiology" and in this final chapter he suggested that soon the enduring social systems of social insects and vertebrate animals would be explained by one common theory. This suggestion became the subject of Wilson's second, best known, book *Sociobiology: The New Synthesis* (1975) and again the sting was in the final chapter: now, an emboldened Wilson argued that the same biological principles explaining animal behaviour could be incorporated into the social sciences. The argument for a new unity of method cementing biology and sociology in turn became the subject of the final book of the trilogy, *On Human Nature* (1978). Wilson's three titles for his books neatly chart the route that the revival of evolutionary social theory would take, a route culminating with the topic of human nature. These were not science books but, rather, books "about science," and their impact owed much to Wilson's penmanship and the fascinating details of animal societies, and of evolutionary science that he made accessible to lay readers. The final part of his trilogy, *On Human Nature*, has at its core "a speculative essay about the profound consequences that will follow as social theory at long lasts meets that part of the natural sciences most relevant to it."[4] Many of Wilson's objectives were mirrored in Comte's ill-starred project: both favored a unity of method between sociology and biology; both men emphasised methodology; both held that biological and societal change were evolutionary. As his title suggests, Wilson's focus is upon human nature, "an essentially biological phenomenon" that can be explained, just like any other natural phenomena, by the methods of natural science.

Science for Comte equalled the discovery of laws; for Wilson, "The heart of the scientific method is the reduction of perceived phenomenon to fundamental, testable principles ..."[5] in other words, the reduction of apparent variety to Malthusian principles. These principles, he speculated, could account for religion, aggression, sexual behavior and much more besides. Even so, the form that our genetically determined, inherited social behavior takes might well, Wilson acknowledges, be channelled by the culture in which we live.[6] Unlike the evolution of our "human nature" our culture Wilson argues, loudly echoing Comte, evolves in a Lamarckian fashion: "Cultural evolution is Lamarckian and very fast, whereas biological evolution is Darwinian and usually very slow." Although natural and cultural evolution are accomplished by two different mechanisms, it's inherited genes that have the upper hand:

> [...] ultimately the social environment created by cultural evolution will be tracked by biological natural selection. Individuals whose behaviour has become suicidal or destructive to their families will leave fewer genes than those genetically less prone to such behaviour. Societies that decline because of a genetic propensity of its members to generate competitively weaker cultures will be replaced by those more appropriately endowed. I do not for a moment ascribe the relative performances of modern societies to genetic differences, but the point must be made: there is a limit, perhaps closer to the practices of contemporary societies than we have the wit to grasp, beyond which biological evolution will begin to pull cultural evolution back to itself.[7]

Wilson's ambitions, so clearly echoing the High Priest of Positivism, aroused predictable hostility. His blend of ethology, ecology, and genetics sounded alarm bells: ethology in particular had a dirty reputation for its founder, the Austrian doctor Konrad Lorenz, had been a member of the German National Socialist Party, had welcomed the Anschluss, and had written articles claiming that "racial degeneracy" was an imminent threat to western civilisation (biographical details Wilson chose not to mention in *On Human Nature*).[8] Nor were the other ingredients Wilson mixed to cook up sociobiology—his picture of naturally competitive individuals and societies and his, vaguely worded, claims that behavior is in some sense governed by genetic inheritances—likely to reassure his more critical readers. Indeed, given the all too predictable furore that accompanied the debutante sociobiology, Wilson's protestations of surprised innocence appeared questionable.

Wilson's army of critics attacked on several flanks, the sharpest fire coming from scientists, students, and teachers, including some of Wilson's own close colleagues from Harvard, who formed the oppositional Sociobiology Study Group. This group waged war on sociobiology, starting their critical broadside with a letter published in the *New York Review of Books* denouncing sociobiology as reactionary, unscientific and comparable to Nazi ideologies. The eminent Harvard geneticist, and Wilson's erstwhile colleague, Richard Lewontin, compared sociobiology's picture of competitive gene-driven individuals to the ideology promoted by the then politically ascendant Thatcherite-Reaganite "New Right." Most damningly, in a renowned paper intriguingly entitled "The Spandrels of San Marco and the Panglossian Paradigm,"[9] two of the leading lights from the Sociobiology Study Group, Lewontin and the palaeontologist Stephen Jay Gould, exposed two Achillean weaknesses in Wilson's arguments. In this paper, published in 1979, Lewontin and Gould attacked two of the props supporting Wilson's reductionism, the enemy of variety, the lodestone of sociobiology, and in Wilson's case, they argued, a reductionism based upon his unbridled "faith in the power of natural selection as an optimising agent."

In a nice conceit, Lewontin and Gould began their paper with a description of an architectural feature of the great dome of St. Mark's Cathedral in Venice, a dome supported by arches whose intersections formed spandrels:

> Spandrels—the tapering triangular spaces formed by the intersection of two rounded arches at right angles are necessary architectural by-products of mounting a dome on rounded arches. Each spandrel contains a design admirably fitted to its tapering space. An evangelist sits in the upper part flanked by the heavenly cities. Below, a man representing one of the four biblical rivers (Tigris, Euphrates, Indus, and Nile) pours water from a pitcher in the narrowing space below his feet.
>
> The design is so elaborate, harmonious, and purposeful that we are tempted to view it as the starting point of any analysis, as the cause in some sense of the surrounding architecture. But this would invert the proper path of analysis. The system begins with an architectural constraint: the necessary four spandrels and their tapering triangular form. They provide a space in which the mosaicists worked; they set the quadripartite symmetry of the dome above.
>
> Such architectural constraints abound, and we find them easy to understand because we do not impose our biological biases upon them.[10]

Sociobiologists like Wilson, argued Gould and his colleagues, looked at the world through the tunnel vision of their "biological biases": just as Voltaire's incurably sanguine Dr. Pangloss held that "everything was for the best in this the best of all possible worlds," so too sociobiologists regarded every human trait as an adaptation selected to optimize reproductive potential. This methodological blinker blinded Wilson and other sociobiologists to the possibility that at least some traits were simply adaptations to local accidental environmental constraints or niche by-products, but were not "adaptive" in the sense that they could be explained as optimal solutions to adaptive problems—a point Gould and his coauthors illustrated by referring to Dr. Pangloss's skewed thinking; the bridge of our noses is not an adaptive design selected for supporting spectacles.

Opposing what they dubbed as the "adaptationist programme," the bias of evolutionary biologists and sociobiologists that led them to explain reductively all traits as the naturally selected heritage of past adaptive solutions, Gould and company championed a pluralist evolutionary approach. Darwin himself, they reminded readers, was angered by contemporaneous misreadings of his work that focused exclusively upon natural selection as the only evolutionary engine and while Darwin's own major alternative mechanism, use-and-disuse-heredity, was as we have seen incorrect there are many alternative evolutionary narratives, some of which, such as "genetic drift," explain generational variety as the consequence of pure chance events. For example, the introduction of an infectious disease for which a human population has no immunity will randomly cause deaths; in a small population this may lead to the frequency of some genetic sequences becoming greatly lessened or extinct. In their paper, they drew up "A Partial Typology of Alternatives to the Adaptationist Programme" and Gould's own key scholarly contribution, the "punctuated equilibrium thesis" that he developed along with Niles Eldredge, proposed that evolution was not a slow, steady incremental business; rather, evolutionary history was written as long periods of comparative stasis punctuated by exceptional episodes of rapid change.[11] By emphasizing evolutionary pluralism the reductionist reins of sociobiology were loosened; Gould and company's other chief argument against the sociobiologists' adaptationist programme slackened them still further by slipping the reins out of the hands of our genes. Although through mutation, "copying mistakes" and the like human reproduction produces a continual variety of genes it is not genes that reproduce, and nor do they get naturally selected: genes only exist as part of the whole organism, it is the organism that reproduces and either individually or as a member of a group gets "selected." Procrustean reductionism to genes was, they contended, unfounded in principle.

The second flank of critics, like Gould and the Boston Study Group, were also sympathetic to evolutionism but this flank sought to retain reductionist explanation by correcting what they saw as the errors and flaws in sociobiology. In his third book, *On Human Nature*, Wilson had argued that religion, and what he presented as religion's secular equivalents such as Marxism, had been "fatally" discredited. Mirroring Comte's prescription for a stoic acceptance of Positivist societal laws, Wilson claimed that lacking sure guidance from religion or secular equivalents, "To chart our destiny means that we must shift from automatic control based on our biological properties to precise steering based on biological knowledge." At the steering wheel will be our brains, our minds. Wilson's view of the mind directly contradicted the empiricists' central tenet that all knowledge comes from experience: "...the human mind is not a tabula rasa, a clean slate on which experience draws intricate pictures with lines and dots. It is more accurately described as an autonomous decision-making instrument...." "....a device for survival and reproduction, and reason is just one of its various techniques."[12] This role for the mind as the captain of our evolutionary predispositions, and Wilson's anti-empiricist picture of the mind as an instrument for survival became two of the main planks upon which the second flank of sociobiology's critics built their corrected version of sociobiological reductionism, "evolutionary psychology."

Prominent in the making of evolutionary psychology were Leda Cosmides, currently the director of the Psychology Department, and John Tooby, the director of the Anthropology Department, at the University of California. The distinctive twist made by evolutionary psychologists, their refinement of sociobiology, was their replacement of the dubious adaptationist program with an "approach to psychology" that, following Wilson, focused upon the evolved "design of the mind." Dismissing the "standard social science model," a model they emblemized by Hume's empiricism, Cosmides and Tooby conceptualized our brains as computers "...designed to generate behaviour that is appropriate to your environmental circumstances."[13] Our brains were "designed" to solve adaptive problems, and only adaptive problems, that we have faced in our earlier species history. For 99 percent of our species history we lived in hunter-gatherer societies and our brains slowly evolved over millions of years bequeathing modern man a "stone age mind." Consequently: "The key to understanding how the modern mind works is to realise that its circuits were not designed to solve the day-to-day problems of a modern American..."[14] Our brains, in this view, are an assembly of specialized circuits designed to meet particular adaptive problems and whereas individuals may differ through chance genetic inheritance they still share the same neural circuitry: evolutionary psychology, as one of its aims, "...seeks to characterise the universal, species-typical architecture of these [information processing] mechanisms." In this way, evolutionary psychologists substitute uniform species neural architecture in place of the older empiricists' blank slate homogeneity. The old nature/nurture distinction becomes redundant: learning from experience is, they reason, only possible if a neural mechanism for learning is already formed, "...three pound bowls of oatmeal don't learn, but three pound brains do." Rather than being an all-purpose tool as traditionally assumed by social scientists, the brain as pictured by Cosmides is more like a Swiss Army penknife with different blades for different tasks.

Explaining behavior, insist evolutionary psychologists, means explaining the present in terms of the past, the long distant past of our hunter-gatherer forebears. For example, in a study published in 2001 John Tooby and colleagues[15] came to the conclusion that our brains are not designed to distinguish other human groups in racial terms because during our long evolutionary history people seldom met other races. Racial categorizing, they argued, is simply a by-product of "coalitional affiliation" and is not a fixed evolutionary inheritance. This explanatory tactic, this imaginative reconstruction of the environment and adaptive problems faced by hunter-gatherers in our dim species history, further distinguishes evolutionary psychology. Their additional explanatory tactics, studying the tiny groups of humans still living as hunter-gatherers, trying to identify universal human behaviors, drawing parallels between human and other species' behavior, also rely upon inferential methodological procedures. This procedural approach is open to one of the chief criticisms levelled by Gould et al. at the adaptationist programme: such inferences may be nothing more than just-so stories of the kind told by Rudyard Kipling, imaginative but untrue Panglossian narratives. Furthermore, inferential evolutionary psychology explanations cannot specify the degree to which a piece of behaviour is genetically influenced; just because we have a particular neural blade in our "Swiss Army brain," this won't tell us how much the blade's design will influence our behaviour. More damningly for evolutionary psychology, neither can it tell us why individuals in the same circumstances will behave differently, why one of us might not use a particular blade, why another might use the blade intended for removing stones from horses' hooves for roasting lumps of cannabis. In other words, even if evolutionary psychology was a sound psychological approach it could not explain variety, why people behave differently, the way people actually are and behave.

Explaining variety became the topic for Behavior Genetics, a further strand of sociobiological thinking distinguished from evolutionary psychology by Cosmides and Tooby in terms of the two approaches' explanatory topics: evolutionary psychologists "… seek to characterise the universal, species-typical architecture of these [neural] mechanisms," behavior geneticists are interested in differences in people's genes leading to differences in their behavior. As a subdiscipline, Behavior Genetics is only some thirty years old but can claim a shady pedigree stretching back to the studies of Francis Galton, the cousin of Darwin whose research persuaded Darwin to abandon his theory of use-and-disuse heredity. As a child prodigy himself, Galton had been fascinated by genius. His comparative studies of pairs of identical twins with pairs of fraternal twins had led him to conclude that identical twins were not simply physically similar but also very alike in terms of their personalities, careers, interests, etc., implying that nurture had little influence. Galton's own reputation was indelibly besmirched by his association with eugenics but, according to the distinguished molecular biologist, chief of gene structure and regulation at the U.S. National Cancer Institute's Laboratory of Biochemistry, and prominent behaviour geneticist Dean Hamer, Galton's methodology was fundamentally correct, for "… by comparing the resemblances and differences between identical twins, fraternal twins and unrelated individuals, it's possible to calculate how much of a difference in a trait is caused by inherited factors. This is known as heritability."[16] Hamer emphasizes that it is not the case that genes simply determine behavior:

> One of the most common misconceptions about genetics is that there are genes "for" things. Some people have the genes "for" breast cancer, shyness, blue eyes, and so they must have the disease, condition, or trait. That is what most people tend to think when they hear about a gene "for" depression, or a "gay gene," or "obesity gene." If this were true, it would be easy enough to undergo testing to see what genes you have, and therefore what you ought to worry about. That is not the way it works. Everyone has a "mood gene," and a "sexual orientation gene," and a gene that regulates body weight. The difference is that genes come in different varieties of flavours.[17]

Hamer in common with sociobiologists and evolutionary psychologists is keen to refute the current view popular among social scientists, journalists and the public that nurture is the chief cause of individuation, "This theory is not only stupid but cruel. People are different because they have different genes that created different brains that formed different personalities."[18] Molecular biology demonstrates "beyond doubt" that "we come ready-made from the factory," but the influence of genes should be seen metaphorically as akin to musical instruments, not musical scores: "Genes don't determine exactly what music is played—or how well—but they do determine the range of what is possible."[19] As we grow, the influence of our genes upon our personalities becomes more pronounced, a growing degree of influence that Hamer holds evident in differences between adult rates of crime and delinquency, adult IQs and in adult personality traits such as novelty-seeking or neuroticism.

Behavior geneticists measure the degree of genetic influence by using a refined version of Galton's methodology, exploiting the natural case study offered by comparing twins. Identical, monozygotic twins share the same genes; fraternal twins are no more genetically similar than ordinary siblings, sharing half their genes. This fixed genetic proportionality is the basis for behavior genetics' explanations for variance in behavior, a natural methodological test used also to understand differing susceptibility to mental illnesses such as bipolar depression and schizophrenia. In an article reviewing the literature on risk to schizophrenia, Ming Tsuang summarises the evidence for a genetic contribution to schizophrenia that illustrates the way in which twin studies can be used to assess inherited vulnerability:

> That schizophrenia and schizophrenia spectrum disorders have a hereditary component is well established. While the general population life time prevalence is about 1%, relatives of schizophrenic probands have a higher risk of schizophrenia and related disorders. The risk of developing schizophrenia in family members increases with the degree of biological relatedness to the patient—greater risks are associated with higher levels of shared genes. For example, third-degree relatives (e.g. first cousins) share about 12.5% of their genes, and show a risk of 2% for developing schizophrenia. Second-degree relatives (e.g. half-siblings) share about 25% of their genes and show

a risk of 6%. Most first-degree relatives (e.g. siblings, dizygotic (DZ) twins) share about 50% of their genes and show a risk of about 9%. Monozygotic (MZ) twins share 100% of their genes, and show risks near 50%.[20]

Large sets of data on twins held in various countries, notably the Minnesota Study of Twins Reared Apart, reveal the astonishing adult similarities of identical twins who were brought up in different families, disturbing similarities that imply a negligible role for nurture, and indeed for parents. Just as Wilson attempted for sociobiology, and Leda and Tooby for evolutionary psychology, so too the psychologist Eric Turkheimer in a recent article[21] gives a methodological manifesto for behavior genetics, a set of "laws" elaborated by Stephen Pinker in his much discussed book tellingly entitled *The Blank Slate: The Modern Denial of Human Nature*.[22] Like Wilson, Pinker's book is a philosophical discourse, rather than a work of science, and much of his discussion contests the empiricists' tabula rasa view of man. Behavior genetics makes its appearance in Pinker's nineteenth chapter in which he begins by elaborating Turkheimer's "three laws." The first of these "laws" states that "all human behavioural traits are heritable" and by measuring correlations between the behavior of monozygotic twins, fraternal twins, ordinary siblings and unrelated individuals:

> The results come out roughly the same no matter what is measured or how it is measured. Identical twins reared apart are highly similar; identical twins reared together are far more similar than fraternal twins reared together; biological siblings are far more similar than adoptive siblings.[23]

It is essential to recognize that what is being measured in behavior genetic studies is the *variance* in a group, the differences the individuals in a group exhibit. This methodological approach cannot tell us anything about what the individuals have in common. So for illustration, if we were to measure the height of two groups of similarly aged women and plotted their variance in height, usually measured statistically using "standard deviation," then although a behavioral genetic study could indicate the extent to which the variance was inherited, it could not tell us anything about how much of each individuals' height was inherited and nor could it say anything more than the variance was correlated with genes. Correlations, as any sociologist will tell you, are tricky, they need interpretation if they are to stand as causal explanations for as Pinker observes:

> We know that tall men on average are promoted in their jobs more rapidly than short men, and that attractive people on average are more assertive than unattractive ones. [....] Height and looks are obviously heritable, so if we didn't know about the effects of looks, we might think that these people's success comes directly from genes for ambition and assertiveness instead of coming indirectly from genes for long legs or a cute nose. The moral is that heritability always has to be interpreted in the light of all the evidence; it does not wear its meaning on its sleeve.[24]

Turkheimer's second law of behavior genetics states that "The effect of being raised in the same family is smaller than the effect of the genes." Measuring the differences between adopted siblings, comparing biological siblings reared together with adopted siblings, permits the influence of a shared environment to be gauged whereas comparing adopted identical monozygotic twins allows the influence of non-shared, unique environmental influences to become apparent. The rather startling implication of all this becomes plain in Turkheimer's Third Law, "A substantial portion of the variation in complex human behavioural traits is not accounted for by the effects of genes or families." Identical twins brought up in the same family, sharing both genes and the same family environment, are not identical in terms of intellects or personalities and so "There must be causes that are neither genetic nor common to the family that makes identical twins different and, more generally, makes people what they are."[25]

Just how startling the implications of this approach are is explored to great effect by Pinker when considering the massively controversial theories of Judith Harris, theories that Pinker had brought to wider attention by a briefer discussion in his earlier book, *How the Mind Works*. Harris, formerly a freelance writer of psychology textbooks, reanalysed copious psychological accounts that held parental influence to be paramount for the formation of their children's adult personalities and concluded that these studies ignored heredity, assuming that a correlation between parents and children spoke of nurture rather than the influence of family genes. Noting that child-obsessed parenting was a comparatively recent practice, a modern practice fuelled by philosophers such as Rousseau and by Freudian psychoanalysis, Harris suggested that what was important for children was their own peer groups rather than adult culture. As any parent knows, the pressure upon children to fit it with their peers may weigh as or more heavily, than parental pressure. Different siblings grow to become distinct individuals, one brother a choirboy, the other an all-night party animal. Children of immigrant parents easily become fluent in the language of their peers, even when this language is not spoken in the home (the observation that persuaded Pinker that Harris was on to something). In published articles and then in her much-debated book, *The Nurture Assumption: Why Children Turn Out the Way They Do*,[26] Judith Harris proposed a radical alternative to the current view of how children's personalities are formed. In Pinker's words:

> In almost every case, people model themselves after their peers, not their parents. This is Harris's explanation of the elusive environmental shaper of personality, which she calls the Group Socialisation Theory. It's not all in the genes, but what isn't in the genes isn't from the parents either. Socialisation—acquiring the norms and skills necessary to function in society—takes place in the peer group. Children have culture, too, which absorb parts of the adult culture and also develops values and norms of their own. Children do not spend their waking hours trying to become better and better approximations of adults. They strive to be better and better children,

ones that function well in their own society. It is in this crucible that our personalities are formed.[27]

Harris's identification of the unique, non-shared environmental influence that shapes children's personalities provoked a storm of often hostile criticism[28] from professionals of all kinds working or researching upon child development, and also from parents disturbed or outraged by what they took to be Harris's wholesale theft of their future imprateur. Pinker was not wholly satisfied either. In his assessment, while Harris may have identified rightly the "crucible" of socialisation, the child's peer group, this may not in itself necessarily explain the development of personalities. Identical twins, sharing genes, family environments and, on average peer groups, only show around 50 percent similarity and thus "… neither genes nor families nor peer groups can explain what makes them different."[29] Harris, aware of this limitation, suggests that differentiation occurs as children fulfil differing roles within a peer group, but her suggestion was still to be tested, and Pinker characterises the process of children filling differing niches in their peer groups as "largely a matter of chance."

As Pinker recognizes, if children slot into peer group niches by chance then we should also consider the implications of chance in other spheres: "But once we allow Lady Luck into the picture, she can act at other stages of life." Lady Luck could intervene throughout our lives, taking us along capricious biographical paths. "Perhaps our history of collisions and near misses explains what made us what we are." Perhaps early chance events in the womb, how one foetus lies in the womb compared to its twin, or the mother's diet for instance,[30] may affect neurodevelopment.

> If the nongenetic component of personality is the outcome of neurodevelopmental roulette, it would present us with two surprises. One is that the "genetic" term in our behavioural geneticist's equation is not necessarily environmental. If the unexplained variance is a product of chance in brain assembly, yet another chunk of our personalities would be "biologically determined" (though not genetic) and beyond the best laid plans of parents and society.
>
> The other surprise is that we may have to make room for a pre-scientific explanatory concept in our view of human nature—not free will, as many people have suggested to me, but fate. It is not free will because among the many traits that differ between identical twins reared together are ones that are stubbornly involuntary. No one chooses to become schizophrenic, musically gifted, or, for that matter, anxious or self-confident or open to experience. But the old idea of fate—in the sense of uncontrollable fortune, not strict predestination—can be reconciled with modern biology once we remember the many openings for chance to operate in development.[31]

Just as Pinker is dissatisfied with Harris's Group Socialisation Theory, so too Harris is unhappy with Pinker's courting of Lady Luck (there only real point of disagreement). Chance suffuses Pinker's hypothesis, it's there in the spin of the genetic roulette, in the baby's biological development, and in the environment. This is a step too far for Judith Harris, a step she's unwilling to take because it would mean abandoning any hope of an evolutionary-psychology/adaptive-reductive explanation for personality development. In reply to my querying the nature of her disagreement with Pinker's position, Judith Harris kindly outlined her preferred alternative to accepting that chance shapes the people we become:

> The puzzle Steve [Pinker] and I are trying to solve has to do with the unexplained, nongenetic variation in the behavioural genetic data. To explain this variation, we have to posit effects that are not directly predictable from the genes, because if they were simply the outcome of genetic differences, they'd contribute to the genetic variance (heritability), not to the non-genetic variance. [....]
> I guess what makes my position different from Steve's is that saying that it's random (as he does) implies that it's not adaptive. If the environment can push you anywhere, willy-nilly, then there's no telling what kind of personality you'll end up with, which means there's no telling whether the personality you end up with is going to be useful to you in adulthood (in the evolutionary psychologist's sense of increasing "fitness") or against your best interests. I, in contrast, assume that the plasticity of personality seen in children has adaptive purpose, and that its purpose is to provide you with a personality that will be useful to you in adult life. Which means, to me, that it isn't random.
> Assume, for example, that a child suffers some biological accident that makes him short and puny. It would not be to this child's advantage to develop an aggressive personality, because if he picks a fight he's likely to get beaten up. So he develops a different sort of personality. The personality he develops is not predictable from his genes—so in that sense it is "random"—but it's not random in the sense of being caused by factors that are irrelevant to the outcome. Though it's not predictable from his genes, it is predictable from his size and strength.
> The problem—the reason it's just a matter of degree—is that the adaptive mechanism I am proposing can easily be misled. How does a child know that he's short and puny and that aggression would be a counterproductive strategy for him? He has to rely upon the experiences he has with other people of his sex and approximately his age, which usually means experiences within his peer group. But "chance" factors can also affect these experiences. Something happens one day that affects the way his peers behave towards him—he trips over a log and falls flat on his face and from then on he's regarded as clumsy. That sort of thing. The mechanism I'm proposing can't tell the difference between relevant things and irrelevant things, so it can be hijacked by the irrelevant things. By chance, in other words.[32]

In her next book, *No Two Alike: Human Nature and Human Individuality*, published in 2006, Judith Harris explicitly rejected chance as a possible cause of the puzzling "unexplained variance" found most notably between identical twins raised together in their parental home. There are quite striking similarities between this book and hers; we discuss and examine many of the same topics and theorists but in sharp contrast to my treatment of the "unwelcome guest", and having rehearsed the chief arguments of her first book, she then explicitly rejects chance as a possible answer to the conundrum of unexplained variance:

One suspect whose modus operandi could fit that description [the cause of growing personality variance] is chance. I'm not even going to count this as one of my red herrings, because if chance—randomness—is responsible, then my mystery would have no solution.[33]

Although she admits that chance, which she calls "randomness", "cannot be ruled out" as an explanation[34] it is clear that she assumes chance is not a fitting explanatory candidate as it cannot be accommodated within the explanatory methodology of psychology, even less so within Harris's favoured neo-Darwinist methodology. In consequence, she reasons that the conundrum of variance can be explained by what she terms the "status system,"[35] her hypothesis that since the dawn of time individuals have sought esteem by competing against each other, the all too familiar neo-Darwinian signature tune, and that in their constant competition individuals distinguish themselves, become less and less alike in their struggle for prestige. "Status," true to its etymology, simply means "one's standing," here one's standing in the social world, but for Harris it has become redefined as competition always to be the best. For her, children aren't in the business of finding out who they are, discovering their own unique character, but rather "... they want to be *better* than the other members of their group—they seek high status."[36] Status is for Harris just a synonym for Spencerian individualistic competition. This notion of a differentiating "status system" is chiefly fostered by Harris's commitment to a reductionist explanation for the unexplained variance in behaviour genetics' data, for the variety routinely found in the way people act, by her hope that there is some way of reducing variance to evolutionary imperatives. As she tells us,[37] her solution is only an hypothesis, a theory waiting to be tested, but it will be the argument of this book that Harris's and similarly minded evolutionists' initial assumption—the assumption that chance is an unsatisfactory explanatory candidate—is unwarranted and that what she playfully refers to as the "mystery" of unexplained variance is merely a chimerical consequence of her misplaced rejection of chance. It is not, contra Harris, that there is no solution to the "mystery" of unexplained variance, rather that there is no mystery.

Despite bold claims and continuing research, there is precious little hard scientific support for the claims of neo-Darwinian social theorists. It may be worth summarizing exactly how little has been discovered thirty years on from the publication of *Sociobiology: The New Synthesis*, starting with Wilson's own life and achievements. In his biographical sketch of Wilson I quoted near the start of this chapter John Gray begins by acknowledging "Chance led E. O. Wilson to the studies that made him one of the greatest thinkers of the scientific age." His chance disabilities led him to choose "... to pursue a life as a naturalist by studying creatures [ants] that could easily be picked up and inspected using his remaining good eye." And it was from studying the social behavior of ants that he developed sociobiology. Wilson's loss of sight in his right eye was the result of a fishing accident that befell him when a child; a simple chance accident, in behavioural genetic measurement from his "unique, non-shared" environment. His second misfortune, a loss of hearing, was the result of a "hereditary defect," again a chance inheritance, this time a poor spin of the genetic roulette wheel. The Professor's biographical path, the path that led to sociobiology, was paved with chance events; if chance had not intervened then maybe Wilson would have joined the army, as he had contemplated when he left college.[38] His new discipline, sociobiology, focused upon universal evolved human nature, cannot explain different biographical patterns and neither can its refined offspring, evolutionary psychology. Both sociobiology and evolutionary psychology depend upon inferences from our long species history for their explanations, these inferences resist refutation, the inferential narratives are vulnerable to the criticisms launched by Gould and others against an adaptationist prejudice, and, and perhaps most damningly, there is no hard scientific support for them, no dependable identification of the genes for our supposedly evolved universal behavior or universal neural architecture.

This absence of hard genetic evidence sits awkwardly with sociobiological narratives. For instance, Dean Hamer and Peter Copeland, in their chapter on "Sex", rehearse the standard sociobiological theory for differences between male and female sexuality, which runs something like this: both men and women have a vested interest in the transmission of their genes; men produce millions of sperms every day whereas women have a limited supply of eggs; therefore, "For men, the optimal strategy to preserve the species is to have as much sex as possible with as many different partners as possible. For women the optimal strategy is to be highly selective and to have sex only with a man who will commit time and resources to children";[39] all notions of romance, love, tenderness, beauty etc. are reduced to masks obscuring the underlying evolutionary impulse to mate; these inherited gender differences are the reason men are naturally promiscuous, women naturally choosy, why men value good looks that denote fertility, while women value wealth and status that signal a good provider.

This evolutionary tale is also told by Pinker and Wilson, and it is a staple of sociobiology. Which is all very well but of course in the real world there are myriad variations in male and female sexuality, inexplicable for sociobiology; the crude sociobiological picture is not of true universals, merely generalizations, and as Hamer and Copeland admitted:

All of these differences in what men and women want—beauty versus money, youth versus age, availability versus commitment—seem like they could be genetic. They are observed across human societies, so they can't be purely cultural. In many cases they are seen in other species, so they are probably evolutionarily conserved. And they are different from one person to the next—not all men are pigs, not all women prigs—hinting at individual genetic differences. But seeming is not proving. *We have no idea what these genes are, how many there are, what they do, or how they are differently expressed in males and females—all of which is necessary to prove a genetic basis.*[40]

Neither sociobiology nor evolutionary psychology can identify the genes supposedly responsible for gender universals or for differences. Behavior genetics, the sub-discipline devoted to explaining differences, variance in groups, fares little better. Twin studies and the other methodological techniques of behaviour genetics suggest, at best, that genes are implicated in 50 percent of the variance found in samples. At least half of the variance has nothing do with genes which as evolutionary psychologists point out are not some sort of tiny wizards conjuring up our actions, merely lengths of DNA that will code for the production of proteins. Most human features and traits are the result of many genes working in concert passed on to the next generation as a polygenic inheritance. Given that polygenic inheritances are expressed in a range (say, of heights) in any sample there will always be variance, and given that at least half of this variance will not be genetic, the cautious language adopted by sociobiologists to describe the effect of genes on behaviour is clearly prudent. Genes are said to "predispose," "incline," or in Wilson's more flowery prose "keep our behaviour on a lead": what genes don't do is cause us to behave in specific ways. Analogously, if I place a steel ball-bearing on the top of a slope, and I then let go of it, it will roll downwards. The cause of its motion is the pull of gravity, plus the properties of the ball-bearing, its roundness, and the slope that is its environment. Ball-bearings have a predisposition to roll about, the slope gives a literal inclination, and the motion is caused by gravity.[41]

When it comes to identifying the specific genes that purportedly lend a predispositional quality to individuals' or to species' behavior sociobiologists have been about as successful as sociologists were in their quest for societal laws. There are very few contenders for the title of "gene identified by a behavior geneticist for behavior X." One highly controversial candidate for this role came along with the claimed identification of what the media carelessly labelled a "gay gene." Dean Hamer, who had lost friends to AIDS, had been examining the possibility of a genetic susceptibility to the deadly Kaposi's sarcoma. This came to nothing when it was found that a virus that struck people, such as AIDS sufferers, who had a weakened immune system, caused this cancer. The research led Hamer to search for genes linked to homosexuality and in 1993, trumpeted in the press, he announced that there was a gene, or genes, that contributed to male homosexuality. To date, this gene has not been reliably identified and as Risch et al.[42] pointed out in a letter to the journal *Science*, there would be a strong selective pressure against any such gene. Even if a gene or genes could reliably be identified for any behavioral pattern, this would simply mean that its bearer had a predisposition, an inclination towards behaving in a certain fashion, not an irrevocable command. Whether any genetic predisposition comes into play depends upon environmental influences, those influences that sociobiologists corral into dubious adaptationist narratives, influences yet to be understood by behavior geneticists. Similarly scientists studying disorders such as schizophrenia and bipolar depression, which are believed to have a strong hereditary component, are still trying to identify the specific genes involved and, along with behavior geneticists, they recognize that it is the unique, non-shared environment that adds and interacts with the genes to produce the disorder:

> [....] even if an individual has an identical twin with schizophrenia, or two affected parents, the risk is nowhere near 100%. In the case of identical twins with one affected member, the genetic predisposition is present in both individuals, but is expressed only in the twin who has undergone certain environmental experiences as well. [...] Components of the environment include psychological, biological and physical factors experienced by the individual from the moment of conception, through development, birth and maturation. Monozygotic twins may experience different perinatal factors such as adequacy of blood supply, position in the womb and birth complications. Later, they may experience different home and school environments, as well as different marital experiences, occupational events or surroundings. Such differences in environment are likely to be meaningful, as non-shared environmental influences accounted for almost all of the variance in liability to schizophrenia attributable to environmental effects in several twin studies.[43]

There is one further twist from twin studies, an unexpected romantic twist that mischievously confounds adaptationist narratives. The logic of behavior genetics should lead to the conclusion that mate selection is influenced by a person's genes and by their unique environment that combine to inform his or her mating criteria, our criteria of who will be a suitable mate. In 1993, in the same year that Hamer announced his discovery of a "gay gene," Professor David Lykken, then the director of the Minnesota Twin Family Study and his colleague Auke Tellegen published a paper that challenged this explanatory presumption.[44] Contrary to expectations, their study showed that the spouses of identical twins were no more alike than the spouses of fraternal twins and not much more alike than any randomly chosen set of partners. Moreover, two-thirds of the male twins said that they were indifferent to, or actually disliked, their twin's spouses. Rather than a uniform, law-like process informed by the individual's genes and unique environment mate selection appears to be better characterised as the unpredictable work of Cupid. As Lykken writes:

> Our findings, that infatuation is largely unpredictable either on genetic or environmental grounds, have to my knowledge never been critiqued in print and certainly they have not been empirically refuted. Neither, however, have they been generally accepted except, perhaps, by poets. Psychologists assume as a consensual predicate that behaviour is lawful and that important human responses are in principle predictable. Lovers, also, at least while walking down the aisle, assume that their mutual attraction was inevitable for a host of reasons that are obvious, at least to themselves.[45]

Just as lovers might be affronted by Lykken's conclusions, so too psychologists and sociobiologists cleaving to reductionist evolutionary theory might bridle at the idea that one of the most important events in our lives, important not just for us personally but also for the genetic composition of our children, is, in the phrase favoured by Lykken, simply "adventitious," down to chance.

It should be evident that the explanatory promises of sociobiology, evolutionary psychology and behavior genetics have not as yet been met and that chance, far from being weakened by contemporary evolutionary social theory, has reemerged as a revitalised contender to explain the pesky matter of variety in our behaviour and personalities. It is this very variety that comprises "human nature" and if sociobiology is unable credibly to reduce this apparent diversity down to underlying uniformities then it must be judged an explanatory failure. There is one more dodgy aspect of sociobiology to consider, the claim made by Wilson, and of course by Comte, that cultural evolution is Lamarckian, faster than Darwinian natural evolution:

> Because it is also far slower than Lamarckian evolution, biological evolution is always quickly outrun by cultural change. Yet the divergence cannot be too great because ultimately the social environment created by cultural evolution will be tracked by biological natural selection.[46]

This argument is, as we shall see in the next chapter, wrong. Cultural change, the social environment, does not evolve along Lamarckian lines—in fact, it doesn't evolve at all. Instead, societies and cultures change for a variety of reasons, some of which are the business of Lady Luck. The environment of human evolution is a social affair, and as in all affairs, chance can and does play a part.

Notes

1. S. Lukes, 1973, *Emile Durkheim.* London: Penguin, ch. 27.
2. J.D. Watson and F.H.C. Crick, 1953, "A Structure for Deoxyribose Nucleic Acid." *Nature,* vol. 171, p. 737.
3. J. Gray, 2003, "E O Wilson" [Great Thinkers]. *New Statesman* 14 July, p. 22.
4. E.O. Wilson, 1978, *On Human Nature.* London, Penguin, p. x.
5. Ibid., p. 11.
6. See ibid., pp. 18-19.
7. Ibid., pp. 79-80.
8. These unsavory details of Lorenz's past, and the following discussion of the reception given to Wilson, are culled from Kenan Malik's fine, critical scrutiny (2000) *Man, Beasts and Zombies.* London: Phoenix, pp. 184-190.
9. S.J. Gould and R.C. Lewontin, 1979, "The Spandrels of San Marco and the Panglossian Paradigm: A Critique of the Adaptationist Programme." *Proceedings of the Royal Society of London,* Series B, vol. 205, pp. 581-598.
10. Ibid., pp. 581-582.
11. Gould's own pluralistic and "punctuated" story of evolution is fascinatingly told in, among his many other equally wonderful writings, S. J. Gould, 2000, *Wonderful Life: The Burgess Shale and the Nature of History.* London: Phoenix (particularly ch.11).

12. Wilson, *On Human Nature*, p. 67 and p. 2.
13. L. Cosmides and J. Tooby, 1997, *Evolutionary Psychology: A Primer*, p. 4. (This "primer" is readily available on the Web.).
14. Ibid., p. 11.
15. R. Kurzban, J. Tooby, and L. Cosmides 2001 "Can race be erased? Coalitional computation and social categorization." *Proceedings of the National Academy of Sciences,* vol. 98, pp. 15387-15392.
16. D. Hamer and P. Copeland, 1998, *Living With Our Genes: Why They Matter More Than You Think.* New York: Doubleday, p. 21.
17. Ibid., p. 19.
18. Ibid., p. 25.
19. Ibid., p. 12.
20. M.T. Tsuang, W.S. Stone, and S.V. Faraone, 2001, "Genes, environment and schizophrenia." *British Journal of Psychiatry,* vol. 178, pp. 18-24, [p. 19].
21. E. Turkheimer, 2000, "Three laws of behaviour genetics and what they mean." *Current Directions in Psychological Science,* vol. 5, pp. 160-164.
22. S. Pinker, 2002, *The Blank Slate: The Modern Denial of Human Nature,* London: Allen Lane.
23. Ibid., p. 374.
24. Ibid., p. 377.
25. Ibid., p. 380.
26. J.R. Harris, 1995, "Where is the Child's Environment? A Group Socialisation Theory of Development." *Psychological Review,* vol. 102, pp. 458-489; 1998 *The Nurture Assumption: Why Children Turn Out the Way They Do* London, Bloomsbury.
27. Pinker, *The Blank Slate*, p. 390.
28. Judith Harris hosts an impressive website that, amongst other items, archives the reception, including hostile criticisms, of her work. The site includes a section concerning the issue of "birth-order," a common objection to Harris's arguments: http://home.att.net/~xchar/tna/
29. Pinker, *The Blank Slate*, p. 396.
30. Some evidence for the influence of diet, here the influence of supplements commonly taken by pregnant women, affecting not only mice offspring's phenotype but also their inheritable genes, is given in: R. Waterland and R, Jirtle, 2003, "Transposable Elements: Targets for Early Nutritional Effects on Epigenetic Gene Regulation." *Molecular and Cellular Biology,* vol. 23, pp. 5293-5300.
31. Pinker, *The Blank Slate*, p. 397.
32. Private correspondence between the author and Judith Harris, 10 December 2002. I am most grateful to Harris for her permission to quote from this correspondence and for her willingness to discuss my queries over her work.
33. J. R. Harris, 2006, *No Two Alike: Human Nature and Human Individuality.* London: W.W. Norton, p. 45.
34. Ibid., p. 47.
35. Harris hypothesises three systems: in addition to the status system there are, she argues, also the relationship and socialization systems, but it is the status system which she presents as the solution to unexplained variance.
36. Harris, *No Two Alike*, p. 246 [italics in original].
37. Ibid., p. 265.
38. This example of chance in Wilson's autobiography can also be made in the case of Judith Harris's life and the route which led her to become a freelance writer; her life too was shaped by chance events and by medical misfortune. Curiously, in her second book Harris uses her own autobiographical progression to illustrate

seemingly chance influences but, like a good Darwinist, in the very next paragraph she restates her evolutionary faith and abandons talk of mere "randomness" (ibid., pp. 47-48).

39. Hamer and Copeland, *Living With Our Genes*, p. 170.
40. Ibid., p. 176 [italics added].
41. More strictly speaking, dispositions are not what Aristotle termed "efficient causes," they do not instigate change.
42. N. Risch, E. Squires-Wheeler, and B. J. B. Keats, 1993, "Male sexual orientation and genetic evidence" [letter]. *Science,* vol. 262, pp. 2063-2065.
43. Tsuang et al., "Genes, environment and schizophrenia," p.20 [italics added, citations in the original have been omitted].
44. D.T. Lykken and A. Tellegen, 1993, "Is human mating adventitious or the result of lawful chance?: A twin study of mate selection." *Journal of Personality and Social Psychology,* vol. 6, pp. 56-68. David Lykken, the late emeritus professor at the University of Minnesota and the world's leading expert on polygraphs died aged seventy-eight in the autumn of 2006. I would like to record my thanks to the professor who willingly gave up his time to answer my, I suspect naïve, questions about his research, research which in the case of this 1993 paper he had found difficult to get published owing to its heterodoxical argument.
45. D.T. Lykken, 2002 ,"How Relationships Begin and End." In: H.T. Reis, M.A. Fitzpatrick and A.L. Vangelsti (eds.) *Stability and Change in Relationships Across the Lifespan.* New York: Cambridge University Press.
46. Wilson, *On Human Nature*, p. 79.

3

A Chancy World

The science that fuelled Wilson's sociobiological speculations is only some fifty years old: just as Spencer, Comte, and other nineteenth-century social theorists were too quick off the mark in their adoption of nineteenth-century natural evolutionary theory, and unwisely dogmatic in their analyses and pronouncements, so too it may be that today's theorists should wait a while before trying once again to found social theory upon fast-changing contemporary genetic science. Fifty years is not a long time in which to unravel the secrets of life and the theories and views currently being proposed may well be proved hopelessly wrong. One illustration of the infancy of genetic science and the fragility of current thinking emerged when the human genome was finally mapped out. Informing the Human Genome Project, persuading governments to grant funds for research, luring greedy commercial organizations to buy up the copyright on as yet unidentified genes, were a set of deterministic assumptions. As Paul Silverman has recently written:

> For more than 50 years scientists have operated under a set of seemingly incontrovertible assumptions about genes, gene expression, and the consequences thereof. Their mantra: One gene yields one protein; genes beget messenger RNA, which in turn begets protein; and most critically, the gene is deterministic in gene expression and can therefore predict disease propensities. Yet during the last five years, data have revealed inadequacies in this theory. Unsettling results from the Human Genome Project (HGP) in particular have thrown the deficiencies into sharp relief.[1]

To the dismay of speculative venture capitalists, to the surprise of scientists, when the first draft of the human genome sequence was published in the spring of 2001 it revealed that, rather than the expected 100,000 genes, we can only boast a measly 30,000, about the same number as lowly earthworms. Some venture capitalists were left holding the copyright to genes that didn't actually exist and scientists were obliged to rethink their basic assumptions and come up with a new non-deterministic mantra that could capture the ability of our measly gene stock to produce our million or so proteins. The old deterministic mantra can no longer be sung for findings from the HGP show, in Silverman's words, that

> Some genes encode more than one protein; others don't encode protein at all. These findings help refine evolutionary theory by explaining an explosion of diversity from relatively little starting material. We therefore need to rethink our long-held beliefs: A re-evaluation of the genetic determinism doctrine, coupled with a new systems biology mentality, could help consolidate and clarify genome-scale data, enabling us finally to reap the rewards of the genome sequencing projects.[2]

In the light of this massive overestimation of the number of our genes, given the challenge presented to deterministic assumptions by the HGP, it may well be prudent to suspend attempts to ground social theory in evolutionary science, at least for the time being.

Even if in the future genetic science were sufficiently robust to license biological determinism then we would still need to explain our development and phenotypic expression, we would still need to explain how our biological selves become the people we are and how this effects our behaviour. The findings discussed in chapter 2 from behavior genetics reveal that the influence of our genes, whatever this influence turns out to be, accounts for no more that 50 percent of certain similarities within groups of individual adults; understanding the other 50 percent, and indeed the ways in which our genes influence our behavior, requires us to understand the ways in which we are affected by our environment, both the natural world and the world we have made for ourselves. In any case, we should not overestimate the explanatory power of genetic coding, our genes only codify within the context of fertilized eggs which in their turn rely upon their context, a healthy womb. Just as the perforations in a pianola roll cannot play a tune when taken out of the instrument, so too genes out of their bodily context count for nought. Unlike pianola rolls, our genes are subtly individual, we all sing the same tune in our own unique ways. Natural evolutionary theory, bolstered by genetic science, is admirably good at explaining how individual physical diversity arises—whereas, as we have seen in the preceding chapter, attempts by sociobiologists and evolutionary theorists to explain purported behavioral similarities are less convincing. In any case, when it comes to behavior, genes are only ever half the story. The other half is scripted by the environment the organism inhabits.

Notwithstanding their other myriad disagreements and spats, all evolutionary theorists recognize the significance of the environment for the understanding of how organisms grow and behave. For us humans, this environment is increasingly of our own making; it is the world of our culture, technology, customs, traditions, social institutions, and so on that we increasingly inhabit. Clearly, because our artificial home changes, and changes usually far more rapidly than the natural world, we need to explain its dynamics, how societal change occurs. The picture of societal change favored by the eighteenth-century Scottish

School and by other Enlightenment philosophers, the picture that was adopted and refined by nineteenth-century social theorists, traced a linear procession of historical stages, each one spawned by its predecessor which in its turn is eventually supplanted by a newly emerging stage. The identified motive for change, the characterization of the stages, the prospects for the future, all these differed but nevertheless theorists of wildly conflicting intellectual and political persuasions couched societal change in the same "supplantist" explanatory framework. National comparisons became expressed within this framework, other societies were judged more or less advanced along the developmental road, a road along which, by the time that social sciences were proposed, societies were thought to take evolutionary steps. This picture of historical stages, of stages supplanting each other, of evolutionary succession, is still painted today by many theorists and social commentators. Current theorists of "postmodernism" or "globalization" still routinely present society as having reached a definitively new stage of development that has purportedly supplanted an earlier era of "modernity." So, for example, in his first 1999 Reith lecture on "globalization" the director of the London School of Economics, advisor to Anthony Blair and prolific sociological theorist Professor Anthony Giddens ventured the following unfortunate judgement:

> Although this is a contentious point, I would say that, following the end of the cold war, nations no longer have enemies. Who are the enemies of Britain, or France, or Japan? Nations today face risks and dangers rather than enemies, a massive shift in their very nature.
>
> It isn't only in the nation that such comments can be made. Everywhere we look, we see institutions that appear the same as they used to be from the outside, and carry the same names, but inside have become quite different. We continue to talk of the nation, the family, work, tradition, nature, as if they were all the same as in the past. They are not. The outer shell remains, but inside all is different—and this is happening not only in the US, Britain, or France, but almost everywhere.[3]

Nine years on, following the attack upon the Twin Towers, then upon Iraq, now upon Lebanon, following the welter of "terrorist" outrages, Professor Giddens' characterization of contemporary nation states appears not merely "contentious" but, rather, profoundly wrong and foolish. All the hallmarks of what I am calling "supplantism" are stamped upon his paragraphs; a societal change, in this case a "global" societal change, is happening "everywhere we look," in all Western countries, in all areas of life, and this ubiquitous change is transformational, nothing will be the same ever again, "all is different." An older way of doing things, in this case "modernity," is being supplanted, dramatically, by "globalism."

Professor Gidden's predictions, albeit erroneous, were theoretically facilitated by supplantism but as events have starkly revealed, this is not how societal change occurs. Just as the salutary lesson of the First World War cruelly refuted Durkheim's sanguine predictions, the slaughter in Iraq reveals all too clearly that it is not the case that institutions, sentiments, and practices are simply replaced or overridden by brand new versions. What the conflict in Iraq reveals, as had been shown previously in the old Yugoslavia, is that religious sentiment, nationalism, communal hatred, and the like are not lost to history but instead remain dormant, quite capable of being reinvigorated if circumstances demand. We should not be surprised to meet again the dangers and problems our forerunners grappled with; regardless of the optimistic predictions of supplantists, religion, territorialism, torture techniques and other such less lovely features of our history are preserved, not lost. History carries forward both the sublime and the ghastly, each change adding to our repertoire, legacies often coexisting side by side. Supplantists, as I have written elsewhere,[4] are like the anguished pundits who worried, needlessly, that when television became a mass commodity it would vanquish conversation, replace wirelesses; they worried unnecessarily, we still chat and nowadays a record number of people listen to the radio. Television did not supersede the wireless, it lived side by side and its popularity is now waning along with its novelty. Similarly, nation-state citizenship did not preclude older ethnic and religious affiliations. Earlier versions, be they ethnic memberships or wirelesses, are preserved as alternatives that may be taken up again in the future.

The analogy with unwarranted anguish concerning the mass viewing of television is not, in practice, fully accurate because part of the appeal of supplantism seems to lie in its, unfounded, optimistic promise of a bright new dawn; the promise that the old world is being superseded by a wholly new order. Since the Enlightenment, this supplantist theory has been linked to a progressive picture of societal change with each superseding stage improving upon its predecessor, a progressivism reminiscent of pre-Darwinian evolutionism. But like the natural world, the social world does not change in a progressive fashion; changes incorporate and build upon the past like the vocabulary of languages, retaining older words, phrases, and spellings. Unlike the natural world, the artificial world does not evolve, simply because it is not the sort of thing that permits of evolution. Society cannot be said to evolve for the logic of Darwinian natural evolution demands that phenotypic features must be either preserved or lost depending upon natural selection: no loss, no evolution. Social theorists tend to use the word "evolution" loosely and promiscuously but properly speaking the explanatory logic of Darwinian evolution—the only current credible explanation—cannot be applied to societal change. Changes and innovations are these days routinely and increasingly preserved in what I am calling the "artificial world," the environment we've made our home. For convenience, we can distinguish three aspects of our artificial world; in no particular order, first, our technology, second our knowledge, third our social practices. In all three of these aspects we find that instead of pseudo-evolutionary supplantism, there is a process of accumulative change with the preservation of earlier changes.

This process is perhaps easiest to detect, and easiest to accept, in the world of technology for it would be truly astonishing if there were no accumulation in technology, if each time there was a new invention the inventor had been obliged to start literally from scratch. One of the key technologies affecting and shaping the artificial world has been the movable type, that is, the modern, printing press. More than any other technology, the press has allowed for the preservation and circulation of ideas, not just the nice ones like the formula for penicillin but also the instructions to build nuclear weaponry.

When the first East India Company ship docked at the bustling port of Surat in Gujarat in 1608, well over 200 million texts had already been printed in European countries, the printing press was to be found in all major European towns, and literacy was a standard requirement for the Company employees (known, appositely, as "writers").[5] By the mid-seventeenth century more than a million copies of the Bible and the New Testament had been sold in England and the level of literacy had reached some 30 percent. In contrast, throughout India the only presses in existence were one or two that had been imported by Portuguese and Dutch merchants or missionaries and there would be no Indian-owned press established until the nineteenth century. The effects of this printing technology upon Europeans are hard to overestimate. In addition to promoting literacy, the introduction of the press had profound effects in many ways. For example, as the historian Christopher Hill has shown,[6] the availability of the printed King James Bible, the edition held in Bunyan's pilgrim's hands, allowed for the first time ordinary Englishmen and women to read for themselves the Word of God, to interpret for themselves the lessons of the Scriptures, scrutiny that fed the schisms that appeared in the seventeenth-century Church. Printing in English, rather than in Latin, the language of both the Church and the social elite, elevated the vernacular and weakened clerical authority. Printed texts allowed for the first time uniform editions to be published, editions that could be uniformly corrected, identical versions rather than the idiosyncratic copies of scribes with their inevitable errors and idiosyncrasies. These impresses were not felt in India until after the Raj had been established, and arguably are still to be felt fully by many of the one billion contemporary Indians; literacy remains dismally low in India and deeply divided along caste, gender and religious lines, both Hindus and Muslims still retain the essentially oral character of their religious cultures, notably illustrated by the continuing respect given by Muslims to the rote learning and memorization of the Koran.

From English booksellers, in the seventeenth century only to be found in London and the major cities, and from itinerant chapmen who hawked their wares in the smaller English towns and villages, could now be bought at reasonable cost printed almanacs, children's alphabets, Classics, smut, journals, political tracts, and, at the end of the century, newspapers. Europeans could now regard themselves as citizens of national literatures, men of means and leisure like Montesquieu could learn of far away peoples and their customs by reading about them in their private libraries, a privilege that was soon to be issued to all with the opening of public libraries. The London Royal Society could publish the latest scientific research in the Society's journal. Knowledge itself was transformed as books existed independently of their authors whom they outlived as authorial authority, like all personalized authority, became undermined by the ever-ripe fruits of the press. Knowledge became democratized, authorities gave way to experts. And all this, this seminal societal change, was accomplished by an accumulation of very simple technologies. For as historians of printing[7] recognise and remark, Gutenberg's technical achievements were modest and could very easily have been made by many of his contemporaries. Gutenberg, about whom little is known, did not of course invent printing; books were already being printed from wood-blocks and engraved metal plates. What Gutenberg's innovations allowed for was the mass printing of editable books, books for which in the mid-fifteenth century there was a proven and lucrative demand. Most of the components he needed were already present: paper from China, where they had been printing from wood-blocks for a thousand years, was available; the wine press had been introduced into his native Rhineland by the Romans; metal-working skills were sufficient (Gutenberg himself had started out as a goldsmith). His only real contributions were the invention of an adjustable type-mould and the formula for the ink allowing an impression to be taken from a printing plate comprising the moulded metal characters, the slugs, held fast in a wooden forme. The adjustability of the mould overcame the problem of characters of different sizes, the letter I is narrower than W, and the slugs could, unlike wood-blocks, be reset and reused. These two small contributions, added to the already existing technologies and skills, were what permitted letterpress printing and the accompanying huge societal changes. All of these incremental steps were accumulative, not evolutionary. The earliest books were indistinguishable in appearance from scribal texts, their typefaces copied the beautiful scribal scripts. There was no loss of earlier technologies, no loss as new innovations came to predominate. Letterpress printing came to dominate but writing by hand did not end. There were no significant technological innovations in printing until, in the nineteenth century, presses became made of metal rather than wood and became powered by engines, as too did the paper mills. Letterpress printing, of the kind pioneered by Gutenberg eventually gave way to lithography and nowadays the old world of print with its skilled compositors and formes of hand-set metal type has been overtaken by rooms of soulless computers from whose keyboards typing is automatically transformed into perfectly justified printing plates. Lithography brought in its train substantial changes to the old masculine, highly skilled, strongly unionized trade that withered in the face of challenges from comparatively unskilled processes that could be done by cheaper unapprenticed typists, including women.[8] Once again, this is not an evolutionary change, we save fountain pens for signing our most important documents, some printing is still letterpress, wood-block technology isn't extinct. The language of the print trade retains the earlier inky feel, trade jargon and phrases resonate the past, an inky past itself built upon other older ways of doing things. So for example, compositors work in "galleys," when I served as a union shop steward in a print company my title was "Father of the Chapel."

The birth of the modern movable type printing press with its consequences for the artificial world is only one, albeit striking example of accumulative development, and only one example of the contrasting historical technological positions of Europeans and Indians. Equally significant, and equally the product of small incremental accumulative innovations, was the steam engine—the driving force behind the growth of modern industrial capitalism. It was steam engines that replaced the water mills that powered the first factory machinery, that vastly increased production, that were as we have seen in chapter 1, ignored by Adam Smith in favor of the productive power of the division of labor. A division of labor certainly does increase production, but nothing like as dramatically as powered machinery: for illustration, in the early nineteenth century the hand-presses printing the *Times* of London produced some 300 sheets per hour; when in April 1811 the *Times* adopted Friedrich Koenig's steam press output rose to 1,100 sheets per hour, and following the invention of the rotary press in 1848 hourly output was over 20,000 sheets. Similarly with papermaking; British national output rose from the figure of 11,000 tons in 1800, all handmade, to 100,000 tons in 1860, only 4,000 tons of which was still handmade.[9]

Gujarat lacked water mills as well as steam engines, engines that had eventually to be imported from England to power the Indian-owned cotton mills of Bombay in the late nineteenth century. The reason for the absence of Gujarati water mills is fairly obvious; there are no promising rivers in the region, and there has always been a plentiful supply of cheap labor power. Nor were there any local spurs to the development of steam engines comparable to those that encouraged eighteenth-century British engineers. Gujaratis did not face the problem of ever deeper mine shafts that had to be kept dry and ventilated, shafts dug to extract the coal needed to replace scarce charcoal. As with the press the invention of the first real working engine, Newcomen's engine of 1713 heralded momentous changes in the artificial world, but along with Gutenberg, what secured Newcomen's place in the history book was a small, ingenious little innovation that allowed his engine to continue running automatically. Each successive new model of the steam engine built upon an existing version, each model facilitating further applications including of course locomotives, whose impact upon those who witnessed the growth of the railways was nicely expressed by William Makepeace Thackeray: "We who have lived before railways were made belong to another world. It was only yesterday, but what a gulf between now and then! Then was the old world. [….] But your railroad starts the new era, and we of a certain age belong to the new time and the old one."[10]

There is an inexhaustible stock of ready examples that could be added to those of the printing press and the steam engine, examples of accumulative technological change that reshaped the artificial world. The effects of accumulative changes to the printing press and to steam engines are striking and obvious but the impact of other technologies may be obscured by their sheer familiarity. Photography, for instance, which had been key to the expansion of lithographic printing from the 1840s onward, also preserved the past and helped to preserve memories: we have become so accustomed to keeping our memories in photo-frames that we may not appreciate the dread our greatgrandparents knew only too well of losing precious memories like sand slipping through an egg-timer—a peril well illustrated by Sebastian Faulkes in his novel of the First World War where one of the British soldiers, Jack, struggles to remember the face of his son who died while he was serving in France and of whom he has no photographs, a struggle he will not win.[11]

Or consider a much older, familiar, technology that allowed our ancestors to weather the extremes of an Ice Age winter, the humble needle, an invention at least 30,000 years old:

> No one knows who first made this simplest of artefacts, a small tool that revolutionised humanity's ability to thrive in environments with extremely cold temperatures. Needle and thread made it possible for humans to handle the kinds of dramatic temperature shifts characteristic of northern latitudes, where icy winds can chill the skin in minutes or sharply warmer climatic shifts can endure for years. For tens of thousands of years, humans had relied on skin cloaks and crudely sewn clothes to survive Ice Age winters. The eyed needle allowed people to fashion garments that not only fitted the individual precisely but also combined fur from several animals, so that the user could benefit from the unique properties of each skin.[12]

Similarly, the introduction of artificial dyes in the second half of the nineteenth century, an invention that nowadays we take for granted, literally changed the color of our artificial world; whereas in the past objects were largely naturally colored, or colored with natural dyes such as the indigo imported at considerable effort from Sarkhej in Gujarat, nowadays the palette for our environment is overwhelmingly of artificial hues, the whole species is following Mr. Pooter's lead.

That technology changed so rapidly in Europe, but not in India, was partly a consequence of chance. As a well-trained sociologist, when I researched the history of the press in Gujarat I worked with the assumption that the reason Gujaratis had taken so long to adopt the press was for sociological reasons and I suggested a number of features of Gujarati religious culture that inhibited its adoption. I now think that I was only partly right in my analysis, the part I omitted was the role of chance. The reason that the press spread so rapidly throughout Europe was because once Gutenberg's model was up and running it could easily be copied. There was no great secret, no dark "printer's art," just a few simple technologies; the only "secret" was that it could be done, much the same as the delusory "secret" of nuclear weaponry that Truman futilely tried to hold in "sacred trust" for America when in fact the all too public detonations over Hiroshima and Nagasaki had demonstrated conclusively that these weapons were feasible, the revelation that spurred Russian physicists to have a nuclear test device ready for Uncle Joe in four short years (in 1949).

Why didn't Gujaratis, and other Indians, simply copy Gutenberg's press? All the skills, all the prerequisites such as paper and ink, were available in seventeenth-century Gujarat, and there was a clear market and demand for printed texts. A successful Gujarati Hindu businessman, Bhimjee Parekh, did, in the 1670s, set out to build a press and had made some progress as acknowledged in this letter written in January 1676 by a Company employee to the Company's London directors:

> Wee have seen some papers written in the Banian characters by the persons employed by Bhimjee which look very well and legible and shews the work is feasible; but the charge and tediousness of these people for want of better experience doth much discourage. If your Honours would please to send out a founder or Caster of letters at Bhimjee's charge, he would esteem it a great favour and honour, having already made good what we could reasonably demand of him for the printer's charge hitherto.[13]

An extremely wealthy businessman from a Hindu caste renowned for their commercial acumen, Bhimjee could well afford the £50 per annum demanded for the requested "caster of letters" annual wage but, as luck would have it, the English printer sent by the Company, one Mr. Hill, turned out not to be able to cast type and most likely an embezzler to boot. Although a significant setback, even without the help of a truly competent "caster of letters," with perseverance, Bhimjee's employees could in all probability have mastered the techniques needed to print the religious texts that Bhimjee had desired but Gujarat in the late seventeenth century had become a lawless, anarchic region, infested by Maratha raiders, fast degenerating as the last "Great Mughal's" regime collapsed. This was clearly not the time to pursue new ventures or to ride inessential hobbyhorses; as a reaction to the worsening local situation, the British decamped from their Surat Presidency to their newly acquired island of Bombay, nothing further was heard from Bhimjee about printing and there are no records of any other indigenous attempt to run a press in Gujarat for a century or so.

Bhimjee's ill luck appears circumstantial, perhaps if he or some other entrepreneur had tried ten or twenty years earlier then by the time the British began their rise to paramountcy there might well have been a thriving print sector in Gujarat, perhaps the introduction of printed texts would have promoted similar societal changes to those that Gutenberg's innovations had forged in Europe (changes the press began to effect in India when it was introduced in the nineteenth century). Bhimjee's ill luck reflects one variety of chance, circumstantial chance, a chance issuing from what is known as "contingency"—a philosophical term definable simply as "the way things are."[14] Thus, Bhimjee's circumstantial ill luck resulted from a chance misfortune, from the launching of his press venture in circumstances that were contingently unpropitious, the way things were in Gujarat in the 1670s. What's of importance in this example is the matter of timing, a universal feature as we shall see of all chance occurrences, a feature also identifiable for example when the East India Company was inaugurated at the start of the seventeenth century. As I remarked at the start of the first chapter, the Company's rationale came from their wish to import profitably goods and spices that were only found in far-off lands, the geographical reason for their monetary value and air of exoticism. That berries, nuts, plants, trees, etc. were unevenly found throughout the world was a consequence of the intrinsic evolutionary drive to diversity. At any one point in time different groups of people face differing natural environmental influences, imperatives, requirements, and problems. Unsurprisingly, their societies take different developmental paths, sometimes reaching the same position by different historical tracks as in the example of food production; some groups initiated settled agriculture, some copied their initiative, some never became farmers at all. The significance of farming goes well beyond food on the plate, Adam Smith along with others from the Scottish School believed it marked the third historical stage of societal development, superseding "agricultural nomads" who had earlier superseded the original "hunters." With the change to settled agriculture it was possible to produce more than was necessary for immediate consumption, food that could be stored up as provision against future shortages, some individuals could be liberated from food production so as to concentrate upon other jobs and in time could become craft specialists. Where on the planet this developmental step was taken depended partly on climatic variations, soil differences, plant and animal distribution; as the biogeographer and evolutionary biologist Jared Diamond notes:

> But most wild animal and plant species have proved unsuitable for domestication: food production has been based upon relatively few species of livestock and crops. It turns out that the number of wild candidate species for domestication varied greatly among the continents, because of differences in continental areas and also (in the case of big mammals) in Late Pleistocene extinctions. These extinctions were much more severe in Australia and the Americas than in Eurasia or Africa. As a result, Africa ended up biologically somewhat less well endowed than the much larger Eurasia, the Americas still less so, and Australia even less so…[15]

According to Diamond, these natural variations of opportunities and challenges led different groups along diverse developmental paths and when these groups met some were better placed to conquer, exploit, and subjugate than others. It is Diamond's contention that these "historical inequalities have cast long shadows on the modern world" and that "History followed different courses for different peoples because of differences among people's environments, not because of biological differences among peoples themselves."[16] Parts of Diamond's thesis are controversial, some parts I regard as mistaken, but in his attempt to revitalize an approach to comparative societal development, an approach that had fallen out of favor with historians, Diamond presents compelling, intriguing evidence, the sort of detailed evidence missing from Montesquieu's exploitation of this approach, evidence far more plausible than Montesquieu's microscopic examination of sheep's tongues and his vague "theory of the climates." Moreover, Diamond's argument opposes biological determinism, opposition strengthened by the arguments of Brian Fagan[17] whose examination of the effects of climatic changes upon human history testifies to chance environmental changes and to the distribution of plant species, herdable species including boar, wild goats and sheep and the useful cereal crops grown in the Fertile Crescent, the site of our earliest cultivation, currently a site of American military occupation. How exactly comparative history plays out is subject to chance factors; India's natural advantages over Europe appeared great, there was little that Indians needed or wanted from Europe but plenty that Europeans desired from Indians. What might have appeared as a natural blessing, the natural wealth of the subcontinent, proved a curse as wave after wave of invaders ransacked, exploited, and conquered. English traders, as I remarked in the first chapter, were unable to sell much of their country's produce to Indians and were obliged instead to purchase what they wanted with hard currency that demanded their ships, laden with bullion, were fortified and the Company employees armed. Having to sail thousands of miles on each round trip, having to carry arms, brought unforeseen advantages to the English, advantages that they could capitalize upon when circumstances changed in the region.

The maritime prowess displayed early on by the British when attacked off the Gujarati coast by their rivals, the Portuguese, had impressed the Mughal rulers of Gujarat: witnessed by the Mughal general Sardar Khan, British crews of the Company's tenth voyage defeated a far larger squadron of Portuguese galleons, revealing to the Mughals that the Portuguese were not invincible at sea and suggesting that the English could be useful in breaking up the Portuguese extortion racket, their system of demanding with menaces payment from trading ships, including ships commissioned by Mughal nobility, and also ships carrying Muslims on the hajj pilgrimage to Mecca.[18] This naval victory raised the standing of the English, eased trade and helped define their relationship to the wholly terrestrial Mughal rulers. Throughout the seventeenth century, '... the English relied on the latent threat of their power at sea to maintain their position in India, while at the same time the Mughals did their best to limit the territorial powers of the Company."[19] The Mughals' own interests in trade and commerce drew them in to the Europeans' disputes, to the eventual advantage of the English and to the detriment of the Portuguese. The English came to act as protectors for Mughal shipping and they were involved with Gujarati trade to the Red Sea ports. Nonetheless for the English, trade in Gujarat was never easy or smooth and more secure alternatives to Surat were continually reviewed. By the second half of the seventeenth century the general currents of stability and prosperity that were shored up with Mughal military rule became threatened by raids upon Gujarat from Maratha chieftains. Surat, at that time the most important port under Mughal rule,[20] was plundered by Maratha raiders in 1664 and besieged for forty days; only the Mughal governor's castle and the Company Presidency resisted. Further raids were visited on the port in 1666, 1670, 1672, and 1700. Other Gujarati cities suffered a similar fate disrupting commerce and everyday life (including hampering Bhimjee's efforts to establish a printing press). The British moved their Presidency down coast to the island of Bombay, for which they paid Charles II a nominal rent, and by 1688 Bombay had grown to become a sizeable, well-fortified Presidency, swelled with members of Gujarati business communities and castes lured to the island by the prospect of greater security.

With the death of the last Great Mughal, Aurangzeb, in 1717 the region lacked a paramount power. Local potentates, chieftains, princes, tried to establish or reestablish fiefdoms. The obvious candidate for paramountcy was the Marathas, the raiders and plunderers who hailed down coast from the Deccan and Western Ghat districts of India. By the early eighteenth century the Marathas comprised a confederacy under the authority of the Peshwa. Their capital and government court were at Pune where in principle they paid homage to the Raja of Satara; in practice, after 1712, the Raja had become a nominal figurehead and the Peshwa (originally a second minister), commanded the government and the Confederacy. During the late seventeenth and the first half of the eighteenth centuries the Marathas challenged the Mughal empire, a role that has earned them an honoured place in modern Hinduistic Indian national history books for their challenge had a religious as well as pecuniary bent: this was a challenge mounted by Hindus against Muslim rulers. The majority of the Marathas hailed from lowly castes but their leaders were Brahmins, giving them, as the historian Edward Thompson observes, "exceptional power and influence" over their troops and followers.[21] By dint of their military prowess, especially their horsemanship, in the opening decades of the eighteenth century they had risen to prominence in Gujarat. By 1723 the Marathas were demanding regular tribute and in 1743 the Gaekwad Pilajee[22] had, having defeated the Imperial forces, established himself in Baroda, the city that was to remain the family seat of this branch of the Maratha Confederacy. In 1754 the mint at Ahmadabad, the chief inland Gujarati city and modern-day de facto capital, ceased to issue Mughal currency and now began to mint coinage with the image of Ganesh, the elephant-headed Hindu deity, on their faces. Two years later Ahmadabad itself, the last Mughal stronghold in the region, surrendered to the Marathas after a lengthy siege. The Marathas were not, however, in the mould of the fading Mughal Empire or the future British Raj. The Marathas' prime interest in Gujarat was in extracting wealth, not in the creation of a colony or in the forging of alliances with Gujaratis to further their partisan political struggles in Pune. Wealth was extracted by two chief devices: first, by simple plunder; second, by demanding *chauth* or *deshmukh* (one-fourth and one-tenth tribute on revenue, respectively). In this respect, the Marathas were simply continuing the general system of revenue collection that had been practised by the Mughals. In areas that they did not control directly, a large portion of the province, revenue was collected by *mulakgiri*, which amounted to little more than crude extortion. An armed force would be sent at regular intervals to threaten local chieftains who, if they were unable to resist, had to pay up. This crude, but apparently effective, method of revenue collection was in line with the Marathas' usual modus operandi.[23]

In the midst of the instability and insecurity which accompanied the decline of the Mughal Empire, traders and merchants found themselves having to choose between rival protectors, between the traditional order and the Europeans. In 1758, the Surati merchants, attracted by the prospect of inalienable property rights, menaced by growing expropriation from local elites,[24] chose the latter in preference to the traditional Nawab and, having opted for the English rather than the Dutch, "...offered to finance the take-over by the British of the Surat citadel. After considerable hesitation, the British made the requested move and, in March 1759, the citadel fell into their hands."[25] Under the joint governorship of the Nawab and the newly appointed English chief, fortified with Company troops, the walled citadel survived as an oasis of commercial security in the midst of turmoil and conflict. Surat prospered, however, as a satellite of Bombay which, as Michelgugiemo Torri notes, marked a reversal of the seventeenth-century relationship between the two centers.[26] During the latter half of the eighteenth century the fortunes of the Marathas soured as internecine struggles weakened and eroded their Confederacy, when they suffered a serious defeat at the hands of the Mughal army at Panipat and as the British by dubious diplomacy and by military means exploited their weakness. With the decline of the Maratha Confederacy the British were, by the late eighteenth century, a rising force in the region who faced few competitors for paramountcy. In 1800 the first British resident, Major Walker, took up residency in Baroda, the Gujarati base of the Maratha Gaekwad who had by then thrown in his lot with the British and was now paying the cost in terms of subordination to his new white masters, a price that in the next century would include British interference in appointing his successors.[27] Finally in 1817, under the terms of the Treaty of Pune, the Peshwa relinquished all his rights over Gujarat and in the same year the subordination of the Gaekwad to the British was formalized under the "Definite" Treaty. The last real obstacle to British paramountcy in the region, the Maratha Confederacy, became a thing of the past and the Peshwa finished his days living on a pension from the British.

The rise by the British, from being insignificant traders to paramountcy, was propelled by various motives, and took different paths in the three British

Presidencies (Bombay, Madras, and Calcutta). Company directors forbade military adventurism, were opposed to involvement in Indian politicking, and forbade missionary work, favouring a steady, unspectacular return on their investments. Until the opening of the Suez Canal and the laying of telegraph lines, communication between the East India Company's London Board of Directors and their employees was slow, letters were carried on the Company's ships and replies could sometimes take years to arrive. Day-to-day decision-making was in the hands of the three Presidencies' executives and the three Presidencies experienced diverse local conditions, different local rulers, faced different commercial competitors. The trajectory to paramountcy in western India, the trajectory followed by the Bombay Presidency, was in the early stages discrete from those issuing out of Madras and Calcutta; Clive's military adventurism did not impinge upon the take-over of Surat and the British rise to power in Gujarat only later became interwoven with the threads from the other two Presidencies, threads that were woven together as the British arose as a national conquering force. In this complex stew of motives, characters, and circumstances, chance played a part. The technological discrepancies evident betwixt England and Gujarat and their concomitant influences, the English adoption of the printing press, the development of the steam engine, the natural discrepancies, the siting of spices, plants such as indigo and opium poppies, were all as we have seen products of chance, of contingent or coincidental factors. The East India Company's military strengths, the unsought for opportunity this gave the English when the Mughal Empire's power waned in Gujarat and they were invited to oversee security in Surat, were similarly chance occurrences.

Although chance did not cause the English to start down the road to paramountcy that led to the Raj, it did play a part, or more accurately various parts, facilitating, prompting, steering the process. Chance helped in the accumulation of the societal changes that shaped both India and Britain, and in part the British had been plain lucky, not the sort of judgment that appealed to either Imperialistic historians, Indian opponents of the Raj or to European social scientists. Rather than acknowledge the hand dealt by chance, their preference was in identifying mysterious, hidden national factors such as the Britishers' superior culture, religion, or national character, or their inherent rationality; or from the other side, the complicity of Indians in permitting their country to be overrun by a disreputable band of foreign traders. The hidden danger of this rejection of chance in favor of other, purportedly more profound, mysterious national causes lies in the attribution of blame and praise; whole nations, whole cultures, become responsible for chance-promoted outcomes; smug British rulers quaffing port served by their Indian servants could turn a blind eye to the brute military exploitation that shadowed the Raj, secure in the awareness of their god-given national superiority. As the estimable author William Trevor has written in a passage describing an unlucky fictional child's reflections upon the chance events that had decisively shaped her sad life, inward recollections she makes to herself when she is sitting with nuns who have paid a visit to console her:

> She might say that chance was in charge again when she noticed the old-fashioned bicycle propped up against the sea-wall, when she looked and saw a figure standing still. It was chance that she was passing them, as it was when her father looked down and saw what the O'Reilly's dog had tired of burying in the shingle.
> But the nuns do not believe in chance. Mystery is their thing. *Take the forest from its mystery and there is standing timber. Take from the sea its mystery and there is salted water.*[28]

As they do with people's characters, good novelists like Trevor have a surer understanding of chance than social theorists, nuns, and neo-Darwinists such as Judith Harris whom as we saw in the last chapter, also prefers mysteries over chance.

There are many reasons why chance can be hard to accept, chance leading either to fortunate or miserable outcomes. Good luck may be welcome but the prospect of chance taking charge seems to trivialize history and belittle biographies, appealing to mysterious forces restores some sense of reason and purpose. In its way, the appeal to such mysterious forces is related to faith in a divine Designer of the world; a faith in a God who designed, planned and oversees the universe, the picture of God favoured by eighteenth-century deists, the picture that was so shockingly challenged by Darwinian evolutionary theory. There seems to be a widespread desire to imbue chance events with extra significance, as signifying a higher intelligence, a divine purpose, a desire illustrated by the epiphany of Yusuf Islam, the pop singer formerly known as Cat Stevens:

> "I went swimming in the ocean" he says. "Then I tried to get back to shore but the current was pulling me out to sea. I had no strength left. I could see my manager on the beach. I couldn't even wave, I was so tired. I said: 'God, if you save me I'll work for you.' At that moment this wave came—just a gentle wave—but suddenly I was swimming back with the energy that I needed."
> Some might call that coincidence.
> "Some might. But I don't believe that the earth and the universe are here by coincidence. When I got back to shore, I was aware that I had made a commitment."[29]

Most social theorists share Cat Stevens' belief that "the earth and the universe," or at least the social aspect of the world they study, is not "here by coincidence." To the secular social theorist chance appears as an affront to determinism, to the belief that the artificial world is fully determined, that everything which happens is the predictable effect of some cause and open to naturalistic explanation, the belief that became an article of faith for Enlightenment philosophers and which underpinned modern social science disciplines. This anxiety is largely groundless for chance and determinism do, indeed must, coexist. If there were no determinism then there would be no such thing as chance, chance would be unrecognizable. As Aristotle had noted, only a rational being can be lucky, and as he also forcibly argued, chance is not something mysterious or supernatural. Chance events are just as much the outcome of causes as are any other occurrence and chance, for Aristotle, is itself a cause of things happening. In his illustrative example:

> Luck and the automatic [spontaneity] are reckoned as causes, and we say that many things are and come to be on account of them. We must see, then, in what way luck and the automatic fit into our causes, whether luck and the automatic are the same or different, and in general what they are.
>
> Some people wonder even whether there are any such things or not. They say that nothing comes to be as an outcome of luck, but that there is a definite cause of everything which we say comes to be as an automatic outcome or as an outcome of luck. Thus when we say that a man as the outcome of luck comes into the market-place, and found there someone he wished but did not expect to find, they claim that the cause was wishing to go and attend the market. And similarly with other things which are said to be the outcome of luck: it is always possible to find some cause for them other than luck; since if there were such a thing as luck, it would seem to be really very absurd, and one might wonder why it is that none of the sages of the past who discussed the causes connected with coming to be and passing away gave any distinct account of luck; but is seems that they too thought that nothing is the outcome of luck.[30]

Unlike the "sages of the past," Aristotle had realised that accepting chance did not lead to absurdity and that chance could easily be accommodated within a picture of the world in which everything has a causal precedent; it was all a matter of timing, a point perhaps more readily illustrated by the nineteenth-century Frenchman Mssr. Cournot. In a rare examination of chance by a sociologist, Professor Boudon writes:

> Cournot, of course, illustrated the idea by means of a very simple example, such as that of a falling slate stunning a passer-by. The fall of the slate was certainly predetermined. It was not properly fastened on the roof and was at the mercy of the slightest gust of wind. The fact that the passer-by was walking just below the roof was also the result of an easily traceable causality. He was going about his business that day as on any other day and was thus bound to pass the roof in question. So we are dealing here with two causal series. The fact that they converge, however, is according to Cournot, not causally determined, since there was nothing to make the slate fall just as the man was passing.[31]

In both these illustrative examples, Aristotle's man visiting the market and Cournot's man going about his everyday business, chance is a matter of timing; the first unexpectedly meets someone, the second is stunned by a falling slate, because unrelated causal sequences *coincide* (in Aristotle's terminology, "concur"). There is nothing mysterious about the causal sequences themselves, nothing that places them outwith ordinary explanation, nothing that is undetermined about them.[32]

Chance, argues Professor Boudon, is a particular "… structure which is characteristic of certain sets of causal chains as perceived by an observer."[33] But as I have argued,[34] the perceptions of an "observer" are irrelevant, and superfluous, because in the case of Cournot's example of the stunned passer-by we could substitute a piece of paper blown by the same gust of wind that dislodged the slate and a chance event—now the falling slate spears the piece of paper—still occurs. Alternatively, in Aristotle's example why not substitute a snail that is crushed underfoot for the man in the marketplace? Coincidences occur regardless of perception, it is a real feature of the world and as Aristotle rightly insisted, a quite legitimate candidate for explaining how and why things happen. Nor am I happy with Boudon's claim that the fall of the slate was "predetermined": rather, the sloppy tiler's workmanship had left a *predisposition*, an inherent weakness that was exposed when the wind gusted. Predispositions and predeterminations are not identical; the former requires to be activated by further causes in order to be realized and they are not predestined to occur (without that chance gust of wind the predisposition counts for nought). Returning to the example of the British rise to paramountcy in Gujarat, we can recast the sequences that led to the British assuming protection of Surat within a Cournot mould. That the English traders were armed, held in high esteem for their military prowess, is quite explicable in terms of the Company's business history, the need to carry and protect bullion, the prestige and political advantages that military strength conferred. Similarly, the parlous state of Surat is equally explicable in the light of the worsening circumstances in Gujarat attendant upon the disintegration of Mughal rule. That the British were invited to oversee Surat's protection was facilitated by the coincidence of the British military disposition being available when the Surati traders felt the insecurity attendant upon the collapse of the traditional order. Coincidence, we might say, occurs when two or more causal sequences collide, when preexisting dispositions are realised. Troubles arise when nuns, theorists and related kinfolk postulate some extra mysterious force, some fictitious cause, or God, in order to avoid accepting chance.

Social theorists have come up with two main strategies for neutering chance; in Boudon's phrase "a very unwelcome guest," a conceptual guest denied a place at the theorists' high table. These strategies of denial are first, the notion of "unintended consequences of action," second, probability. The first strategy used to ostracize the very unwelcome guest, unintended consequences of action, has a quite proper place in theory, but not when it is used strategically as a veil to hide sheer luck. Whilst it is clearly worth bearing in mind that intended actions can have unintended, unforeseen, or unwanted consequences, some of these consequences are chanceful and their chance character has nothing to do with intention except in the sense that they were not intended outcomes. Whereas all cases of (human) chance occurrences are unintended, because intention demands some foreknowledge of the future, not all cases of unintentionality equate with chance. Likewise, not all chance occurrences can be dealt with by the modern theorists' second strategy for shunning the very unwelcome guest, by subsuming them to probabilistic analysis for as A.J. Ayer had noted, "The word 'chance' is commonly used in several different senses. [....] In some of these senses, although not in all, 'chance' is a synonym for 'probability.'"[35] In order for probability to be judged, there must be prior knowledge of the possible number of outcomes and it must be possible to replicate the event: thus, in the ever-popular example, when I toss a two-sided coin I cannot know whether it will fall to heads or tails, but I can judge that if I were to toss that coin many times, or toss many such coins simultaneously, then in all probability they would show roughly half heads, half tails. Probability cannot be applied to one-off occurrences—such as the examples I've drawn from the history of the British in India—and not can it be applied to events or things that are not identical, or are too dissimilar. I'd like to emphasise that second, banal, criterion demanded of probabilistic subjects, the need for what is being probabilistically analysed to be sufficiently similar: if we were tossing dice with varying numbers of faces, of subtly different shapes, weights, materials etc., then we could not judge the probability of throwing a six. Probability is useful for it gives us analytical purchase on sets of otherwise wholly chanceful individual phenomena (tossing that coin), it is part of our ordinary thinking, and it has helped greatly with social scientific analysis,[36] but it should not mask the reality of chance occurrences that do not fall within its analytical orbit.

Different forms of chance need carefully to be distinguished, nonetheless some varieties of chance may be considered as members of the same family.[37] Coincidences, the first of the two types I have distinguished (the other type being "contingencies"), can I think be seen to encompass serendipity, the happy knack of making fortuitous discoveries. Discoveries are of course integral to all sciences and also, as inventions, instrumental in advancing technology. All new scientific discoveries seem to be purely chance findings but a moment's reflection suggests a distinction between genuine accidental discoveries and those discoveries that are made in the course of a scientific quest for some solution or other to a problem or puzzle. This distinction is nicely made by Professor Royston Roberts, a distinction he draws between two types of serendipity:

> I have coined the term *pseudoserendipity* to describe accidental discoveries of ways to achieve an end sought for, in contrast to the (true) *serendipity*, which describes accidental discoveries of things not sought for.
>
> For example, Charles Goodyear discovered the vulcanisation process for rubber when he accidentally dropped a piece of rubber mixed with sulphur onto a hot stove. For many years Goodyear has been obsessed with finding a way to make rubber useful. Because it was an accident that led to the successful process so diligently sought for, I call this a pseudoserendipitous discovery. In contrast, George deMestral had no intention of inventing a fastener (Velcro) when he looked to see why some burs stuck so tightly to his clothing.[38]

As a working distinction Roberts' two types of serendipity does service and it highlights some common feature of true coincidental chance, of true serendipity: accidental discoveries occur, as the etymology of "accident" reveals,[39] when something unexpected—for example, the accidental ingestion of lysergic acid diethylamide (LSD) by Dr. Sidney Cohen—"befalls," when it occurs without expectation or intent. The first commercially produced artificial dye, the color we've come to call by its French name of "mauve," was a truly serendipitous discovery made by the young William Perkin whilst he was trying to synthesize quinine. Perkin abandoned academic research and went on to build a factory and business, producing for the first time cheap synthetic dyes. Without these artificial dyes, chromosomes, as their name implies, would have been undistinguished. The Sutton-Boveri Theory depended upon an accumulation of technologies, an accumulation of improvements to instruments such as microscopes, an accumulation colored by at least one serendipitous discovery. Our artificial world would have remained colored by nature, Sarkeji processors would have supplied jeans manufacturers with their indigo dye.

Similarly, chance may aid and abet social research, although the researchers routinely fail to acknowledge or analytically recognize its influences. Bucking the usual disciplinary reluctance to acknowledge that social researchers are often licked by luck, Gary Fine and James Deegan examined the ways in which researchers carrying out qualitative, ethnographic, anthropological field-work are vulnerable to chance, for instance a serendipitous alliance with someone who facilitates entry into a social network, someone who grows to become a "key informant":

> Who one knows is, within bounds, a matter of chance. A rich corpus of contemporary field research has addressed relational and personal processes in fieldwork. While there are categories of individuals with whom one is relatively likely to establish relations, our specific contacts cannot be predicted in advance. One's true love was selected from a pool of eligibles, most of whom one never gets to compare. Ethnography is preeminently a methodology that depends on relationships. The relationship between the researcher and the subject of the research is less significant in experimental, survey or historical research, while little could be more central in ethnographic research.
>
> The direction of a course of analysis and the research questions asked can be influenced by the alliances a researcher makes in the early stages of a project. Central to Whyte's study was his friendly partnership with Doc and his boys. Doc grasped his role as a sponsor and gatekeeper who facilitated Whyte's rapport with other community members. Whyte's alliance with Doc led to others in the community who were largely ignored as well as to those who were disliked in the community. Ultimately, this friendship with Doc led to a greater understanding of community patterns that might have remained opaque, and we recognise such alliances by enshrining the concept of "key informant." But how did this "key informant" relationship develop? In most cases, it did not develop through a conscious selection by the observer. This image may be cynically romantic (as in narratives of strategically manipulating one's

future spouse to fall in love), but the reality often seems a good deal messier—based on happenstance, luck, or mistaken identity.[40]

That chance meetings, alliances, friendships, quarrels, missed appointments, and the like steer the course of qualitative social research, and flavor the findings of such studies, should surprise only the truly naïve. But why exactly chance can play these roles in social research, why we "hit it off" with some people rather than others, and why we "fall" in love, are questions that deserve to be answered. Before attempting to give an answer, I think it may be helpful just to summarize the chief points I have made in this chapter concerning chance's roles in the processes of societal change, in facilitating technological developments, and in aiding the growth of knowledge.

Contrary to Edward Wilson and most other social theorists, I have contended that the artificial world cannot evolve and that rather than the "supplantist" picture of societal change promoted by the eighteenth-century Scottish School, lasting societal change is actually accumulative, the accumulation of usually small, incremental steps. Because these changes are often small and incremental they resemble the sort of generational changes made by the natural selection of phenotypic features, and this delusory resemblance is strengthened by the disproportionately large effects small changes may achieve in the artificial world: just as small physical changes may make the difference between an animal's life or death, so too small technological steps such as those made by Gutenberg can yield enormous societal consequences. Further, accumulative changes to the artificial world appear to be retained, preserved, if they lead to 'improvement' and this aspect of artificial change may feed the belief in an overseeing blueprint, drawn either by nature or god, which ensures historical progress. All three of these resemblances between Darwinian, and pre-Darwinian progressive natural evolution and change in the artificial world, are delusory—there is no mechanism of natural selection in operation, no automatic loss of unselected technologies or knowledge, no automatic drive toward improvement. Earlier versions of technology and knowledge are routinely preserved, not lost. What accumulative change does bring about is a growth of alternatives from which selections may be made and it is this widening of alternatives that yields the *potential* for improvement. Accumulation enriches the world inherited by our children, but that doesn't imply that they will necessarily select the better alternative, nor that later versions are inherently superior, inherently "improved." For illustration, the page you are reading is clearly printed, not inky or smudged, the typeface is regular, each letter distinct, each line properly justified, and the text centred on the page, all thanks to computerised printing technology that has helped, alongside earlier accumulative developments in print, in the production of affordable books. If, instead, this book you are reading had been hand copied by a scribe then mistakes in copying would have occurred, bits might be difficult to read, and you may well not have been able to afford to buy it in the first place. But, which book would you rather read, or own? Accumulation doesn't simply equal linear progress and as I have argued in this chapter how accumulation comes about, and how change occurs, is vulnerable to chance, either coincidence or contingency. The implications of these arguments are wide, sometimes profound (as in the case of the Gujarati episode in the processes leading to the British Raj in India), but before considering these implications, in the next chapter, we need first to examine the tunes to which chance dances in the final, third aspect of what I am calling the artificial world, the world of our social practices. For it is this aspect to the artificial world, the accumulated social aspects, that regulate the inheritance of knowledge and technology, that steers societal change.

Notes

1. P. H. Silverman, 2004, "Rethinking Genetic Determinism." *Scientist,* vol. 18 (10) (published online at www.the-scientist.com).
2. Ibid.
3. A. Giddens, 1999 *Runaway World* [BBC Reith Lectures], Lecture One, p.6 (published online at: http://news.bbc.co.uk/hi/english/static/events/reith_99/week1/week1.htm).
4. J. Mattausch, 2003, "Chance and Societal Change." *Sociological Review,* vol. 51, pp. 505-527, [p. 518].
5. The following discussion of the printing press in Gujarat is drawn from my article, J. Mattausch, 1996, "'A Penury Of Bookes': The Printing Press and Social Change in an Indian setting." *South Asia* [NS], vol. X1X, pp. 59-83.
6. C. Hill, 1993, *The English Bible and the Seventeenth Century.* London: Allen Lane.
7. The fascinating story of the printing press is well told by both S. Steinberg, 1955, *Five Hundred Years of Printing,* Harmondsworth: Pelican and E. Eisenstein, 1993, *The Printing Press in Early Modern Europe,* Cambridge: Cambridge University Press.
8. Cynthia Cockburn has examined the gendered politics accompanying the introduction of technological innovations to the print process in her book, 1991 (Revised edition) *Brothers: Male Dominance and Technological Change,* London: Pluto Press.
9. Steinberg, *Five Hundred Years of Printing*, pp. 191, 192.
10. Quoted in K. Sullivan, 1997, *Steam Trains.* London: Brockhampton Press, p. 11.
11. S. Faulkes, 1994, *Birdsong.* London: Verso.
12. B. Fagan, 2004, *The Long Summer: How Climate Changed Civilization.* New York: Basic Books, p. 27.
13. I quote this Company letter in Mattausch, "A Penury of Bookes," p. 67.
14. Something is contingently true without there being any necessity it should be; so for example, it is contingently true that there are 425 characters in this footnote, unlike the truth of the statement that $1 + 1 + 1 = 3$ which is necessarily true by definition, by the definition of the number 3. If I were to deny that 3 is the sum of three 1s then I would contradict myself, whereas if I deny there are 98 words in this footnote I may be wrong, I might have miscounted, but I'm not making a self-contradictory statement.

15. J. Diamond, 1997, *Guns, Germs and Steel: A Short History of Everybody for the Last 13,000 Years.* London: Vintage, p. 406.
16. Ibid., p. 25.
17. Fagan, *The Long Summer*, p. 93.
18. This discussion of the British rise to paramountcy is taken from J. Mattausch, 1993, *The Gujaratis and the British: A Social and Historical Survey with Special Reference to the Gujarati Tradition of 'Arranging' Marriages* Centre for Ethnic Minority Studies, Royal Holloway College, Occasional Papers No.1, pp. 6-12.
19. I. Bruce-Watson, 1976, "The Establishment of English Commerce in North-western India in the Seventeenth Century." *Indian Economic and Social History Review,* vol. 13, pp. 375-391, [p. 384].
20. Surat was not in fact a true port, it lies some eight miles upstream of the natural harbor then known as Swally Hole. Local "country" boats carried the cargoes up the River Tapi to Surat.
21. E. Thompson, 1978, *The Making of the Indian Princes.* London: Curzon Press, ch..2.
22. "Gaekwad" was an honorific title.
23. P. Mason, 1986, *A Matter of Honour: An Account of the Indian Army, Its Officers and Men* London: Macmillan, p. 54.
24. I. Bruce-Watson, 1978, "Between the Devil and the Deep Blue Sea: Commercial Alternatives in India, 1750-1760" *South Asia* [NS], vol. 1, pp. 54-64, [p. 64].
25. M. Torri, 1982, "In the Deep Blue Sea: Surat and Its Merchant Class during the Dyarchic Period (1759-1800)." *Indian Economic and Social History Review* [NS] Vol.19, pp267-299, [p. 268].
26. Ibid., p. 292.
27. M. Kamerkar, 1980, *British Paramountcy: British-Baroda Relations, 1818-1848.* Bombay: Popular Prakashan.
28. W. Trevor, 2002, *The Story of Lucy Gault.* London: Penguin, p. 225 [italics in original].
29. R. Chalmers, 2003, "Back on the Peace Train" *Independent On Sunday,* 12 October, p. 12.
30. Aristotle [trns.W. Charlton], 1992, *Physics, Books 1 & 11.* Oxford: Oxford University Press bk. 11, ch. 4 [pp. 31-32]. Aristotle also explicitly accepted chance as a causal factor when philosophizing about ethics, for example, 1974, *Ethics* Harmondsworth: Penguin, bk. 3, ch. 3.
31. R. Boudon, 1986, *Theories of Social Change: A Critical Appraisal.* London: Polity Press, p. 178. In his "appraisal" Boudon argues that chance must not be ignored by social theorists but that Cournot's simple illustrative examples of his eponymous Effect suggests that he had not refined sufficiently the concept.
32. In a rare examination of chance by sociologists, Jerome Manis and Bernard Meltzer, in their otherwise engaging article, start from the postulate that "True chance contravenes determinism, a fundamental postulate of science." They miss, I think, the distinction I make between each component sequence being fully, causally, determined yet coinciding with other sequences through chance, and the all-embracing notion that all events are predetermined. See J. G. Manis and B.N. Meltzer 1994 "Chance in Human Affairs." *Sociological Theory,* vol. 12, pp. 45-56; J. L. Martin, 1995, "Chance and Causality: A Comment on Manis and Meltzer." *Sociological Theory,* vol. 13, pp. 197-202.
33. Ibid., p. 179.
34. Mattausch, "Chance and Societal Change," p. 521.
35. A. J. Ayer, 1965, "Chance." *Scientific American,* vol. 213, pp. 44-54, [p. 44].

36. The impact of probability and its amalgamation into the sciences is exhaustively examined in G. Gigerenzer et al., 1997, *The Empire of Chance.* Cambridge: Cambridge University Press.

37. It is partly because I think that chance occurrences can and should be distinguished by their types that I part company with Roger Sibeon who, in his agreeable advocacy of "anti-reductionist" sociology plumps for Mike Smith's undifferentiated umbrella definition of chance as "social happenings." Moreover, although I too shall be arguing in this book that neither one-off chance events, nor people's characters, can be considered by a logic of reductionism, my understanding of these subjects and the roles they play in social life is incompatible with what I understand of Sibeon's theorizing over "agency" and "structure." See R. Sibeon, 1999, "Agency, Structure and Social Chance as Cross-Disciplinary Concepts." *Politics.* vol. 19, pp. 139-144; R. Sibeon, 1999, "Anti-Reductionist Sociology." *Sociology,* vol. 33, pp. 317-334.

38. R. M. Roberts, 1989, *Serendipity: Accidental Discoveries in Science*, New York: John Wiley & Sons, p. x.

39. I owe this etymological observation to John Austin, 1961, "A Plea for Excuses," *Philosophical Papers.* Oxford: Clarendon Press.

40. G. Fine and J. Deegan, 1996, "Three Principles of Serendip: Insight, Chance, and Discovery in Qualitative Research." *Qualitative Studies in Education,* vol. 9, pp. 91-101 [p. 97, citations in the original have been omitted]. Fine's and Deegan's definition of serendipity—chance with insight—is close to Roberts' notion of "pseudoserendipity." The study they refer to, Whyte's *Street Corner Society*, is a well-known piece of social research often cited as an exemplar of good ethnography.

4

A House for Mr. Mandela?

In the last chapter I reasoned that rather than subject to evolutionary patterns of selection and loss, developments and innovations in technology and knowledge are routinely preserved, that there is a strengthening trend toward preservation, and so the history of these two aspects to what I am calling the "artificial world" is more rightly seen as accumulative. In this process of accumulative development, I argued, chance has and can play a role, sometimes a starring role, sometimes just a walk-on part. The script for chance's role is written either as coincidence or as contingency. If this is true, then some interesting implications emerge. First off, this history cannot simply be judged either progressive or degenerate; accumulative change is both *potentially* progressive as well as *potentially* decadent. Accumulative change offers us a growing stock of alternatives, a greater cultural wealth, but it does not hold up the prospect of earlier evils becoming extinct. So for example, the catalogue for the technology of warfare is vastly greater than it was just a century earlier, if desired we can now arm ourselves with both blunderbusses and vials of botulism or, we might choose to decommission our nuclear weaponry, but we cannot eradicate the knowledge of how to build the Bomb. We are permitted increasing progress by accumulative change but whether such progress is realized depends neither upon our technology nor our knowledge per se but in the use we make of them. This brings us to the third aspect of our artificial world, the social aspect, our customs and practices, our cultures, our societies, the political world we have built for ourselves. In this social aspect of the artificial world chance, and here at last character, play a tune to which technology and knowledge must dance because chance and character influence the social mechanisms that pattern the distribution and the inheritance of technology and knowledge—who gets what, who inherits it, what we may know. Identifying the roles of chance and character requires the identification of the social mechanisms of inheritance and property, how for example it's arranged for millions of people living particularly in sub-Saharan Africa and in India afflicted with HIV or AIDS to be denied medicines available in the West. This brings us to the topic of political economy; it will also bring us up against the issue of "human nature," the topic at the top of the evolutionary psychologists' agenda.

There is a curious, distinctive note played by evolutionary psychologists when they discuss political matters: an avowal of what they take to be "political realism," along with a repudiation of progressive, Left, and especially Marxian theory. Steven Pinker offers an autobiographical illustration of this common realpolitik posturing:

> Come on, people now, smile on your brother! Everybody get together, try to love one another right now. This is the dawning of the Age of Aquarius: harmony and understanding, sympathy and trust abounding; no more falsehoods or derisions, golden living dreams of visions, mystic crystal revelation, and the mind's true libera-tion. Imagine no possessions; I wonder if you can. No need for greed or hunger, a brotherhood of man. Imagine all the people sharing in the world. You may say I'm a dreamer, but I'm not the only one. I hope some day you'll join us, and the world will be as one.
>
>   Incredible as it may seem, many of us used to believe this treacle. A leading idea of the 1960s and 70s was that mistrust, jealousy, competitiveness, greed, and manipulation were social institutions due for reform. Some people thought they were unnecessary evils, like slavery or the denial of the vote for women. Others thought they were hidebound traditions whose inefficiency had gone unnoticed.[1]

Now Steven has grown up he's washed off that Sixties treacle, he's come to accept that evolution has "designed" us to be competitive and unfit for the Aquarian Age, and he even offers his readers a rueful apology for including a discussion of such "trite" issues, the discussion from which these quotations are taken.[2] In any case, Pinker reminds his readers, American students who had shared the Aquarian dream quickly swapped their love beads for credit cards after graduation:

> Those students, of course, were the most privileged individuals in the history of humanity. With Mom and Dad paying the bills, everyone around them coming from the upper classes, and Ivy League credentials about to launch them into the expand-ing economy of the 1960s, it was easy to believe that all you needed is love. After graduation day, Reich's generation became the Gucci-wearing, Beemer-driving, condo-owning, gourmet-baby-breeding urban professionals of the 1980s and 90s. Universal harmony was a style as ephemeral as the bell-bottoms, a status symbol that distanced them from the rednecks, jocks, and the less hip preppies. As the post-60s rock musician Elvis Costello asked, "Was it a millionaire who said 'Imagine no possessions'?"[3]

Which is all very well, but hold on one moment, what *precisely* has Pinker grown out of? Oddly, Professor Pinker appears to think that the abbreviated lyrics from two songs by the uncredited John Lennon and, even less plausibly by Tim Rice, exemplify the spirit of the 1960s and 1970s.[4] In truth, the spirit of the sixties was far more varied, diverse, complex, playful, and often incoherent, than Pinker's crude characterization suggests. And, what precisely does Pinker mean by "many of us used to believe"? How many? Equally strongly? They all thought that the Age of Aquarius was equally imminent? They all grew up and became cynical Masters of the Universe after graduation? No, of course not. Young, and not so young, people had differing dreams, differing angers, differing commitments to the sixties' counterculture. Not everybody forsook afghan coats for pinstripe suits, not all of those who did go to work on Wall Street did so happily, some remained true to their hippy principles, some like Cat Stevens turned to religion, some took overdoses, some went on to work for Médicins sans Frontières.

What Pinker is really disavowing is his own youthful hope, his own youthful expectations which he now presents as naivety. This sort of youthful hope may be, in retrospect, naïve, but it is neither homogenous, it is not felt with equal force by all young people, and nor was it specific to the 1960s. As Pinker recognizes, "The Woodstock generation was not the first utopian dream to be shattered," but ironically he fails to recognize that countercultures do not arise as blank slates with no history or precedent; the sixties' version built upon earlier movements and cultures—the Beats, the anti-nuclear weapons protests, etc. –and was responsive to issues specific to the sixties--the Vietnam War, mutual assured destruction, the invasion of Czechoslovakia, the civil rights struggle, and so on. Countercultures are part of an accumulated history and youthful hope is genetic, not cultural. This is not to say that genes in any sense cause some young people to feel hopeful, rather that our genetically given pattern of maturation allows young people to feel especially hopeful. Nor do genes affect all young people, all members of particular generations, all American college students or whomever, in the same way. As Pinker's example shows, the relationship between genes, the social environment, and behavior is not always straightforward and sweeping generalizations will never do justice to the variety inherent in natural evolution and the artificial world, the variety that comprises our experience and which itself requires explanation.

For Professor Pinker, the only credible explanation for our social behavior comes from evolutionary psychology. All other theories are, for him, disproven. However as my friend and teacher Professor Simon Clarke has noted,[5] "for the past two hundred years economic theory has played a pivotal role in social thought," all social theory must incorporate some version of political economy and so Steven Pinker is obliged to confront Marxism, only quickly to dismiss it as comparable in its consequences, but not in its content, to Nazism.[6] In his belief that there is one, and only one, credible explanation for social behavior, Pinker's views match those of sociobiology's founder Professor Wilson, who similarly judged Marxism to be a failed ideology. Indeed, in the rush to embrace neo-evolutionary social theory many a writer has also embraced right-wing political economy, and in particular the arguments advanced centuries ago by Adam Smith, seduced by the apparent symmetry of Smith's arguments with neo-evolutionary theory. Predictably, these writers prioritize genetic explanation

over cultural; culture, including political economy, is analyzed, in reductionist
fashion, as an expression of genetically determined motives, naturally selected
dispositions, rather than as an autonomous environment in which genes are
expressed. Further, "human nature" is distinguished in terms of our genetic
inheritance, rather than in the light of the cultural environment we inherited
from our parents. And, and as usual, this genetically given human nature is
written in generalizations with no true allowance for individual variety and no
recognition of chance factors. One uncontroversial mental capacity we share
to varying degrees is our imagination, the sister of hope, and a capacity not
easily subsumed to reductionist evolutionary psychology. When John Lennon,
who Pinker quoted, asks us to "Imagine there's no possessions" he may have
been naïve, he may have been as Elvis Costello observed hypocritical, but
these shortcomings do not render his question invalid. Answering his question
cuts to the quick of the matter, for it addresses not only the political slant of
evolutionary psychology, it also bears upon distribution and inheritance in the
social world via the issue of private property, the crux of political economy and
the key to understanding Marx's work.

"In this sense," wrote Marx in *The Communist Manifesto*, "the theory of the
Communists may be summed up in the single sentence: Abolition of private
property." Understanding "the sense" of this summation and why it encapsulates
Marx's revolutionary theory, may be easier if we begin by briefly examining
Adam Smith's political economy, the eighteenth-century Scot's theory that
we've already met with in the first chapter when I introduced Smith's pseudo-
evolutionary view of societal change. In the first chapter, I noted that the
modern view of individuals as personalities formed by their experiences has
origins in the empiricist philosophy of John Locke and his belief that we are
born without any innate ideas, that the newborn baby's mind is a *tabula rasa*
waiting to be inscribed by experience, the "blank slate" philosophical position
currently opposed by evolutionary psychologists. In the eighteenth century,
Empiricism gained ground invigorated by the work of the Scotsman David
Hume, the most important member of what came to be called the "Scottish
School," and the reworking of Hume's philosophy by his friend and disciple,
Adam Smith. Smith accepted Hume's argument that the "morals" of a society
or nation, their customs and culture, were the chief reason for the differences
in national and individual character:

> The difference between the natural talents in different men is, in reality, much less
> than we are aware of; and the very different genius which appears to distinguish
> men of different professions, when grown up to maturity, is not on many occasions
> so much the cause as the effect of the division of labour. The difference between
> the most dissimilar characters, between a philosopher and a common street porter,
> for example, seems not to arise not so much from nature as from habit, custom and
> education. When they came into the world, and for the first six or seven years of
> their existence they were perhaps very much alike, and neither their parents or their

play fellows could perceive any remarkable difference. About that age, or soon after, they came to be employed in very different occupations. The difference in talents comes then to be taken notice of, till at last the vanity of the philosopher is willing to acknowledge scarce any resemblance.[7]

Clearly written by a childless bachelor (few parents would agree with his views about imperceptible differences in their young children), Smith's explanation for why individuals become dissimilar betrays his empiricist leanings and his overemphasis upon the effects of the division of labor, the ways in which work becomes divided into increasingly more specialized tasks and corresponding occupations. According to Smith, it is the growth in the division of labor which is the main cause in the increase in productivity of early Industrial Revolution factories (an analytical myopia which, as we saw in the previous chapter, blinded him to the astonishing productive potential of steam engines).

Writing before the French Revolution, and incapable of imagining any improvement upon the gross political and social inequalities of his day, Smith welcomed the growing material prosperity which he believed the division of labor produced. Nonetheless, Smith also recognized the pernicious consequences of the growing division of labor: if "the understanding of the greater part of men are necessarily formed by their ordinary employment" (as empiricism would lead us to believe), and if work becomes restricted to a few small repetitive tasks then: "The man whose whole life is spent in performing a few simple operations [...] becomes as stupid and ignorant as it is possible for a human being to become."[8] Whereas in the past a low division of labor ensured that work was varied and thus "invention is kept alive, and the mind is not allowed to fall into drowsy stupidity," in modern "commercial society" with a high division of labor, when work has become highly specialized, monotonous, and hence unchallenging:

> The torpor of his [the worker's] mind renders him not only incapable of relishing or bearing any part in any rational conversation, but incapable of conceiving any generous, noble or tender sentiment, and consequently of forming any just judgment...[9]

Smith's own, tawdry, solution to this unpleasant paradox—the greater the material wealth the greater the moral and intellectual impoverishment—was to recommend publicly funded elementary education for the children of the poor, public diversions such as fairs and other entertainments, and the promotion of a moral elite to give political guidance for a society whose members were increasingly unable to think or to make judgments for themselves.

Adam Smith had accepted the progressive, quasi-evolutionary view of societal history, the view that societal history progresses through distinctive stages that I have suggested is wrong and misleading. Rather than a process of accumulation, often incremental, occasionally steered by chance events, Smith held that society had passed through three distinct stages and that the eighteenth-century society in which he lived was on the cusp of the fourth, final stage that he christened "commercial society." Each of these historical stages is distinguished by the organization of material production. Government arises not from people coming together to form a social contract, nor from lofty political ambition, but rather from the simple desire to protect property:

> "...the appropriation of herds and flocks [...] introduced an inequality of fortune which first gave rise to government. Till there be property there can be no government, the very end of which is to secure the wealth, to defend the rich from the poor.[10]

"Commercial society," the final fourth stage, represented for Smith the pinnacle of societal development because in addition to the greatest material wealth, it also allowed for the greatest liberty, the greatest freedom for individual owners of property. The true beauty of commercial society, in the opinion of Smith as for his latter-day followers herded under the double misnomer of the "New Right,"[11] lay in the natural, self-regulating ways that capitalism functioned. Individuals, argued Smith, had a natural propensity to "truck, barter and exchange," and were naturally acquisitive and self-interested. By pursuing their natural self-interest, driven by the need to acquire more and more material wealth through trucking and bartering, they unintentionally benefited "even the lowest ranks of society" who came to enjoy the increasing national prosperity that even the greediest individual capitalist could not consume all by himself. In a commonly quoted passage from his first book, the book that actually secured his reputation, *The Theory of Moral Sentiments* (1759), Smith offers a flowery illustration of how the unintended consequences of individual greed might benefit us all: a "proud and unfeeling" landlord surveys his well-tended acres of crops and in his "imagination consumes himself the whole harvest that grows upon them." However, in reality the "proud and unfeeling" landlord cannot consume much more of the harvest than his poorest serf and so he is obliged to "divide with the poor the produce of all his improvements." In this way, the seemingly anti-social natural human qualities of avarice and self-interest *unintendedly* yield common, material benefit:

> They are led by an invisible hand to make nearly the same distribution of the necessaries of life which would have been made had the earth been divided into equal portions among all its inhabitants, and thus without intending it, without knowing it, to advance the interests of society.[12]

In commercial society, the "Invisible Hand" is still at work, now aided and abetted by the "laws" of supply and demand that purportedly match consumer wishes to productivity. If, counseled Smith, we keep government to a minimum, if we do not interfere with the natural workings of the capitalist market, then we will all benefit, albeit only in terms of material prosperity.

Smith's use of unintended consequences of actions to explain the general benefits of seemingly anti-social natural individual self-interest signals a tension in his theory, a tension between his belief in innate human qualities as against his views on societal development and the historically specific need for government. Smith was unwilling to accept a radical implication of philosophical empiricism: if we have no innate ideas, if all ideas come from experience, then individuals are born naturally similar and equal and are made dissimilar and unequal by their experiences in life. Smith, however, introduces supposedly universal species characteristics into his theory—everyone is naturally self-interested, we all have a "trucking and bartering" disposition—that are more powerful than mere ideas gained through experience and that will motivate and guide behavior. Thus, the Smithian picture of what people are like comprises two elements; unchangeable uniform "human nature" and malleable ideas about what we are like. Consequently, Smith's political economy could only foresee an intensification of the intellectual and moral deterioration caused by the unintended result of our unchangeable acquisitive, self-interested actions. The future was simply the growth and maturation of "commercial society," capitalism.

Importantly, for Smith "commercial society" produced desirable outcomes—increased productivity, greater material wealth and freedom—despite, not because of the character and motives of its citizens. Indeed, for a man commonly thought of as the champion of capitalism, Adam Smith held a harsh, and crude, opinion of the rich and privileged; capitalists were no better than landlords in Smith's estimation. Just as the landlord in the passage quoted above from *The Theory of Moral Sentiments* is "proud and unfeeling," so too capitalists are equally unpleasant being in Smith's judgment "greedy, rapacious, selfish" individuals out to fool and deceive the public. Like Pinker's caricature of hippies, this just won't do at all: not all capitalists are fiendish, some have quite admirable, or at least unobjectionable, motives including the not to be gainsaid wish to produce some product or service that they believe to be of real benefit or worth. Some capitalists are morally despicable. Despicable or not they, like us, will often have mixed, conflicting motives, will at times act unthinkingly, or against their normal inclinations. Capitalists are as varied as any other social group, Smith's characterization is wrong not simply because it is too derogatory, but because in addition it allows for little variation, certainly not for subtlety. And yet, curiously, none of this affects the integrity of Smith's explanation of capitalism because of course it is his argument that the dubious benefits of capitalism, greater material wealth and freedom, occur *despite* these sordid motivations, as an unintended consequence of actions mediated by the laws of supply and demand. His explanation identifies a *social mechanism* and this mechanism operates despite people's self-regarding motives: if we substitute a saint for Smith's "greedy and rapacious" capitalist, and have our saint motivated by insatiable "curiosity" (an alternative that Smith himself toyed with only to reject it in favor of self-love), and if our saint is driven to manufacture exquisite crucifixes, then providing they're manufactured in a factory with a high division of labor, and providing the crucifixes are sold on the market, capitalism will continue as if our saint had been Rupert Murdoch in disguise. This is the aspect to Smith's political economy that seems to provoke some ambivalence in Professor Pinker who on the one hand praises the "explainer of capitalism" for his "realistic" picture of commerce and his ingenious explanation for how, as with selfish genes, selfish motives can lead to selfless outcomes,[13] while on the other hand disparaging social scientists for presuming that social life can be explained in terms of social phenomena divorced from the "universe of individual minds," the site of explanation for evolutionary psychologists.[14] His latter criticism is misplaced, it is quite acceptable to explain some, not all, but some social phenomena without reference to either minds or motives. By identifying explanatory social mechanisms—the unintended consequences of self-regarding actions, the market laws of supply and demand, the division of labor—Smith's analysis also identified a subject matter that, as Sir Karl Popper recognized,[15] was autonomous from explanations based upon psychological reductionism, including evolutionary psychology's reductionism. If actions have unintended consequences, then we should not expect to ground our explanation for them on the actors' intentions.

In order for Smith's social mechanisms to operate, they first require private property to be established for without private property there could be no buying and selling, no privately owned factories with high divisions of labor, no capitalism. Although in most respects scornful of Smith's political stance, Karl Marx shared his belief that the division of labor shaped and stunted personal development, quoting Smith approvingly in the first volume of *Capital*—though neither man offered any evidence for this claim and neither had actually worked in a factory. Similarly, both thought that private property was not a timeless, natural human instinct, but rather an historical development. We will revisit Smith's analysis of the division of labor in the final chapter, noting here that his views on the origins of private property echoed those of Hume who had reasoned that the rules and laws governing property, along with other rules of social justice, were the consequence not of our ancestors forming a social contract, not of any grand plan, but rather by a gradual cementing of conventions and agreements made between naturally self-interested individuals who expected reciprocity by their equally self-interested neighbors.[16] Because we are naturally, and now we would have to say genetically programmed, to be self-interested, we should not in the Smithian view of things, expect to transcend private property.[17] And it is of course on this point that Smith and Marx part company because one of Marx's and Engel's sharpest lines of attack was made chiefly against the assumption of natural human qualities; the alternative they proposed rested on the notion that all human qualities can only be understood in the light of the specific historical circumstances in which they are expressed. Smith, as we've seen, believed that private property was a historically evolved relationship; on this point Marx was in agreement with Smith, but unlike the Scotsman, Marx believed that this relationship was inherently harmful and that it could be superseded. In this respect, Marx's treatment of private property is of a piece with the rest of his theory, a revolutionary theory marked by its belief in redemption.

Karl Marx's father, Heinrich, had entertained high hopes for his son, hoping that he would "... become what I might perhaps have become had I been born under such favourable auspices."[18] Marx's first year at Bonn University, a not untypical freshers' year of drinking, dueling, and writing poetry, suggested that these hopes were in jeopardy and so Heinrich transferred his son to Berlin, at that time, 1836, the preeminent German academy. At first Marx remained a romantic, as did his poetry (three volumes of which he sent to his muse and recently engaged fiancée, Jenny von Westphalen), but in 1837, partly as a consequence of studying jurisprudence with its accompanying philosophical concerns he succumbed to the lure of Hegel. As a romantic, Marx had resisted Hegel's curious rationalism but having succumbed he became an ardent enthusiast for a philosophy that appeared able to bridge the gap, first highlighted by David Hume, between what *is* the case (statements of fact), and what *ought* to be the case (statements of value). This famous problem, now known as "Hume's Fork," had been addressed philosophically by Kant but the Kantian solution raised new divisions, divisions for which Hegel sought a remedy in history.

"We shall not," Hegel cautioned his students, "occupy ourselves with general reflections abstracted from world history and illustrated by concrete historical examples, but rather with universal world history itself."[19] Individuals, societies, nations, inventions, all the contents of the past were subsumed by Hegel to the maturing of reason[20] itself, and thus the study of history became the identification of the historical stages through which reason struggled to become realized in human affairs. The proper focus for such a philosophical history was, argued Hegel the state for only the state can embody universal rational principles that transcend particular, individual desires or aims. The "general direction of world history" flowed from the East to the West, with the first rays of reason shining from the East where reason is still in its "boyhood." Exploiting this worryingly anthropomorphic metaphor, Hegel argues that reason starts to mature in classical Greece for, unlike in Oriental societies, the Greeks founded the first true state in which universal principles of reason might, to a limited extent, override individual, particular interests. But, the limited scope of the Greek city-state, limited by the influence of non-rational customs and citizenship for only the privileged few, stunts the growth of reason. With the rise of the Roman Empire, reason is able to mature from its "adolescence" in Athens and reach its "manhood" but, once again, the limited nature of the Roman state inhibits reason's full maturation. Only with the rise of the "Germanic world," in the modern "Germanic nations," is reason at last able to reach "old age," full maturity. The process by which reason grows, however, is unlike the ways in which a man matures through boyhood, adolescence, manhood into old age: reason's history, Hegel suggests, is initially similar to the myth of the Phoenix, but when reason becomes expressed in the West it does not, unlike the Phoenix, simply reappear in replica but in a stronger, purified guise:

> Its Western counterpart is the realization that the spirit too rises up again, not only rejuvenated but also enhanced and transfigured. Admittedly, it becomes divided against itself and destroys the form it earlier occupied, but in so doing, it rises up to a new stage of development. But when it abandons the shell of its former existence, it does not merely migrate into a new shell; it emerges as a purified spirit from the ashes of its earlier form.[21]

Whether or not the Germanic state should have been judged as the final resting home of reason in its "old age" was a question that divided the conservative "Right" Hegelians, who judged that it did, from the more youthful "Left"-leaning followers, who thought otherwise. Marx threw his support and enthusiasm in with the Left, becoming a prominent member of the "Doctors' Club," a group of radical intellectuals who weighed upon his decision to abandon a career in law in favor of university teaching. His doctoral thesis having been accepted in 1841, Marx's hopes of a post at the University of Bonn were dashed by the dismissal of his friend Bruno Bauer, a fellow member of the Doctors' Club whose influence Marx had been counting upon to secure his university post. With a fiancée, without financial help from his family (his father having died in 1838), Marx was obliged to find work and, like many other Left Hegelians, he turned his hand to journalism, writing first for the *Rheinische Zeitung*, a new daily newspaper published in Bonn, financed by liberal industrialists who hoped that their paper would promote free trade. But the paper's tone went well beyond modest free-trade liberalism, offering its readers criticisms of religion and politics that drew disapproval from rival papers and which alarmed the authorities. The paper's financial backers had not allowed its founder Moses Hess, Germany's first communist, to become editor and a string of incompetent appointments were made until, in October 1842, Marx assumed control of the paper which, under his editorship, doubled its circulation within one month.

In the offices of the paper Marx had debated with Hess and others the merits of communism, then a novel departure from socialism, but he was not yet himself a communist and nor was it the paper's political line. Defending his paper against the charge made by a rival, the *Augsburger Allgemeine Zeitung*, that it was a communist rag, Marx wrote:

> The *Rheinische Zeitung*, which cannot even concede theoretical reality to communistic ideas in their present form, and can even less wish or consider possible their practical realization, will submit these ideas to thorough criticism. If the *Augsburger* wanted and could achieve more than slick phrases, the *Augsburger* would see that writings such as those by Leroux, Considerant, *and above all Proudhon's penetrating work*, can be criticised only after long and deep study...[22]

In contrast to the respectable, bourgeois family backgrounds to the German Left Hegelians, Pierre-Joseph Proudhon was born into rural French poverty. Lacking the funds to complete his university education, he turned to the print trade. At first forced to tramp from one temporary job to another, in the autumn of 1832 he landed the editorship of a Fourieriste newspaper and then, having taught himself Latin, he specialized as a compositor of Latin texts, then a lucrative specialism. With two partners, he founded his own printing press but his own first book he had published by another firm. This book, *What Is Property? or, an inquiry into the principle of right and of government* (1840), secured the reputation of Proudhon, the first self-proclaimed anarchist, as the most significant radical thinker of his day. With an initial print run of 500, swollen to 3,000 for the second edition published in the following year, the *Inquiry* quickly became notorious. Its opening paragraph offered a slogan, a battle cry for the oppressed in an age when property had come to be revered by the wealthy and sanctified by political economists such as Adam Smith:

> If I had to answer the following question, "What is slavery?" and if I should respond in one word, "It is murder," my meaning would be understood at once. I should not need a long explanation to show that the power to deprive a man of his thought, his will, and his personality is the power of life and death. So why to this other question, "What is property?" should I not answer in the same way, "It is theft," without fearing to be misunderstood, since the second proposition is only a transformation of the first?[23]

Proudhon's definition of property as theft involved two revolutionary ideas: first, and more obviously, the idea that by claiming an object as "mine" I am necessarily depriving other people of possession; second, perhaps less obviously, that property is a social relationship between people and not, as it might appear, a relationship between individuals and objects. If you say, for example, that this is "your book" then you are not expressing a relationship between you and the physical object but between you and other people whom you wish to prohibit from reading, playing with, defacing etc. "your" book: if there were no other people, say you were living alone on the proverbial desert island, then nothing could be your property. This key Proudhonian insight was retained by Marx as an ingredient for his own theoretical recipe, as was the distinction Proudhon drew between two forms of property relations; proprietorship and possession, the former an unjust exploitative social relationship protected by legal rights, the latter "a matter of fact":

> The tenant, the farmer, the shareholder, and the usufructuary [temporary possessor] are possessors; the owner who rents and lends for use and the heir who waits for the death of the usufructuary to come into possession, are proprietors. To venture a comparison, a lover is a possessor, the husband a proprietor.[24]

In his first important article as the editor of the *Rheinische Zeitung*, a critical examination of the laws on the petty theft of timber, Marx was already adopting Proudhon's chief insight over property,[25] but he did not advocate Proudhon's political solution of securing justice[26] by abolishing a society founded upon private property in favor of a free federal association of "possessors." Nor, as yet, did Marx present any other radical alternative. When, later, in 1847, Marx did publish his response to Proudhon (*The Poverty of Philosophy*) he did so in the light of his critique of Hegel, by means of his fledgling critique of orthodox political economy, and as a committed communist.

Predictably, the increasingly radical tone of the *Rheinische Zeitung* under Marx's editorship caused the Prussian government to close down the paper as part of their wider campaign to suppress the liberal press. This government censorship split the Left Hegelians with one faction, led by Bruno Bauer, retreating from political engagement whilst the remainder, centred around Arnold Ruge, continued their political involvement. Marx moved to Paris and accepted the editorship of Ruge's *Deutsch-Franzosische Jarhrbucher*. As the editor of this new political review, Marx was obliged to refine his own views, in particular, his reception of Hegel's politics. It is from this critique of Hegel that Marx devised what became known as the "materialist conception of history," the reconception that allowed Marx to break with Hegel's statist vision and the conception that underpinned his entire revolutionary theory. Marx owed this theoretical progress to Ludwig Feuerbach whose assault on Christianity had elevated him to the status of the Left Hegelian's favorite philosopher. In *The Essence of Christianity*, Feuerbach proposed that, rather than God having created man, man had conjured up the idea of the Divinity. The God whom Christians worshipped was all powerful, all good, all just, all loving. Although on earth sinners and the ungodly might seem to prosper, their prosperity was dearly bought for hell awaited the wicked man, heaven the true believer. Justice was merely postponed: "For thou hast maintained my right and my cause; thou satest in the throne judging right"; "And he shall judge the world in righteousness, he shall minister judgement to the people in uprighteousness"; "For the needy shall not always be forgotten: the expectation of the poor shall *not* perish for ever."[27] Christians, reasoned Feuerbach, had projected their finest human qualities onto a fictitious being and had sacrificed hopes of betterment in the real world for the delusory promise of perfection in the afterlife. Rather than worship the fictitious projection of our own best qualities, we should reclaim these qualities and use them to build a paradise on earth, not in heaven. In 1843, in his *Preliminary Theses for a Reform of Philosophy*, Feuerbach used the same analytical strategy he had used to attack Christianity for an assault upon unworldly philosophy, a philosophical movement he saw as culminating in Hegel's perverse logic of history. Just as Christians had misrepresented the relationship between the subject, man, and his predicates by making man subservient to his own estranged qualities, so too Hegel had made man subservient to the historically developing spirit, to the idea, of reason. The proper starting point for philosophy was not the abstract, universal idea of reason, but instead real individual men and women: "… the true relationship of thought to being is this: being is the subject, thought the predicate. Thought arises from being—being does not arise from thought."[28]

Enthused by Feuerbach's arguments, Marx set about his own critique of Hegel. In 1843, he produced a lengthy, detailed critique of Hegel's *Philosophy of Right* from a Feuerbachian perspective. This critique remained unpublished but in his second article for the *Jahrbucher* Marx wrote an *Introduction* to the unpublished critique; in the opinion of the Marxist scholar David McLellan, "…one of the most scintillating pieces that he ever wrote." Contained in this *Introduction* are many of the chief ideas which Marx was to weave together for his revolutionary theory, as well as his famous remarks on religion:

> The foundation of irreligious criticism is this: man makes religion, religion does not make man. But man is no abstract being squatting outside the world. Man is the world of man, the state, society. [....]
> Religion is the sigh of the oppressed creature, the feeling of a heartless world and the soul of soulless circumstances. It is the opium of the people.... The first task of philosophy, which is in the service of history, once the holy form of human self-alienation has been discovered, is to discover self-alienation in its unholy forms. The criticism of religion is thus transformed into the criticism of earth...[29]

Whilst the criticism of religion was the "presupposition of all criticism," in order for criticism to have real practical effect if must be rooted in the real world. Rather than Hegel's maturing universal Idea of reason saving mankind, what needed to be identified was a real-world social group—a social group that suffered universal injustice the righting of which would have universal significance for everyone. This social group was identified, in the *Introduction*, as the proletariat (at that time a rapidly expanding social class commonly championed by French socialists). By overcoming their "unholy," real-world self-alienation, the proletariat would end the self-alienation of all humanity.

Marx's "materialist conception of history," his insistence upon finding solutions to political problems in the reality of practical life rather than in speculative philosophy, led him to quarrel, criticize, and refute the arguments of his former German companions, especially Feuerbach, and also the then highly influential writings of Proudhon. The basic objection lodged against the Germans was that they failed to grasp the true relationship of ideas and consciousness to life, they continued with their speculative philosophising, refusing to acknowledge that "consciousness does not determine life, but life consciousness." As men and women produce first food, then increasingly sophisticated things, they enter into "definite social and political relationships, into a "definite mode of life," which exist "independent of their will." Like Adam Smith, Marx reasoned that it is modes of life, the changing ways that material production is socially organized, which governs individuals and their ideas: the history of such modes of life therefore are the proper focus for explaining the history of the species and, unlike for Smith, sufficient in themselves without the addition of supposedly innate "natural" qualities. How this history unfolds must be understood not by the imposition of some abstracted ahistorical logic, the charge Marx laid against Proudhon, but by an examination of how real men and women had made their own history "under conditions and circumstances not of their own choosing."

By the time that these critiques were penned, in the early 1840s, Marx was collaborating with Engels, his life-long supporter, friend, and financial backer. The contribution brought by Engels, whom Marx eventually befriended in 1844 (having cold-shouldered him when they had first met two years earlier), was far greater than the continual bailing-out of the spendthrift Marx for which he is vulgarly remembered: it was Engels who focused Marx's studies on economics, the critique of which was the last ingredient in Marx's revolutionary recipe. In the second of a pair of articles published in the *Jahrbucher*, Engels offered a polemical critique of the contemporaneous science of "political economy" as written by the "economic Luther, Adam Smith." For Engels, already a committed communist (converted by Moses Hess), familiar with the actual conditions of industrial manufacture, and with Proudhonian thinking, "In the present circumstances that science ought to be called private economy, for its public connections exist only for the sake of private property."[30] In a world of private property, terms such as "national wealth" are mere fiction. The consequence of private ownership is trade founded upon the competitive, antagonistic, mutually mistrustful relationship of buyer and seller, each seeking to maximize their individual advantage. Scornful of Smith's attempt to reconcile this antagonism brought about by private property, Engels argues that capital (simply "stored-up labor") and labor are really two sides of the same coin, only artificially divided by the social convention of private property:

> Labour—the main factor in production, the "source of wealth," free human activity—comes off badly with the economist. Just as capital has already been separated from labour, so labour is now split for a second time: the product of labour confronts labour as wages, is separated from it, and is in its turn determined by competition [....] If we do away with private property, this unnatural separation also disappears. Labour becomes its own reward, and the true significance of the wages of labour, hitherto alienated, comes to light—namely, the significance of labour for the determination of the production costs of a thing.[31]

The thrust of Engel's critique of orthodox political economy was hugely sympathetic with Marx's own thinking at the time. Marx had rejected Hegel's belief that an impartial bureaucracy could mediate between the competing interests of individuals in civil society, instead identifying the proletariat as the social group holding the key to the overcoming of all human self-alienation. In the "Paris Manuscripts," notes written by Marx for the purpose of self-clarification, mainly critical commentary upon the writings of political economists, he specified the chief elements of alienation which afflicted workers in a world of private property. Marx extends Feuerbach's critique of religion to the realm of economics but these dimensions of alienation he discusses are of a general nature, rather than specific to any actual mode of production. In this early formulation, it is free creativity that becomes lost to the workers, work has become "forced labour":

> …labour is *external* to the worker, i.e. does not belong to his essential being; that he therefore does not confirm himself in his work, but denies himself, feels miserable and not happy, does not develop free mental and physical energy, but mortifies his flesh and ruins his mind. Hence the worker feels himself only when he is not working; when he is working he does not feel himself. He is at home when he is not working, and not at home when he is working. His labour is therefore not voluntary but forced, it is *forced labour*.[32]

Forced labor was for Marx a "fact," as was the conclusion he drew that the more workers exerted themselves, the more they produced, the greater was their alienation: "The worker becomes poorer the more wealth he produces [.…] The *devaluation* of the human world grows in direct proportion to the increase in value of the world of things."[33] Just as Christians alienated their own best, real human qualities the more religious they became, so too the workers became further and further alienated from their true humanity as their enforced productivity grew. The solution to the problem of alienation demanded the ending of private property, a conclusion Marx had reached in the "Paris Manuscripts" and which he and Engels baldly restated four years later as a slogan in the *Communist Manifesto*. But "private property," as they noted in the *Manifesto,*[34] assumed different forms in different periods of history, in different modes of production: the way to understand private property, its underpinning of alienation, and the opportunity for its abolition by the proletariat, was not by "… repeating the mistake of the political economist who bases his explanations on some imaginary primordial condition. Such a primordial condition explains nothing."[35] Instead, the proper intellectual strategy lay in grounding analysis in the real contemporary world of capitalism, in the dissection of alienation as it actually affected real living people. This task occupied Marx, beset by debt, ill-health, and family tragedies, for the next twenty years, eventually partially realized in 1867 with the publication of the first volume of *Das Kapital*.[36]

Das Kapital includes the mature expression of Marx's revolutionary theory of alienation, now incorporated within and comprising part of his analysis of the capitalist mode of production. This volume that had cost Marx his health, and upon which his wife and admirers pinned so much hope, was not an immediate run-away success. Largely ignored in Germany and not published in English in Marx's own lifetime, it has long been popularly considered a dry, incomprehensible, technically difficult text on economics. This poor estimation, often held by those who haven't actually read the volume, has however recently been challenged in Francis Wheen's sparky biography of Marx. According to Wheen,[37] Marx's style of writing reflects the nature of his subject matter; the style of writing Marx adopted was geared to the nature of his analysis, an ironic, mocking tone befitting to the essential absurdity, or as Wheen put it to "the deranged logic," of capitalism. Wheen, I think, makes a plausible case for this ironic interpretation but even so the first volume of *Das Kapital* is no page-turner (except, if you're like me, in the sense of having to turn back again to reread parts you didn't properly understand the first time). Luckily, the actual section that contains the mature version of the theory of alienation as it is specifically experienced in capitalism is short, unlike the section's glorious title, "The Fetishism of Commodities and the Secret Thereof." As the title to this fourteen-page section indicates, understanding capitalistic alienation involves understanding the production and valuing of commodities, the topic of the first part of *Das Kapital*. To help, I hope, explain Marx's thinking on these subjects, their relation to his revolutionary project, and the ways in which Marx's thinking emerged from the critiques we've looked at briefly so far, I'm going to use an imaginary example, the example of Nelson Mandela attempting to retire to a nice little home in the English countryside.

Even heroes need homes and so, in our imaginary example Nelson Mandela, remarried and largely retired from active political life, decides to spend the rest of his days in leafy southern England. But, in a capitalist society such as England, homes have become houses, commodities to be bought and sold in the marketplace. Hence the surprise, the pleasure on the face of Mr. Perfidy when one Monday morning Mr. and Mrs. Mandela unexpectedly enter through the door of Perfidy & Sons., Residential and Business Estate Agents. Recovering his composure, Mr. Perfidy invites his illustrious visitors to take a seat and asks how he might be of help? "Well," explains the great man, "my wife and I are looking for a small home, just three bedrooms, a garden, in the country but not too far from London, somewhere where I can write in peace but still be able to travel up to town easily." "Certainly, an honour Sir; I'm sure we have many properties on our books that will suit" replies the still stunned Mr. Perfidy, signaling an office junior to get the details of likely houses. "Just one small point," adds Mr. Perfidy in a diffident voice, "er, what sort of price range are you considering?"

True to his name and to his profession, Mr. Perfidy has been less than straight; the price is no "small point," for it is, in the capitalistic artificial world, the principle way by which all commodities, including basic commodities such as houses are valued. Every commodity—and as capitalism ages more and more of the world is commodified—has a monetary price: medicines, works of art, childcare, education, food, water, cars, cannabis, land, all come with a price tag. All human needs and desires become satisfied by purchasing commodities.[38] The cost of a commodity, determined simply by the price it can realize in the market, comes to override other values which the commodity might hold for us. This potentially "double value" attached to commodities had been emphasized by Engels in his article published in the *Jahrbucher*,[39] a distinction as Engels put it between "abstract or real value and exchange value," later rephrased by Marx as the distinction between the "use value" and "exchange value" of commodities. By use value, Marx had in mind simply the many, many ways that a commodity could be valued as it was used, in our example the ways in which the Mandela's new home could afford a peaceful refuge from the strains of world diplomacy, somewhere for their grandchildren to play hide-and-seek, for old comrades to spend time visiting, an object of pride for their neighbors, a place of pilgrimage for admirers, etc., etc. None of these "use values" can be properly measured, or compared (what value can be placed on a child's delight in finding a new hiding place under the stairs? To what may their delight be compared?). But, in capitalism, such use values become subsumed or restrained by the blunt exchange values, the cost, of things.

Let us suppose that, in an act of consistent charity the Mandelas have, before arriving in Britain, donated all their money to an orphanage in South Africa: what will Mr. Perfidy do? He cannot simply give them the house of their choice for all the houses on the agent's books are private property, they all belong to somebody, as do all other commodities. Given the exceptional circumstances, perhaps Mr. Perfidy will discretely 'phone his wealthy business acquaintances suggesting that they have a whip-round to raise the necessary sum; or, perhaps the Mandelas' international supporters raise the money; or, maybe, Mr. Perfidy shows the Mandelas the door, regretting that can he be of no service to them. Whatever the outcome, the Mandelas' desire to settle down in leafy southern England runs up against the exchange valuing of commodities, a value protected by the law which upholds the right of individuals to own commodities.

As our environment becomes transformed into a world of privately owned commodities each with its own price tag, work becomes a question of producing commodities or of facilitating their production; some jobs, for instance estate agents, can only exist when "commodification" is established, other jobs, such as teachers, are infiltrated by commodity values which turn pupils into consumers in the same way as homes are turned into houses. The mechanism for pricing commodities may appear to be governed by the laws of supply and demand, as Adam Smith had proposed, but somehow or other this exchange mechanism has to yield a profit for the seller. The commodity has, by some mysterious means, to realize a profit; the seller demands more than the commodity actually cost to produce or buy. In the short term, commodities may be sold at or below cost but capitalism won't tolerate loss in the long term. The basis of profit cannot be inherent in the commodity itself for it possesses no inherent value of any sort, only the values we ascribe to it. The price of the commodity, its exchange value, has to be greater than its production cost and, according to Marx, it is the amount of labor time needed to produce the commodity that will be the key variable in determining its price. Consequently, in capitalism employment is usually rewarded and organized in terms of time, with factory workers clocking-in, with wages, salaries supposedly reflecting time spent at work.

Wages, salaries are paid in money, the intrinsically useless commodity, the universal currency of value that permits all other kinds of different commodities to be compared (this book, for example, costs roughly the same as three litres of strong cider, or sixteen operations to remove cataracts from the eyes of poor Africans). With the arrival of money, all manner of otherwise absurd comparisons can be drawn and commodities come to assume a life of their own. In capitalism, ordinary folk are obliged to sell their labor, measured in time, and are rewarded with the currency to buy commodities; they sell their creativity and are rewarded with commodities. In addition to buying commodities, money as capital can be used to buy what Marx refers to as the "means of production," the equipment, factories, tools, offices etc. that are used to produce commodities. This distinction between capital, money that will yield a profit, and mere cash, is the basis of the great divide between the two social classes that will, in Marx's view, predominate in capitalism: on the one hand, capitalists who own and/or control the means of production; on the other hand, the proletariat who, in the course of history have become separated, alienated from the means of production and now possess, control, only their own labor, their "labor power." Whereas in the past, when land was still the main source of production and wealth, ordinary people still enjoyed some rights over the means of production (say, a small strip of land they could farm), in capitalism the means of production becomes the private property of a small societal minority of capitalists.

History, the succession of modes of production, is portrayed by Marx as similar to Hegel's analogy of the mythical Phoenix: just as Hegel's Phoenix of Reason is reborn time and again in a stronger, more purified form, so too are the social classes which characterize a mode of production. With each rebirth, from slaves and slave masters in the Classical world, through feudal landlords and peasantry to proletariat and capitalists the division between the two classes becomes sharper, as does the degree of alienation experienced by the subject social class. The workers, the proletariat, have less and less say in the conditions in which they work, fellow workers become competitors rather than colleagues, what is produced, how it is produced, how it is sold, and to whom, all become governed by the market. Only profitable enterprise will persist, and profit depends upon exploiting the workforce, paying them less than the value of the time they have sacrificed. The more the workers produce, the greater their alienation. Certainly, as Smith had welcomed, there will be mass ownership of commodities, nearly everyone in rich countries will have more consumer goodies, but the price to pay, a rising cost for the proletariat, will be the loss of freedom and the loss of a social identity that transcends individual ownership. In order to survive, to improve one's lot in life, it becomes necessary to work for the money that will buy commodities that can offer only transitory pleasures. In the England in which the Mandelas hoped to settle down, the single greatest regular expenditure of most people is on housing, on monthly mortgage repayments. England is popularly, but mistakenly, thought of as a nation of home-owners but this is a fiction as most houses are actually owned by financial institutions whose name remains on the title deeds of the property for twenty five years by which time the borrower has given the best years of their life to repaying the massive interest on the advanced capital. The cost of housing, always high, periodically soars and crashes, its wild fluctuations the perennial worry and tedious conversation topic for home "owners." Where we live, who we live alongside, if we can move, what sort of job we do, all this and much more is currently dictated to us by the housing market. Fathers commute ever longer distances to work on perilous roads (British traffic fatalities now exceed 3,200 a year, our roadsides are decorated with wreaths), first thing in the morning mothers on their way to work bundle reluctant children into cars taking them to their childminders, British working weeks are currently the longest in Europe. People have become slaves to "their" property, it seems as though houses, mere assemblages of bricks and mortar, have a value, a life of their own. For the sake of an illusory rise in the "value" of "their" house, parents sacrifice the futures of their children who themselves will never be able to gain the lowest rung of the housing ladder. Property developers build "executive" houses, houses with strong metal gates to exclude the poor. It may be clichéd, but more than any other commodity or market I can think of, housing represents, currently acutely for the British, most clearly what Marx meant by the "fetish-ism of commodities," the ways in which the private ownership of commodities makes men and women victims of their own creations.

Marx's solution to ending alienation, ending commodity fetishism, is to be found in the nature of capitalism itself. Put very baldly, his argument was that *capitalism itself* would generate the opportunity for the proletariat to put an end to their own, and hence humanity's self-estrangement. It is the proud boast of every child, every empire, every nation and every mode of production that it will live for ever. None of them do. Similarly capitalism makes claim to immortality but for it to persist, production must be continually profitable. So far, no capitalist country has ever enjoyed consistent profitability, instead they lurch from boom to slump, sometimes with periods of stagnation thrown in for good measure. In the past, when the pulse of profitability and the price of economic failure could move from nation to nation this erratic economic performance could be blamed upon specific failings (poor British manage-ment, superior German work force or whatever) but in a world of stark global interdependency this sort of fudge becomes less credible. To restore profit-ability companies may pursue a number of strategies, such as lowering wages, increasing the length of the working day, intensifying production, sacking one labor force in favor of a cheaper foreign alternative, and the state in the service of capitalism may enact protectionist legislation, lower wage policies, etc. but such measures will only work as temporary palliatives, they will not solve the chief problem, the tendency of capitalist production to decline in profitability as the labor force becomes unable to buy the commodities which it has created. There is, for example, no shortfall in the demand for houses in England, nor is there any reason in principle why new houses should not be built, but people's ability to build and buy houses, and their opportunities to move to areas where houses are available, are curtailed or prohibited by the valuing of land, houses and of their labor: this valuing, the exchange value, is itself a consequence of the capitalist system which elevates profit over other considerations.

Political remedies, working through the established legal and political channels, may alleviate specific exploitations but they cannot address its underlying cause. Agreements, deals, compromises, reached between unions, or by political parties with employers may improve the conditions in which the proletariat work but these victories, often as Marx emphasized of real worth, are open to attack when the economy falters and the proletariat become politically weak; moreover, these reformist agreements are powerless to eliminate exploitation, alienation once and for all. Exploitation, alienation, rides on the back of private property and the right to ownership is enshrined in law: I might contest the right of an individual to own a particular house but I cannot challenge the right to own property per se for this right is the bedrock of the law. Only when the right to privately own property is abolished will the division between capitalists and proletariat, and the exploitative relationship between the two classes, cease. Thus, all political movements working within the established framework are only able to achieve partial, precarious victories; profound betterment requires a revolutionary change, a challenge to the very basis of capitalism.

This challenge emerges from the contradictions of capitalism, from the inability of capitalism to realize its own rationale. Capitalism promises all its citizens freedom, growing material prosperity, employment, legal rights, peace, and equality but these promises are not met. Instead, as capitalism ages, the essentially *non-rational* effects of private property become ever clearer, no longer veiled behind the ideology supposedly justifying capitalism. Injustices arise from the non-rationality of the valuing of commodities. Abolishing private property abolishes this non-rationality and its sibling injustices: in its place the proletariat build a society whereby the social usage of things produced by the community becomes the basis of value. The proletariat, uniquely, can accomplish this task because they have no personal stake in capitalism, they are fully alienated, and so by abolishing private property they at the same time abolish the conditions under which exploitation, alienation, can exist. By abolishing private property the proletariat: abolishes the Proudhonian proprietor, all men become Proudhonian possessors and they reclaim their best qualities, their real sociable nature, their unmatched creativity, just as Feuerbach's radicals reclaimed their alienated best qualities from God.

This hurried sketch of Marx's revolutionary theory is just that, merely a sketch drawn for the purposes of this book's investigation of chance and character. I would hope that even this poor outline will illustrate the merits of what, in several respects, is still the most seductive piece of social theory ever written. That most people spend most of their lives working, if they're "lucky," that most working people would retire tomorrow if they could afford to, that wealth is increasingly unevenly distributed, that money is the chief concern of most people, that political power, opportunities in life and money have become inseparable, that wars nestle nastily with economic interests—all this and much more rude economic reality is still too often conveniently overlooked by many a salaried social scientist following the academics' flight from Marxism and the separation of the old "political economy" into discrete disciplines of economics, sociology, politics, etc.

But, should we allow ourselves to be seduced by Marx's analysis? How could chance and character fit into his explanatory mechanism? And would their reinstatement somehow extinguish the embers of Hegel's Phoenix? If it were put into practice, in the real chancy world, would Marx's revolutionary recipe replace capitalism's "deranged logic" with the sort of ordering of society that would allow Mr. Mandela to occupy the house he deserves?

Notes

1. S. Pinker, 1998, *How The Mind Works.* London: Penguin, p. 429.
2. Ibid., p. 425.
3. Ibid., p. 426.
4. This is perhaps an understandable cultural lapse of Professor Pinker who by chance happens to be my age, we were both born in 1954 and so missed Woodstock and all but the tail end of the Sixties counterculture.
5. S. Clarke, 1982, *Marx, Marginalism and Modern Social Theory.* Macmillan: London, p. 6.
6. Pinker, *The Blank Slate*, pp. 154-158.
7. A. Smith, [1776], *The Wealth of Nations*, bk. 1, ch. 2. In: R. Heilbroner (ed.), 1986, *The Essential Adam Smith.* Oxford: Oxford University Press, p. 170.
8. A. Smith, *The Wealth of Nations*, bk. 5, article 2. In: Heilbroner, *The Essential Adam Smith*, p. 302.
9. Ibid.
10. A. Smith, *Lectures on Jurisprudence*. In: Heilbroner, *The Essential Adam Smith*, p. 40 (this theme is retained by Smith in *The Wealth of Nations*, e.g., bk. 5, part 2).
11. A key difference between Smith and the so-named "New Right" is that whereas Smith despised and distrusted entrepreneurs, today's anti-state champions of capitalism have elevated entrepreneurs to the status of heroes. Whereas for Smith it was only the *unintended* consequences of their actions which benefited society, the "New Right" claim that it is the intended aims of entrepreneurs which should be imitated and encouraged.
12. A. Smith, *The Theory of Moral Sentiments* [1759]. In: Heilbroner, *The Essential Adam Smith*, p. 123.
13. Pinker *The Blank Slate*, p. 161.
14. Ibid., p. 285.

15. K. Popper, 1945, *The Open Society and Its Enemies*. London: Routledge & Kegan Paul, ch. 14.
16. The pedigree for Hume's arguments, and his empiricist philosophy, reaches back to John Locke who, in his *2nd Treatise on Civil Government*, had opposed Hobbesian "social contract theory" and in addition had proposed a labor theory of property.
17. For a defence of Smith's views on the origins of private property, see A. Flew, 1986, *David Hume: Philosopher of Moral Science*. Oxford: Basil Blackwell, ch. 10. Professor Flew presents Smith's picture of historical development and of the origin of private property as "evolutionary" without, as is so often the case, explaining how precisely evolution could operate in these spheres.
18. Quoted in: D. McLellan, 1972a, *Marx before Marxism*. Harmondsworth: Pelican, p. 60.
19. G.W.F. Hegel, 1987 [1822/28], *Lectures on the Philosophy of World History: Introduction*. Cambridge: Cambridge University Press, p. 11.
20. For the sake of this discussion, and hopefully for the sake of clarity, I am using "reason" to embrace Hegel's notions of the "Idea" and the "Spirit" captured in the German word "*geist*." English does not have a synonym for "*geist*" which conveys the dual meaning of "spirit" (as in zeitgeist, the spirit of the age) and also "consciousness."
21. Hegel, *Lectures on the Philosophy of World History*, pp. 32-33.
22. Quoted in: McLellan, *Marx before Marxism*, p. 124 [latter italicization added].
23. J-P. Proudhon, 1994 [1840], *What Is Property? or, An inquiry into the principle of right and of government* (Cambridge Texts in the History of Political Thought). Cambridge: Cambridge University Press, p. 13.
24. Ibid., p. 36.
25. McLellan, *Marx before Marxism*, pp. 126-127.
26. For Proudhon, justice was the supreme ethical and political goal, "...the general, primitive, categorical law of all society" that proprietorship offended (Proudhon, *What is Property?* p. 31).
27. Psalms 9, Vs. 4, 8, 18.
28. Quoted in McLellan, *Marx Before Marxism*, p. 142.
29. Quoted in D. McLellan, *The Thought of Karl Marx*. London: Macmillan, pp. 21-22.
30. F. Engels "Outlines of a Critique of Political Economy." In: Marx & Engels, 1975, *Collected Works, vol. 3*. London: Lawrence Wishart, p. 424.
31. Ibid., p. 431.
32. K. Marx "Economic and Philosophical Manuscripts." In: K. Marx, 1975, *Marx Early Writings*. Harmondsworth: Penguin, p. 326.
33. Ibid., p. 324.
34. K. Marx and F. Engels, "Manifesto of the Communist Party." In: L.S. Feuer (ed.), 1969, *Marx and Engels: Basic Writings on Politics and Philosophy*. London: Fontana, p. 62.
35. Marx, "Economic and Philosophical Manuscripts," p. 323.
36. We will revisit this point about the inherent incompleteness of Marx's work in the next chapter.
37. F. Wheen, 2000, *Karl Marx*. London: Fourth Estate.
38. We will return to Marx's views on "constant" and "relative" desires in the final chapter.
39. Engels, "Outlines of a Critique of Political Economy," p. 425.

5

The Currency of Comparison

So, after the revolution, will Nelson Mandela get the house he deserves? Let's just recap on Marx's revolutionary recipe, sloganized in the *Communist Manifesto* as "the abolition of private property," a slogan which as Marx emphasized—in order to preempt his critics and to allay fears that communists would deprive the poor of even their last few possessions—meant the abolition of the private ownership of the means of production, not simply the abolition of all private property. In capitalist society, this would mean the abolition of the private ownership of the factories, the agricultural land, the newspapers and everything else that at present is used to produce commodities for a profit, including of course the labor of the workers. It was Marx's and Engel's belief that such private ownership led to the exploitation of the majority working class by the minority capitalists and so led classes and individuals to form competitive, exploitative social relationships with one another. End private ownership of the means of production and we would remove the wellspring of antagonism, competitiveness and social strife. For Marx, private ownership of the means of production is, as we saw in the last chapter, a social relationship between people, a key to analyzing society, and an explanatory locus for understanding how society works, comparable in this sense to the Darwinian explanatory mechanism of "natural selection." If, reasoned Marx, we abolished private ownership of the means of production then the manufacture of the artificial world, the environment in which we live, would no longer be distorted by the drive for profit and could instead be organized for our mutual benefit: exchange values would become use values and Nelson Mandela could move into his new home—not his new house, note, his new home. The most common, vulgar, criticism of Marx's vision is that he neglected "human nature," the kind of criticism Professor Pinker makes against his parody of the hippy Aquarian dream. This criticism of Marx is, I think, valid, but not in the way that it is usually understood and not because, contra Pinker, our human nature is made nasty through evolutionary adaptive pressures.

Marx's work remained unfinished. Only the first volume of *Das Kapital* was completed by Marx. In the sixteen years he lived after its publication in

1867 Marx, who became the leading light of the International, wrote largely upon matters concerning practical socialist politics, mainly shortish pieces sometimes co-authored with Engels. The second and third volumes of *Das Kapital* were compiled posthumously by Engels from Marx's copious notes with a fourth volume, known as "Theories of Surplus Value" compiled by Karl Kautsky and published later on. Quite why Marx failed to complete at least the second volume remains puzzling, quite possibly he was just too busy with more pressing political matters, but even if he had completed at least the remaining three volumes this would still have left his ambitions unfulfilled for Marx had originally intended to write a six-volume study that would have considered all aspects of political economy. Naturally, when Marx died Engels became the guardian of and the authority upon his friend's legacy but Engels was keen to present Marxism as a science and to interpret history in evolutionary terms.[1] The revolution, in Engel's version of history, was no longer a flowering of Hegelian logic, now it had become a product of evolutionary development: Hegel's Phoenix changed from a mythical bird into a creature of evolutionary development and history became a predictable, law-governed science. In his "Speech at the Graveside of Karl Marx"[2] Engels told the handful of mourners that: "Just as Darwin discovered the laws of organic nature, so Marx discovered the law of development of human history…" And of course Engels appears a paragon of circumspection in comparison with the Russian socialists' reverence of Marx and their dogmatic faith in iron laws of history, a reverence and dogmatism that buried millions in the grave of certainty. Like all certainty, their iron conviction was stoked by ignorance.[3]

The Russian leaders, in company with their European comrades, had no or very little knowledge of Marx's early philosophical writings which were not published until after the Second World War:

> A whole generation of Marxist theorists knew next to nothing (through no fault of their own) of Marx's early philosophical writings: it is vital to keep this fact firmly in mind, if one wishes to understand one decisively important circumstance. The first generation of Marxists approached Marx via *Capital* and his other published writings (mainly economic, historical or political), and were unable to understand fully the philosophical precedents and background underlying them.[4]

Not only were pre-Second World War Marxists ignorant of this background and these precedents, a gap in the historical record that partly accounts for Engel's influence, neither were they aware of the intellectual process that had spawned *Das Kapital*. They did not even know of the existence of the drafts Marx had made for *Das Kapital*. Indeed, the history of these drafts illustrates only too well the confounding role that chance may play, confounding any notion of predictability in the history of ideas. Now known as the *Grundrisse*, the "groundwork," Marx's draft sketches for *Das Kapital* comprised seven notebooks, written during the winter of 1857-58, that became lost in unknown circumstances and which had to wait a century for proper publication (in German in 1953). An earlier limited two-volume edition had been published in Moscow in 1939 and 1941 but this edition was hardly circulated[5] and anyway by that time Stalin and the Politburo had more pressing concerns and were now busy ordering the execution of "traitors" to the Soviet war effort rather than as they had before for "crimes" of political dissent or for impeding the guaranteed new socialist dawn. This was no small academic issue for the *Grundrisse* notebooks indicated that Marx had, by the late 1850s, reformulated his earlier romantic, philosophical ideas: in particular,[6] his youthful, romantic views on what exactly would be liberated by the revolution appeared to have changed fundamentally and in ways quite foreign to the tragic Russian creed. The notebooks contain new ingredients for the revolutionary recipe; passages and remarks in the *Grundrisse* showed, contrary to the common understanding, that Marx's communist society would be enjoyed by people now freely pursuing their own self-fulfillment, a society of individual differences, with each of us still wearing our own clothes, not one in which we would all wear the same uniforms (in Russia, as in China, too often prison uniforms).

In the transition from his youthful, romantic theory to his mature analysis, Marx's approach to the question of "human nature" remained unchanged. He remained scornful of attempts to base social theory upon some version or other of a fixed, primordial, human nature that supposedly makes us behave in prede-termined ways and which distinguishes us from other species: in his opinion, "Men can be distinguished from animals by consciousness, by religion or by anything else you like."[7] What is distinctive, he reasoned, was our capacity to produce things, first our food and then increasingly sophisticated goods, the furniture of our artificial world. This distinctive capacity for production was realized in the company of other people, it was a social achievement and could be understood only as it was actually, historically achieved. As a young man, grappling with Hegelian philosophy, forging his own ideas, Marx had analyzed this capacity in abstract, philosophical terms but by the time he came to write the first volume of *Kapital* he had apparently refined his ideas, become familiar with economics, focused specifically upon capitalist society, and had introduced the concept of "social labor."[8] It is thus *social labor* that becomes mutated in capitalist society and his refined aim for the proletariat is for them to reclaim their capacity to labor socially, free at last from the damaging consequences of the private ownership of the means of production. With improvements to productivity through improved technology, and with social labor now steered by social needs rather than captained by the ceaseless drive for profit, individu-als would have increasing time to spend upon their own personal interests and development, personal development which in turn comes to inform their social labor. Communism becomes a synonym for true individuality. Marx's unfinished recipe was for a dish of individuality, not for a meal of equality thought of as uniform equality—the fatal misreading of the theoretically undernourished Russian leaders, intellectually starved of Marx's notebooks that had been mislaid by chance, who dressed equality in uniforms.[9]

Our capacity for social labor, and the means to individual fulfillment can, however, only be understood in the light of all our other human capacities; for example, our capacity for language. We cannot make, or understand, our artificial world without language, we cannot work and produce in the company of other people if we keep silent. Arguably, we cannot think without language and language is, of course, made possible for us by a combination of our biological make-up, our voice boxes, our mental mechanisms, etc. and by our accumulated lexicon. It is this joint heritage, part biological part cultural, that in tandem facilitates social interaction and which preserves our accumulated history. When precisely we first became language users, whether or not we have an inbuilt language instinct, how language impacted upon our evolution, these and similar questions remain unresolved and disputed. Until recently, from at least the seventeenth century, our use of language was commonly held as a mark of species distinctiveness, a unique and defining human attribute. Durkheim and others presented language as an example of a social reality that could not be reduced to explanations about individuals; it was, he thought, a collective, supra-individual phenomenon:

> How many ideas or sentiments are there which we obtain completely on our own? Very few. Each of us speaks a language which he has not himself created: we find it ready-made.[10]

Both these ideas—that language is uniquely human, that language comes "ready made"—are we now know wrong. An accumulating body of studies on animal language, particularly communication by our ape cousins, reveals that other animals do use language, some with sophistication. You can't hold a conversation with a chimp, it doesn't have a voice box, but chimps can be taught sign-language, they do communicate with each other, albeit in a comparatively limited manner. And there's the rub, language use, like many another topic of intra-species comparison, is a matter of *degree*, not of simple presence or absence. Language is, properly, a *range* of abilities. Nor could it mark definitively an individual as a member of our species: if a baby was born with no aptitude for language then we would not think of the baby as belonging to another species, simply being able to use language doesn't make you human. Durkheim's point about language being "ready made," a ready-made gift for the new baby, won't stand up to scrutiny either. If we were to accept that babies maturing from slobbery gurgles to speaking their first proper words may, as Noam Chomsky believes, have an inbuilt language instinct, a mental grammar circuitry activated by hearing others speaking, then this could explain how the baby acquires language, but it won't explain what precisely the baby, then child and later adult will actually say, sing, write or indeed read. Each of us has an individual, distinctive voice (babies recognize their own parents' voices),[11] it's heard when we sing, and some can't sing in tune, we write distinctively enough for lecturers easily to spot plagiarism in student essays, some of us struggle to achieve even clarity (as a quick read of anything written by Hegel will immediately confirm), and not everyone shares my taste for Kipling's poetry. Sorting out what's involved with using language, and how we come to use language in our own distinctive ways, is a good means for correcting the improper expression of the fundamentally sound objection to Marx's, but also a good means to challenge the equally dodgy evolutionary psychologists' pictures of "human nature."

Language, contrary to what Durkheim had supposed, does not come "ready made." What is there awaiting the new-born baby is a community of language users and, for the luckier ones born by chance into a literate society, an accumulation of texts. The baby will need, and this is the crux of the matter, to use language in new situations, for novel purposes, in innovative ways. Our biological, genetic heritage of linguistic proficiency has to be able to facilitate innovation in unfamiliar circumstances. To understand how this could be done, a brief excursion into the mature philosophy of Wittgenstein is necessary, an excursion centred upon his key concept: individuals, particular examples, become members of a group not by virtue of them all sharing some single, common, uniform, defining essential quality, but instead because they share a range of similarities and differences. This key concept, which Wittgenstein borrowed without acknowledgment from his unaccredited philosophical muse, the nineteenth-century philosopher Arthur Schopenhauer (about whom more later in this chapter), is the best available theoretical tool—and as we shall see "tool" is most appropriate—for a proper understanding of human nature, and much else besides.[12] It's a simple, but profound, idea best illustrated by Wittgenstein's own example of the activities we group together under the common heading of "games."

"Games" is both an illustrative example and also a metaphor running through the first part of Wittgenstein's *Philosophical Investigations*, the only part he himself compiled, and the book that was his best, but as he himself says in his Preface, nonetheless unsatisfactory effort at explaining his philosophy. The reason he chose to use games as an illustrative example and as a master metaphor is partly because games are played, in a huge variety of ways, and often, but not always, with other people. It is the variety of what we call games, the diversity in how they're played, that needs always to be kept in mind. We might unthinkingly presume that, just because they are all called "games," they share some essential feature in common, but, and most emphatically, this is not the case:

> Consider for example the proceedings that we call "games." I mean board games, card games, ball games, Olympic Games, and so on. What is common to them all? –Don't

say: "There *must* be something in common, or they would not be called 'games'"—but *look and see* whether there is anything common to all. For if you look at them you will not see something that is common to all, but similarities, relationships, and a whole series of them at that. To repeat: don't think, but look! - Look for example at board-games, with their multifarious relationships. Now pass to card-games; here you find many correspondences with the first group, but many common features drop out, and others appear. When we pass next to ball-games, much that is common is retained, but much is lost.—Are they all "amusing"?

Compare chess with noughts and crosses. Or is there always winning or losing, or competition between players? Think of patience. In ball games there is winning and losing; but when a child throws his ball at the wall and catches it again, this feature has disappeared. Look at the parts played by skill and luck; and at the difference between skill in chess and skill in tennis. Think now of games like ring-a-ring-of-roses; here is the element of amusement, but how many other characteristic features have disappeared! And we can go through the many, many other groups of games in the same way; can see how similarities crop up and disappear.

And the result of the examination is: we see a complicated network of similarities overlapping and criss-crossing: sometimes overall similarities, sometimes similarities of detail.

I can think of no better expression to characterize these similarities than "family resemblances"; for the various resemblances between members of a family: build, features, color of eyes, gait, temperament, etc. etc. overlap and criss-cross in the same way.[13]

In these central "remarks" we come up against the "great question that lies behind all these considerations": the question of how we should best understand the business of categorising individual examples of things, people, etc.—how we come to recognize them as members of a common family, in Wittgenstein's illustrative example the family of activities we call "games." There is no one, common essential quality that all activities we call games must share that allows us to call them "games," anymore than there is one common feature necessarily shared by all members of the same family. It is true that the members of some conceptual families do all share some feature or other: for example all humans breathe oxygen, but this is a universal feature, not a defining, core essence of humanity; many other species breathe oxygen, if we met a boy who did not breathe oxygen then we might be astonished, but we would not axiomatically label him as non-human. Universals and essences need to be distinguished; Wittgenstein's argument and his "family resemblance" theory are addressed only to essences. The uniformity of the names we use for these activities, here "game," misleads us into the presumption that such essences exist and has often misled social theorists to search for non-existent essences which seem to offer the promise of properly grasping the true nature of the topic under investigation. This belief in essences nourishes reductionism for surely we should explain superficial diversity in terms of more fundamental commonalty, reducing variety down to the true core of the phenomena? But such essences are chimerical and social theory's back catalogue contains many a fruitless quest for them. For instance, in the case of religion it is tempting to believe that all religions must share a common, defining essence of religiosity and that this essence is the core of all religious activities whose apparent diversity is analytically superficial. Religion is found in all human societies and this ubiquity suggests that some fundamental human need or existential predicament is being surreptitiously voiced, the argument of Feuerbach adopted and refined by Marx. Less revolutionary nineteenth-century thinkers also produced analyses that claimed to have identified the true function of religion; Durkheim for example claimed that in worshipping gods, we were really worshipping our collective social spirit. Although their identification of the purported true essences of religion differed, what Feuerbach, Marx, Durkheim, and others fell for was the dangerous analytical implication that accompanies the belief in essences, essentialism's fellow-traveler, the seeming implication that variety is less significant than commonality. Wittgenstein's family resemblance approach, quoted above, is intended to combat this delusive implication; categories are woven with both differences and similarities, each just as real and significant. It is not, contrary to Feuerbach and company, that the differences between religions are necessarily less vital than the things they may share, the universal features of religion: which is more significant at any one time is an empirical issue, not answered by pre-given religious essences. We can happily accept that religions may on occasion help communities cohere, or may offer refuge from dissatisfying, cruelly capitalistic life, or from absurd suffering, just so long as these and similar aspects of religious practice are presented as *additional* features of religion, not as their defining, core feature. For illustration, one of these universal component features found inhabiting religions is of course Satan, in his different costumes, a fiendish subject neglected by Feuerbach and thus by Marx; presumably, just as we project our best qualities onto a mythical God, so too we project our worst onto a mythical Lucifer—suggesting that ending religious fetishism may liberate aspects of our true humanity that are best left alienated.

Wittgenstein's family resemblance proposal, borrowed from Schopenhauer, is preferable to the alternatives[14] and one strength of Wittgenstein's borrowed solution to the question of how we group particular examples of things into collective categories such as "games" is the compatibility of this solution with Darwinian theory: the metaphorical comparison of the similar and different features shared by members of the same linguistic family is precisely the picture of generational inheritance that Darwin painted, the sketch of how siblings share similar and different family features, the sketch now fleshed out by genetic science. The notion of "family resemblances" allows us to rethink what we mean by "individuality," what we mean by "human nature," and this rethinking will expose shortcomings in Marx's revolutionary recipe. Before we can clear up these topics, we need to first consider what children must learn in order to become linguistically proficient, a proficiency marked by an ability to use language in novel situations.

Contrary to what Durkheim had supposed, each of us does indeed create our own language; that is to say—or write, or sing, or chant, or carve, or mimic—we use language in new, creative ways as circumstances demand. Words, argued Wittgenstein, were metaphorically similar to tools and our vocabulary comparable to a toolbox. This metaphor, thought Wittgenstein had the virtuous implication that just like tools, words could be seen to have different functions, they were used in different way, and so required different skills to be learnt in order for them to be used proficiently. A child becomes linguistically proficient when she is able to *use* words acceptably in new situations in the same way that an apprentice becomes proficient in the use of the tools of his trade. "Acceptably" here means in line with social convention: just as private property is not a relationship between individuals and things, so too words do not get their meaning from their correspondence to objects, but like private property from social relationships. So, for instance, I am walking through the countryside with my younger son and he asks me "Dad, what's an oak?" I raise my arm and point to a gnarled old oak tree and reply, "That's an oak, over there." Later that evening, we're having dinner and my wife raises her arm, points to a nasty damp spot she's just noticed on the kitchen wall, and asks us "What's that?"—to which my son confidently answers, "It's an oak." What my son has misunderstood is the social convention of pointing-and-naming; he wrongly thinks that "oak" refers to the physical action of raising an arm, he doesn't yet understand the, in Wittgenstein's phrase, "language game" that is being played. Only training in the language game will allow him to become proficient, and learning the language game, like any other game, requires we learn its rules. "Rules" is Wittgenstein's own term but as he himself recognized it's liable to mislead for it may wrongly be equated with "laws" or hard-and-fast rules. The rules of language, to cut a long controversy short, are better thought of as *principles*: no linguistic principle could possibly tell you precisely how to reuse a word or phrase, nor could it prepare you for unfamiliar situations.[15] Indeed, the inappropriate use of language, the foundation of many jokes, is a good test of fluency and the fact that we never run out of jokes is a tribute to our language's inherently flexible, open-ended nature. We learn to use our language by applying the principles appropriate to the circumstances, we are proficient when those to whom we are speaking are not baffled, confused, do not misunderstand or snigger, but rather continue along with the conversation. The changing circumstances are not a series of wholly unique situations; rather, and this goes back to the notion of family resemblances, a succession of situations that are partly similar to and partly different from previous cases: similarly, each new game of snooker is different, none are replicas, but none are wholly different from those that you have played before. The rules of snooker easily manages this diversity, and so too do the guiding rules, the principles, of language games.

It is not, as Wittgenstein's followers often mistakenly presumed,[16] that words change for ever their meaning depending upon their circumstantial usage; rather, that we learn new usages which we add to our personal dictionary, our accumulating semantic stock. How a word or phrase is understood will be dependent upon circumstance, but the earlier meanings are not automatically lost; like other social innovations they are routinely preserved. This accumulative process may explain the strengths of English which, compared to other languages, including its major European rivals, enjoys a far larger vocabulary, a vocabulary built by borrowing words and phrases from other languages, permitting finer distinctions to be drawn, subtler points to be made. It is not that there is anything intrinsically, essentially superior about English; there is no superior essence, just an accumulation of borrowings, purloinings, and adoptions from other languages that have accrued to offer English speakers greater linguistic riches.

This Wittgensteinian picture of language sheds light upon the real nature of novelty, upon what we should mean by individuality, and also upon the topic of "human nature." The prominent evolutionary psychologist Leda Cosmides, as I mentioned in the third chapter, argues that our brain should metaphorically be compared to a Swiss Army penknife, with different blades shaped and honed by evolutionary pressures. Each blade performs different mental tasks, we don't just have one blade for doing everything. One problem with this analogy, that I illustrated earlier on, was that you can use the same blade for different tasks (in my example, the same blade is suitable for roasting cannabis as well as for removing stones from horses' hooves). Indeed, the device intended to help horses in distress is in fact not a "blade" in the sense that it has a cutting edge, rather, it's a tool which slots back into the Swiss Army penknife in the manner of a conventional blade. These blades, like the tools in Wittgenstein's metaphorical linguistic tool box, have differing natures, differing uses, the range of which cannot be specified fully and which require a range of differing skills. Preserving differences, recognizing diverse usages, siting usages in various contexts, and avoiding reductionism, especially attempts to reduce variety to some mythical defining "essence," are the lessons of Wittgenstein that easily become lost in the evolutionary psychologists' explanatory strategy. A good illustration of this common failing is to be found in certain neo-Darwinist explanations for patterns of human mate selection, an issue clearly central to the process of gene transmission.

As we saw in chapter 3, identical twins seem as vulnerable as anyone else to the capriciousness of Cupid's darts; their choice of partners is, in Lykken's phrase, "adventitious," not "lawful," seemingly a matter of chance and not the outcome of evolutionary targeting. Nonetheless, it is not the case that human mate selection is wholly random, even Cupid's darts fall in a broad pattern that is seemingly universal, the same the world over. Charles Darwin had proposed, in *The Descent of Man*, that competition by both men and women for the best mate played a key role in evolution. "Sexual selection" was a means to reproductive success, a strategy to maximize the opportunity for having healthy children, and as we might now say, a strategy for passing on our genes. When *The Descent of Man* was first published in 1872 the idea of women, or at least respectable middle-class women, actively making sexual selections offended Victorian sensibilities and the idea may still offend modern feminists for it implies that standards of beauty, criteria of physical attractiveness, are underpinned by biology, not patriarchal power, an implication that Nancy Etcoff, an American psychologist, has vigorously upheld in opposition to some feminist theorists who argue that what counts as "beauty" is a changing, patriarchal cultural ideal, not a measure set by our biology.[17] One piece of research evidence cited by Etcoff is Professor Davendra Singh's identification of the apparently universal male preference for the hour-glass female figure. That there are some universal patterns (but not essences) of human behavior should really come as no surprise given our species similarity and those who find such similarities objectionable do so often because they believe that progressive politics must be founded upon a view of human behavior as wholly malleable, wholly within our control. This was not Darwin's own view, in *The Expression of the Emotions in Man and the Animals* he had argued that we have a set of universal species expressions, for instance the facial expression of happiness or revulsion, much as one would expect given our evolution from a common ancestor. His argument has been revived by Paul Ekman[18] who had originally set out to disprove conclusively the Darwinian view and found, to his own surprise, that evidence for cultural plasticity was sorely lacking and that when shown pictures of individuals expressing say happiness or aggression, people from very different cultures readily identified the emotion expressed. What makes us happy or aggressive will of course be culturally influenced, and whether or not we express an emotion may too be culturally steered, but nonetheless how our facial expression of emotions appears is the same the world over.

One difficulty in making the Darwinian case stems from the problem of isolating cultural influences, in this case mass media images of facial expressions, a difficulty Ekman tackled in 1967, borrowing a technique developed originally for studying children who could not yet read, by showing photographs of facial expressions to the South Fore people of Papua New Guinea and asking them to match one of the photographs to short scripted scenarios that were read aloud to them (for instance, "She is angry and about to fight"). As these South Forean subjects did not have a written language, had never or very rarely seen film or television, nor seldom seen any pictures or photographs, they were almost untainted by any external cultural stereotypes yet they readily matched expressions to scripted emotional responses: "These stone-age people, who could not have learned expressions from the media, chose the same expressions for each emotion as had the people in the 21 literate cultures."[19] Similarly Davendra Singh has, in a recently published article, used a comparable strategy to avoid cultural contamination when asking male subjects to rank the attractiveness and attributes of line-drawings of women who differ in their weight and in their waist-hip ratios. The line-drawings, the silhouettes, show rows of female body shapes in three rows of weight (underweight, average, and overweight), and in each row there are three waist-hip ratios (0.7, 0.8, 0.9). In a series of articles,[20] Professor Singh has reported findings showing men from many different cultural backgrounds overwhelmingly prefer the silhouette of the average-weight woman with a 0.7 waist-hip ratio (i.e., a waist seven-tenths the width of the hips) and both men and women ranked the silhouettes for attributes such as desire for children, good companionship, being interesting to talk to, in line with the silhouettes' body shapes. Recently, respondents for this exercise were sought from the Azore Islands and Guinea-Bissau, from peoples who have only started watching television in the late 1980s, and even then the programming they had watched was very limited and local.[21] These comparatively culturally distinct subjects also honed in on the average-weight silhouette with the 0.7 waist-hip ratio. The reason why physical attractiveness plays such a large part in mate selection, reasons Professor Singh, is because it signals reproductive good health. The waist-hip ratio signals fertility in pre-menopausal women and the seeming universal male preference for the 0.7 waist-hip ratio may explain why both Marilyn Monroe and Twiggy were successful models (they both had desirable ratios), it may account for the Victorian fashion for waspish waists, the Indian outfit of saree worn with a tummy-exposing short blouse, and the ubiquity of bare tummies currently displayed by pre-menopausal European women. Muddying the picture slightly are a number of studies that suggest a female's body-mass index (BMI), her height compared with her weight, is a stronger variable affecting judgments of attractiveness but Singh sticks to his guns, arguing that of course if the range of BMI is treated as an independent variable and shown in a wide range, then it will be paramount but his studies show that female attractiveness is a combination of a normal BMI and a low waist-hip ratio:

> It is more important to identify the indicators of attractiveness and their adaptive significance than to demonstrate that some variables such as age (using 10- to 80-year-old range) or obesity account for more variance than, for example, fluctuating asymmetry does.[22]

Singh's response to studies emphasising BMI, from which the above quotation is taken, reveals his allegiance to evolutionary psychology: it's the evolutionary significance of human physical attractiveness which he holds to be the chief analytical goal. The argument boils down to the claim that evolution has honed a mental blade which leads us to respond, perhaps unknowingly, to physical signals of reproductive health, a blade in our Swiss Army penknife that predisposes men to prefer hour-glass figures and encourages women to mould, diet, starve their bodies into this shape. While this may be mildly interesting, or maybe if you're a woman disturbing, it is important to recognize that what is being identified in this example of mating preferences are universal predispositions—but not anything that simply causes us to act in predetermined ways. One reason this predisposition won't necessarily lead a man to choose a mate with the best waist-hip ratio is simply because in real life women will never resemble the silhouette line-drawings that Singh's experimental subjects are presented with: real women are immensely varied, unlike Singh's silhouettes which vary only by weight and waist-hip ratios. In the real world other female traits will be relevant for mate selection, some of which may also be evolutionary dispositions, for example height which, as a recent study suggests, also influences women's as well as men's perceptions of other women's characters, with tall women judged to be more intelligent, assertive and ambitious than their shorter sisters.[23]

Singh's female silhouettes are all identical in height, people in the real world never are. Height, how tall or short we are, is like all aspects of individuality only knowable, only measurable, comparatively: height is a measure of something real that can only be known by comparison. Our height is the product of both nature and nurture, a phenotypic expression of our genotype. The sharpest influence upon our growth is environmental, an influence that starts at the moment of conception including factors such as the nourishment received by the fetus, our mother's stress levels, her drug habits, the quality of the air she breathes, etc. Environmental factors will be influential up until we stop growing, until we reach our genetically determined maximum height at about the age of sixteen for girls, twenty for boys. The pattern of our growth is erratic; we measure roughly half our eventual adult height by our second birthday and then we grow in spurts, especially during puberty. Throughout our species men are on average taller than women. Height may be a surprisingly important variable affecting many areas of our lives,[24] including our selection of sexual partners; women the world over prefer taller mates, and men shorter, preferences displayed in social psychological research,[25] evident in Lonely Hearts' advertisements, and observable by looking out of your window at the couples strolling by. Height may also be implicated when it comes to job interviews,[26] in pay with taller workers taking home bigger pay-packets,[27] and it may also be correlated with how long we live, taller people enjoy greater longevity.[28] The winners of American presidential elections are most usually the taller candidate, a trend that was of some interest in 2004 for John Kerry towered over Bush by seven inches, but as the election results cruelly confirmed, only a trend, not an unvarying law. (Bush's media minders went to some trouble to disguise their candidate's comparative shortness in the televised presidential debates, as did Prince Charles's PR posse when he was photographed standing next to his taller first wife). In the past height was correlated with social class and status, with the less advantaged "looking up" to their social superiors. Short rulers sat above their subjects on their raised thrones. Nowadays, with, at least in the West, an abundance of food and its more equitable distribution, you can look your social superior straight in the eye.

The range of heights in any human population displays the same pattern of distribution: if the incidences of heights of individuals are plotted from the shortest to the tallest then a classic bell-shaped curve will be seen. Most people's height will cluster around the top of the curve, around the arithmetic mean average of the total heights in the sample—in other words, most people are roughly the same height and there is not that much difference between the shortest and the tallest, "...95% of all heights of individuals fall within a range of 10 to 11.2 inches (25.4 to 28.4 cm) distributed symmetrically around the average height of the group to which they belong."[29] For example, the stature-for-age percentiles for American women in 2000 showed the 50th percentile, the top of the Bell Curve, as approximately 64 inches (163 cm), the 3rd percentile as 59 inches (151 cm) and the 97th percentile as 69 inches (175cm).[30] Most people we meet will not be that much shorter or taller than us and only those few at the furthest extremes of the height range will turn heads as they walk down the street.

Height is then, a "continuum of tallness" measured comparatively. All of us are of some height or other, unlike those features we may or may not exhibit such as premature male baldness, left-handedness, or blond-hair coloring. These latter features are "discontinuous" genetic inheritances; unlike your height, you either display them or you don't. As we saw in the earlier chapter on genetics, the mechanisms by which we inherit universal features like our height that are ranged in a population, and those such as blond-colored hair which you either do or do not display, are different. Height, like other phenotypic features expressed in a continuum, is a product of many genes acting in concert. Known as polygenic inheritance, the height bequest from your parents is a potential, fixed at conception, a ceiling which you may or may not reach depending on the environment in which you grow up. Whether or not you reach your potential height is chiefly down to environmental factors, including chance factors (for instance, the monsoons fail for three years as you reach puberty), environmental variables whose influence is demonstrated by the increases in the heights of Occidental men and women since the Industrial Revolution, signaled by bumping your head on the low ceilings of old houses or the inadequate length of standard-sized beds: the period since the Industrial Revolution is far too brief for any natural evolutionary changes to have produced this truly upward trend, a trend that may now be stalling as we reach our genetically imposed species ceiling when children will no longer routinely grow to be taller than their parents.[31]

A mating preference for a particular comparative height, like the male preference for an hour-glass female figure, appears to be a universal—but not a core, essential—human predisposition. That we use these and similar universal measurements of attractiveness is hardly revelatory, much what everyday experience and Darwinian theory teaches us (what would be truly surprising would be the discovery of wholly discrete criteria of attractiveness). The danger comes, I think, from the ways that such universals are slotted into reductionist explanations where they take on the guise of the real, essentialist underlying cause of our behavior. There is nothing disconcerting in the Darwinian recognition of universal facial expressions if we just keep in mind that the evolutionary processes that led to our universal species repertoire of emotive facial expressions were the same processes that gave each of us our own smiles, or more rightly our own personal repertoire, both similar to and different from anybody else's. Evolution literally put a smile on your face, in fact a huge number of smiles: just think of the smiles you need for "amusement"; wry, rueful, habitual, malicious, surprised amusements all need their own special set to your mouth. Evolution facilitates these repertoires that others can readily recognize, chiefly because as members of the same species we are highly similar. Perhaps it is your involuntary, spontaneous smile of delight that attracts a stranger who becomes your lover. Darwin believed that there was no facial expression corresponding to love itself because, although he held the emotion of love to be "one of the strongest of which the mind is capable," it is not accompanied by any action and hence there were no distinctive movements from which a characteristic expression could have evolved (unlike, say, the wrinkling of the nose at the smell of something disgusting which evolves into the generic facial expression for "disgust").[32] In contrast to Darwin, Paul Ekman argues that love is not a true emotion for "emotions are brief and episodic, lasting seconds or minutes," whereas "parental love, romantic love, [in common with] hatred, envy or jealousy last for much longer periods."[33] Whichever of these two accounts is correct, just because love doesn't have its own lasting face this does not mean that it is a lesser emotion, nor a less compelling reason for mate selection, (similarly, snowdrops are no less beautiful nor real just because they only flower briefly). Love may play a part that is less, more, or equal to brute sexual attraction when it comes to mate selection. The explanatory danger lies in the mistaken belief that mate selection could be explained solely in terms of physical attractiveness, the ever-present temptation to reduce a host of different factors down to just one core reason, here to those "hidden signals" of reproductive health.

Darwinism, in explanatory terms, is something of a one-horse trick with everything explained in relation to reproduction, and this explanatory poverty promotes reductionism which in turn impoverishes our understanding of events, such as falling in love. This illegitimate theoretical move has parallels in the "supplantist" pseudo-evolutionary picture of societal change we met with in the first chapter wherein a wholly new form of society, say capitalism, is held to wholly supplant its predecessor (in this case, feudalism). Just as no such supplantism actually occurs—instead, innovations in the "artificial world" are added on in a procession of societal accretion—so too sexual attraction is merely one factor among many that may influence who we sleep with, propose to, yearn after, cry over. Love, and the other feelings and criteria which grace our actions, are not some sort of thin varnish applied to sexuality in the reductionist thinking of evolutionary psychology. The golden analytical rule suggested by

Wittgenstein is not to seek a chimerical essence of human attraction, but instead to see each component joining with others in the family of attractive features, as an "and," rather than as a superficial offshoot of some core, essential feature to which it must be reductively linked.

Which feature, or more likely features, we find attractive in other people is an empirical issue, neither one predetermined by our evolved biology nor one reducible to some essence of human attractiveness. Height is just one of the varying physical features we would need to add to Singh's female silhouettes if we were to bring them to life, to life as real, varied, individual women. We could start to flesh them out with differing body mass indexes, symmetries of features and other physical differences that are susceptible to the logic of Darwinian explanation, but these additions would barely turn the silhouettes into cartoons; far more detail, far greater subtlety is demanded if they are going to resemble real women. Even in the case of nature's "hidden signals," her signaling is subject to chance: for illustration, let us retake the example of Aristotle's visitor to the marketplace and now let him unexpectedly meet, instead of some known acquaintance, an unknown woman whom he bumps into beside a market stall. He apologizes, she acknowledges his apology and then, just as she turns away, glances at him again, this time with an involuntary smile, a delightful, dazzling smile that lights up her face—but Aristotle doesn't see it, for his attention has been diverted by a display of tempting plump aubergines. Or, Cournot's hapless passer-by who, rather than stunned by a falling slate, becomes instead stunned by an unusually tall, handsome man walking along on the other side of the road; she slows down so as to get a better look, meanwhile the slate falls harmlessly before she's reached the house with the dodgy roof.

Those two examples are crude, but nonetheless perhaps good enough to illustrate the point that universal evolutionary predispositions are, like all other aspects of life, susceptible to the machinations of chance coincidence. Indeed, it may be that chance and romantic love have become increasingly intimate: just as Aristotle had noted that recognising chance is only possible against a background of rationality, so too romantic love becomes highlighted, made more precious, when it is placed against rational scenery. It is maybe for this reason we speak in English of "falling" in love, the supreme goal for citizens of those Western societies which, from the Enlightenment onward have championed reason, a sovereign whose authority, as Pascal knew, does not run to matters of the heart. Often, we do not act on the basis of just one "hidden signal," nor just on the sum of all such signals; rather, we see the whole person, and we form estimations of their whole character, what they are like as people (echoing Stephen Jay Gould's criticism of gene-centred sociobiology, his important observation that only whole organisms and not genes, reproduce and thus the unit of explanation must be the whole person, their whole character). Each person, each character, is unique and we don't choose whether or not we find their character attractive, any more than we choose to like the taste of aubergines. Perhaps it is that girl sitting coincidentally at her desk alongside yours at school who will, by chance, demand you coin a new metaphor for early-flowering love, as had happened to Edward Prynn, an illiterate Cornish farmworker in 1949, when he was a thirteen years old schoolboy:

> I had a girlfriend. At that young age, yes. "Tis what I call *snowdrop love*. I give it that name because snowdrops are about the first flowers in spring. They're young and tender and they soon go, unnoticed. She was called Diana Curragh. She was a darling. In school when I didn't know the answer to the question, Diana who sat to the left of me in another desk, would try and whisper the answer to me. I suppose all females like to see their boy friends getting on a bit, not coming behind the rest. That was most probably why she tried to help me. Diana also used to send me love notes. I couldn't read what she had written on the love note, but we all know the cross. What a symbol the cross is: the Lord Jesus; in the medical profession for care; from a woman it means love! And there were always a few crosses on the letters. I didn't know what the words were, but I knew what they meant all right. I'd smile. I'd keep my piece of paper. I'd never ask any of the other boys to read it to me, so they wouldn't keep on. I'd just give her a smile, as good as to say: "All right, I know."[34]

Diana left Edward's Cornish village when her family emigrated to Australia, Edward himself went blind when he was thirty, but her story, he tells us, had a "happy ending" because "she's married and got a family."

Reductionism, which pulls the petals off snowdrops, provokes a curious ambivalence; it's always tempting yet at the same time oddly dissatisfying. We shy away from reductionism, especially when thinking about ourselves and our own behaviour, instinctively aware that it somehow doesn't measure up, that it somehow isn't up to the explanatory mark. These natural reservations over reductionism are well founded because *we are constituted by variety*; reductionism strips away just those differences that make us who we are. Stripped of variety we become mere silhouettes. To turn silhouettes into people we must add further features, features that will most usually be shared to some degree by us all. These varying features are what bring us to life as real individuals, they are what make silhouettes into characters. If Cosmide's Swiss Army penknife turns out to be a reasonable metaphor for our adaptive mental mechanisms then we will need to factor variety into the metaphor, not squeeze it out from the procrustean bed of reductivist evolutionary psychology. We need to start from the premises that each blade of the universal mental penknife will have to cope with a ceaseless variety and that how the blades are wielded will in turn be affected by the unique characteristics of the person who is using it (sharp blades need more careful handling by clumsy, or inexperienced, people). To appreciate how our characteristics make us whom we are, how we might become aware of them and what part they may play in shaping our behavior, let us revisit the example of height.

I want to claim that our characteristics, our individual qualities such as for example our kindness, patience, etc. are inherited but because this claim has a dark history, because it is likely to meet with righteous opposition, the details of the claim need some careful specification. A useful way to clarify the claim, and some of its implications, is by drawing a parallel between one particular illustrative characteristic, how talkative we are, and our height. All of our characteristics share with the example of height a comparative element; just as we can only know our height by comparison with other shorter or taller people, so too we can only know how talkative we are by comparison, there is no other route to awareness of our individual characteristics, to this sort of self-awareness. For this reason, Marx and other theorists were correct to stress the undeniably social nature of our lives. Characteristics, like height, are in a range, tall to short, mute to verbose, with the differences between the individuals in the range usually small. The fact that such individual differences in the range are usually small does not mean, however, that the consequences, their effects, will not be large: as Darwinists are keen to point out, small differences may have significant impact; having, for instance, slightly drab coloring may mean you escape that hungry predator's attention, you live long enough to breed, whereas your more flamboyant neighbour ends up in the predator's stomach, as do her genes, and similarly being a rather poor talker, but a good listener may, in the right company, be just the edge you need to hold the attention of that beautiful boy. Individuals do not have unique, one-off, characteristics, we share them to a greater or lesser degree with everyone else: when, for instance, I say "He's quiet" I mean something like "He's unusually quiet, uncommonly taciturn," that he is toward a far end of the range, not that he possesses some wholly unique quality. Whether or not, and how, we come to know our own character, in full or in part, is like everything else open to the capriciousness of chance; if you live in a small, isolated community then you will not be aware of the wider range of species characteristics, you may think, as you're taller than everyone else in your small community, that measuring five feet, nine inches is outstanding.

Our character is a question of discovery, it is revealed to us; how much is revealed, and when, is down to circumstances, circumstances that are sometimes swept by the "skirts of chance."

Of course, all such comparative knowledge is open to changing evaluation ("I'm sick and tired of being only average height") and there are other kinds of characteristics that we experience *as* evaluation, those we group together as "tastes," what we do and do not like. If, as in my example of Aristotle's visitor to the marketplace, we like aubergines we have not chosen to enjoy relishing this vegetable any more than we choose to be of average height, nor any more than we may detest its slimy flesh but admire its gorgeous purple skin. We learn that we enjoy, or perhaps have now gone off, the taste of aubergine. If we've never tasted aubergine then we won't know whether it's to our liking, and whether or not we get the opportunity to taste it may be a chance affair. And again, there is a range of aubergine flavours—as when it is baked in moussaka, or roasted then mixed with yoghurt, or fried and garnished with wedges of lemons, pickled with garlic, and so on. Chance experiences may reveal some aspect of our character, some peculiar taste or other: here there lies the danger of imagining that unfamiliar, extreme, testing circumstances would reveal what we are "really like." Perhaps we too would break the bones in our own arm, then cut it off with a knife if we had had, by ill-luck, our arm trapped under a heavy boulder when mountain climbing as, with almost unbelievable fortitude, with no water and as little hope of survival, did Aspen mountaineer Aron Ralston, who used a pocket-knife to amputate his own self-broken arm and free himself from a boulder weighing 800-1,000 pounds that fell and trapped him for five days in a remote desert canyon in eastern Utah.[35] Perhaps on the battlefield we too could discover, through our reactions to carnage and killing, what we are "really like." Imagining ourselves in such circumstances is difficult, it's part of the lure of this sort of mental experiment, for if only, we think, we too were really up against it, then we would know what we are truly like, and we may secretly envy those who have been tested by severe circumstance. Fortunately, most of us never will be placed in these extreme conditions, conditions that may reveal some startling, unsuspected side to our character, some dark, disturbing lessons, such as those revealed to a young American serving in the Vietnamese War:

> Watching guys die is a drag, but there's a weird educational side to war, too. Like the first time I seen a guy's guts laying on top of him, as disgusting as it was, I said to myself, "Oh, wow, So that's what they look like." If you want, you can go in there and help yourself to a handful, you can wash them off and keep them. You can perform major surgery, right there.
> The whole world gets absurd after a while. You can do things that seem not right now, but which seem right at the time. I used to love to go over to guys who would catch rounds in the chest or the guts and pretend I was a doctor. You had the license to do whatever you wanted. I'd go over there and I'd take my hand and stick it inside their guts, pick it up, wash it off or do the old chest routine. I would sort of experiment. You know, I couldn't do anything to hurt these guys, they were dead. But there was something about sticking my hands in warm blood that I used to love especially during the monsoon seasons.[36]

These sorts of truly disturbing discoveries about ourselves—here, an unsuspected capacity or liking for DIY surgery—reveal a further side to our characters, but not our true or base nature. Vegetarians are often, and tediously, challenged by aggressive questioning from guilty carnivores that runs something like "Ah, you *say* you're a vegetarian, but suppose you were on a desert island where no veg grew, then you'd soon start sharpening a spear, hunting wild pig, breakfasting on bacon." Well, yes, you probably would, but all that you would discover about yourself is that in highly unusual circumstances you behave in highly unusual ways, not that you're true self, stripped of its civilized veneer, has been exposed red in tooth and claw. How we behave in extreme circumstances may reveal the range of our character, but the extremes of the range are no more or less real than those in the middle, just less familiar. From extreme circumstances we learn more about ourselves, and in this sense *more* of what we are truly like, but we don't get a lesson identifying some new facet of our selves that reductively explains all our routine behavior.

Just because our character, how we resemble and diverge from other people, is inherited this does not mean that it is immutable, nor that it is unchanging. This is a common, mistaken view that fed the old nature-nurture debate and a mistake which marred the work of Arthur Schopenhauer, Wittgenstein's unaccredited muse.[37] As evolutionary psychologists have usefully noted, the physical features we inherit change over time and can be modified if we so desire. I certainly used to have more hair, we grow two sets of teeth whose appearance and health we can do something about, if I go out running every morning then my leg muscles will strengthen. "Inherited" does not equal "fixed for all time." Similarly, I can improve my singing voice, temper my rash judgements, resist my weakness for bad puns, just as I can learn to lower my head so that I won't hit it against those ancient ceiling beams. If I'm below average height then those low ceilings won't be a constant problem, I won't have to stoop, I perhaps won't even notice them. Like height, our characteristics are not the cause of our behaviour: characteristics do not cause us to do anything at all, there is no causal relation between actions and characteristics. Characteristics, as Schopenhauer had recognized, are *what* we are and we cannot sensibly claim that they determine our actions because we cannot be said to determine ourselves—for this reason, all concerns that free will would be jeopardized by inherited characteristics are simply misplaced, characteristics have nothing to do with free will (a topic much chewed over by evolutionary psychologists and other neo-Darwinists). Characteristics, like height or talkativeness, shape *how* we behave, but not why: similarly, letters on your computer keyboard do not determine what you must write, they are tools for expressing yourself.

In his epigrammatic remarks upon human psychology Schopenhauer insisted, wrongly, not only that character is unchanging and immutable but also, and equally wrongly, that character was always more important than mere personality. Drawing support from etymology, as Hobbes had done earlier, Schopenhauer noted:

> There is an unconscious appositeness in the use of the word *person* to designate the human individual, as is done in all European languages: for *persona* really means an actor's mask, and it is true that no one reveals himself as he is; we all wear a mask and play a role.[38]

Schopenhauer's latter observation, that we hide our genuine character behind the mask of our plastic personality, became taken up in Erving Goffman's sociological study *The Presentation of Self in Everyday Life* (1959). Like Hobbes and Schopenhauer, Goffman also highlighted the etymology of personality, but unlike his predecessors Goffman focused upon the ways in which our personality masks are made and maintained and his own reference for the word's etymological history was to another contemporary American sociologist, Robert Park.[39] Like Park, Goffman argued that our characters are "achieved" in social performances, performances he likened metaphorically to social theatre. In this sense, Goffman crested the growing academic wave which saw character swept aside to be replaced by the Cult of Personality (indeed, the older meanings of character and personality, the sort of usage made by Schopenhauer, has all but disappeared and nowadays psychologists commonly use the two words in the reverse sense, talking of "core personalities" where older writers would have used "character"). Goffmanesque accounts of personality lack explanatory power (as they cannot explain why one person rather than another dons a particular personality mask, rather than another), they are also, I think, instinctively dissatisfying, but such dissatisfaction may tempt us falsely to promote our enduring sense of ourselves, the feeling we have, in Schopenhauer's words, that "...however old we become, we yet feel within ourselves that we are absolutely the same as when we were young..."[40] We need to resist this temptation, we are not "absolutely the same"; we naturally change as we grow older and we may modify our character.

Clearly, being able to present ourselves in various social roles, assuming different personality masks, is a commonplace, the stuff of much routine social life: in some circumstances, this ability may be crucial, it may save your life when there's a heavy, officious knock on your door late at night, it may land you that prized job, help win over that surly boss. Whether personality or character is of greater significance is not a question answerable except with reference to circumstances, circumstances that may be unfamiliar, unexpected and may be the product of chance. The enduring sense we have of ourselves is not, contrary to Schopenhauer, our recognition of an unchanging, essential self, not a fixed face masked by contrived personality. Rather, it is our *accumulated* understanding of the range of our characters, what we are capable of, what we like, etc. revealed to us in our behavior. We are of course aware, to different extents, of the masks we wear, the playing out of our social roles, but equally we do not think that these masks comprise our full selves; what masks we wear, how well we wear them, reflects our character like the engravings on say a metal vase reflects the tools the engraver used and her engraving skills. Characteristics, the comparative range of inherited similarities and differences distinguishing individuals, have effects in the same way as Wittgenstein understood our use of language: blades in penknives do not determine what exactly we must cut, nor whether we use the blade for cutting rather than as an improvised screwdriver, their usage requires we learn the principles of using penknives (for example, always cut away from yourself), and unlike the blades in Swiss Army penknives our inherited characteristics are a set of unique (in the Wittgensteinian definition), tools.

In the past the distinctive impress of character—whose etymology, not examined by Hobbes, Schopenhauer, Park nor Goffman, is from the Greek *Kharakter*, an "engraved mark" —was more readily observable whereas nowadays machine-made, mass-produced commodities are to all intents and purposes identical, and hence characterless. Evolution, however, does not mass-produce characterless penknives: she may bequest us with a repertoire of species instincts, but she never replicates individuals; instead, evolution produces unceasing variety, in our own case an unceasing variety of individuals with their own distinctive set of characteristics, a set very nearly, but never perfectly, the same as other people's. Unlike blades in Swiss Army penknives, our characteristics are varied, varied by chance genetic heredity and chance biological factors. We have, metaphorically, a "character default": a tall woman, a six-foot-tall woman, a height achieved by her chance genetic height potential achieved in the equally chancy environment in which she grew to adulthood, is also naturally shy but this does not mean that she will always hit her head on that low door in her bedroom anymore than she must always be crippled by embarrassment in social gatherings. Just as she can stoop to avoid banging her head, so too she can learn to overcome her natural shyness. In unguarded moments, caught on the hop, taken by surprise, she may act unthinkingly and then her behavior will be an expression of her character defaults (for instance, she unexpectedly is introduced to an attractive man at a party, or, she is being shown a new property by an estate agent, an old house with low ceilings). Character defaults are not causes of behaviour nor motives for behavior, but they are part of what we understand of our own selves, how we understand other people, and they are partly the product of chance. Character defaults are the starting point for character development; as we all differ subtly so too we all start off from differing starting blocks.

Which is all very well, but where does this leave the Mandelas, whom we had left standing outside the offices of Perfidy and Sons, Residential and Business Estate Agents?

Written in a tasteful maroon faux-copperplate script against a light cream background, the name of our fictional estate agents is also a title for the patterns of inheritance that reproduces the world in which you and I live: a world in which creativity becomes commodities owned as private property, property that may be passed on, inherited, by our children. When he comes of age, Mr. Perfidy's son may inherit the family business, a business which both exploits and owes its own existence to the social conventions of private property (if homes were not private property they would not be houses, without houses to buy and sell for a profitable commission estate agents could not exist and so there would be no family business for Mr. Perfidy's sons to inherit). The transmission of genes and property to future generations follow different routes, but along both routes chance lays in wait generating an endless variety of individual characters who inherit a world shaped by the accumulation of past achievements, an accumulative process that includes chancy ingredients (Mrs. Perfidy is only blessed with daughters; the property market in the southeast of England overheats and collapses, estate agents go in to receivership). Clearly, the social world, the artificial world we make, depends upon some system or other of inheritance for its survival, its continuity. We can change the ways past social achievements are inherited, there's plenty of species variety in the conventions of inheritance both across cultures and through history, and in chapter 7 we will examine the importance of these inheritance rules for shaping culture and characters, but the Mandelas have pressing housing needs and so let's effect a hypothetical Marxian revolution and discover whether or not Nelson Mandela moves into the home he deserves.

Having suffered poor health since returning from the *Beagle* voyage, Darwin died from a heart attack in 1882, a year before Marx. In contrast to Marx, Charles Darwin left a considerable estate and regarded the generational inheritance of property as a beneficial social institution. In the fifth chapter of his *Descent of Man* where he considered, in "an imperfect and fragmentary manner," the development of our intellectual and moral faculties, Darwin remarked that "Man accumulates property and bequeaths it to his children, so that the children of the rich have an advantage over the poor in the race for success, independently of bodily or mental superiority."[41] There were drawbacks—for instance primogeniture unfairly favored elder sons even though their younger brothers might be superior in respect to "body or mind"—but on the whole, reasoned Darwin, "... the inheritance of property by itself is very far from an evil; for without the accumulation of capital the arts could not progress; and it is chiefly through their power that the civilized races have extended, and are now everywhere extending their range. Nor does the moderate accumulation of wealth interfere with the process of selection."[42] Darwin's treatment of property inheritance was subject to the, as he saw it, higher logic of natural selection.

In contrast, and appropriately, Marx died intestate leaving just books and furniture valued at £250 –which presumably would have come as no surprise to his daughters given their father's hopeless mismanagement of money, along with his habit of squandering any new funds on family extravagances or in donating them to revolutionary causes. Marx's own political position on inheritance was subject to his analysis of the causes and dynamics of capitalism and as with evolutionism, he was somewhat at odds with Engels. Engels, in his *Outlines of a Critique of Political Economy*, the article that had so impressed Marx and which Marx as editor had published in the *Deutsch-Franzosische Jahrbucher* in February 1844, equated private property with antagonistic competitiveness, a competitiveness that "penetrated all the relationships of our life." As the organizer of the Brussels Correspondence Committee, a committee working to unite German with English and French socialists, Engels secured support for a definition of communism that included the abolition of private property and although the *Communist Manifesto* was credited to Marx, Engels had actually drafted the first version.[43] The program of ten communist aims outlined in the

Manifesto included the abolition of property inheritance but this was, in common with the rest of the *Manifesto* programme, only an aim, not an article of faith, and when shortly afterwards Marx and Engels hastily compiled *The Demands of the Communist Party in Germany* with the intention of adapting the *Manifesto* to the German workers' immediate political needs, this aim, along with three of the other aims from the *Manifesto* had been tempered and rephrased as a demand for a limitation on inheritance rather than as had originally been proposed, its complete abolition. (The four aims retained in the *Demands* were less revolutionary, more easily acceptable to German workers and peasants, intended to hasten and effect a bourgeois, and not a socialist, revolution). Much later in Marx's life he again tackled the question of inheritance, this time in opposition to the Russian anarchist Bakunin's attempt to persuade the General Council of the International to support the abolition of the right of inheritance. In opposition to Bakunin, Marx once again argued that the "...first task was to change the economic organisation of society of which the inheritance laws were a product and not the cause."[44] This "cause," the real fulcrum of capitalism, was the conflicts between the two social classes of capitalism, capitalists and proletariat, whose antagonistic relationship with each other provided the dynamic of societal change and the potential for communist revolution. These two classes were distinguished by their social relationship to the means of production, their ownership or alienation from the means of production, the key form of private property that Marx insisted in the *Manifesto* needed abolishing. Questions over the right of inheritance could not, thought Marx, be answered until this mainstay of capitalism had been destroyed by a proletariat revolution.

Marx's reluctance to demand communists abolish inheritance was prudent because questioning the conventions of inheritance raises sensitive hackles: calls for abolition run up against the deeply held belief that parents should be able to pass on to their own children their property as a natural right. Do we not have a duty to provide for our children? If children or relatives are not to inherit, then how should we share out the estates of the departed? Answering these and similar questions require us to examine not only how we put a value upon our creativity, but also how we value individuals. Marx, at least in the reading I am following, is not intending to replace capitalism with a society of uniform equals but instead with a community of individuals who are freely pursuing their own self-fulfillment. Private ownership of how we produce our artificial world is an impediment to this goal, it is the social convention that fosters social classes having an antagonistic, exploitative relationship, a convention which informs decisions over what we make (only profitable production), and one which distorts our understanding of ourselves and other people whom we come to value at least in part in terms of their material possessions. In short, the social convention of capitalistic private property systematically distorts our artificial world and Marx's political objective is to eradicate this distorting force in the same way that Feuerbach counseled us to eradicate delusory religion.

Feuerbach placed his faith in man's intrinsically good human nature, a nature whose best qualities had been erroneously projected onto mythical gods, which if reclaimed from the heavens could be used to build a paradise upon earth. Marx, rejecting Feuerbach's prescription for an earthly paradise, needed an alternative to cement the building blocks for communism. Simply eradicating the evils of capitalism will not automatically lead to a better future. It is dangerously tempting to think that if we get rid of some evil or other then the outcome must be always good. This is the sort of temptation that leads to foolish politics; for example, like many on the Left,[45] I welcomed the overthrow of the Shah of Iran without stopping first to consider whether or not his successors would actually be an improvement. I had forgotten that there is no guarantee that simply ending an evil regime or practice must automatically lead to a brighter future; some beneficial quality, some helpful resource should be identified if good is to triumph. This resource must be universal if it is to command respect and for Marx it was, arguably, the Enlightenment dream of men at last being able to act freely in accordance with our species capacity for creativity that would allow the proletariat to build the New Jerusalem. Marx was alert to the differences between people and argued that with the overthrow of capitalism, during the temporary dictatorship of the proletariat preceding communism, a false measure of equality would prevail: despite the fact that "one man will excel physically or intellectually" the workers' labor would be treated as though it were of equal value, with each worker having a right to take goods from the "funds for social consumption" equivalent to the amount of labor, measured in time expended, that he had contributed. During this transitional period between the overthrow of capitalism and the establishment of communism, the workers' rights would be based upon a convenient fiction of equality, the fiction that all labor was of equal worth, a fiction that was "unavoidable in the first phase of communist society when it is just emerging after prolonged birth-pangs from capitalist society." "In a higher phase of communist society..." when the old capitalist patterns of the division of labor had unraveled, when the distinction between mental and manual labor had disappeared:

> [...] after the powers of production have also increased and all the springs of coopera-
> tive wealth are gushing more freely together with the all-round development of the
> individual, then and then only can the narrow bourgeois horizon of rights be left far
> behind and society will inscribe on its banner: "From each according to his capacity,
> to each according to his need."[46]

Marx stubbornly focused his revolutionary analysis upon production, the social production of our artificial world, neglecting what was already there, what we had already made. He believed that reorganizing social production would in itself lead eventually to the reorganization of everything else, including distribution and thus inheritance. What we presently call "rights," for instance the right to own property, are nothing more than synonyms for privileges, privileges given by "the economic structure and the cultural development of society" and when the non-rational distribution of privileges produced by capitalism had been overthrown then the very idea of "rights" would cease to have meaning. So where does this leave the Mandelas? The problem lies, I think, in the incommensurability of individual characters; just as we cannot reasonably compare the value of commodities we have made, say medicines with books, so too we cannot properly compare the authors who wrote them, say Pascal with Kipling. Capitalism is founded upon a false currency of comparison that permits commodities to be valued in terms of a universal, but inherently valueless commodity, money. Writing in Paris, when young, when he was still shaking off German metaphysics, Marx observed that:

> Money's properties are my, the possessor's, properties and essential powers. Therefore, what I *am* and what I *can do* is by no means determined by my individuality. I am *ugly*, but I can buy for myself the *most beautiful* woman. Which means to say that I am not *ugly*, for the effect of *ugliness*, its repelling power, is destroyed by money. As an individual, I am *lame*, but money procures me twenty-four legs. Consequently, I am not lame. I am a wicked, dishonest, unscrupulous, and stupid individual; but money is respected, and so also is its owner.[47]

Marx believed that if we were to destroy the capitalistic basis of commodity comparison, then instead of using the debased currency of capitalism we would come to value ourselves and the artificial world in truer, kinder, more accurate ways.

But, when we have removed all the price tags we will have no currency of comparison, we won't have better standards for comparison. Indeed, it is difficult to see how individual characters ever could properly be compared and evaluated: using Marx's example in the above quoted passage, if we eradicate money, if the "wicked, unscrupulous, and stupid individual" can no longer buy respect, then how precisely should she be respected? Further muddying the waters, characteristics are not necessarily consistent. We may have a set of characteristics that are not in harmony, with each characteristic out of line or in conflict with its fellows (the "wicked, unscrupulous and stupid" woman may be a fabulous singer). Creativity, the core of Marx's analysis, may not be consistent with the moral worth of our character; great artists are not always great men or women, what we produce can be wholly at odds with who we are, there is no simple correspondence between art and artists—for this reason the personal lives of artists can be hugely disappointing, as fans of rock stars watching their fallen heroes advertising credit cards, or Tolstoy's wife, could testify. Mandela's character, tested in his phrase in the "crucible" of Robbens Island may be exceptional, both in quality and strength, but how are we justly to compare it with another person's character? If we owe Mandela more than admiration, then what would be the currency of gratitude? Does he deserve to be given a home anymore than Mr. Perfidy's underpaid secretary? Both their characters are chance-given sets of similarities and differences, both live in a world washed by chance. We may admire one over the other but we cannot recompense or reward chance nor uniqueness: egalitarianism, talk of equality, equal rights and the rest have no real place in progressive politics; we might champion egalitarianism not because people truly are equal but because they cannot be properly compared, because there is no yardstick with which to compare the worth of individual characters. Acting out of gratitude, grateful for the sacrifice Mandela made in the fight against injustice, we may well happily give or build him a new home as a gift but this gift will not be one he "deserves" for we have no currency to measure properly his just deserts.

But we don't live in a world where we can act freely out of love and gratitude, or spite and contempt. In our current artificial world, with its "narrow bourgeois horizon," we are obliged to buy and sell with the currency of capitalism and adjudge other people with the currency of personality. In a tellingly capitalistic tribute, a century after his burial Darwin's image was printed on British ten pound notes, on the currency of capitalism, the currency of inherited property, the currency used by estate agents. This currency allows incommensurable commodities, the materials from which they are made, the labor that went in to their manufacture, and the finished items, to be given a common price tag: similarly, personality may obscure our chance individual differences, the chance differences of our incommensurable characters which make us what we truly are. Unsurprisingly, in this mismeasured world we are misrepresented and vulnerable to corruption. How this occurs, and what might be done to counter the misreckoning of commodities and personality, are topics for the next chapters. And as a prelude to these remaining chapters I think it might be useful to summarize the arguments over chance and accumulation.

In summary: we live in a world increasingly of our own making, the artificial world, and it is subject to chance events, chance coincidences. As much of our lives are now spent in the artificial world it has become the environment in which most of our natural evolution will occur. The artificial world changes but does not itself evolve; lasting change is a matter of accumulation –of technologies, ideas, customs, etc.—and so the past is not lost but, and also increasingly, preserved. Technology, for instance the printing press, computers, photographs and the like has facilitated the preservation that allows for accumulation. Both the good and the bad are preserved, with earlier technologies, customs, beliefs etc. often lying dormant waiting to be reused, replayed, as circumstances demand: there is no guarantee that the future will be an improvement on the present, but there is a growing wealth of accumulated alternatives to choose from. The ambivalent potential of accumulation was nicely recognized by the composer Arthur Sullivan who, upon being invited to listen to recordings played on an experimental phonograph in the 1880s, remarked: "I am astonished and somewhat terrified at the results of this evening's experiments—astonished at the wonderful power you have developed, and terrified at the thought that so much hideous and bad music may be put on record forever!"[48] Whether or not we like, or come to like, the song being played is down to our characteristic taste in music. We are each of us unique individuals with our own character, a set of characteristics that we share to a degree and in differing measure, with everyone else and which we are born with. What character we inherit is down to chance, it is revealed to us as we grow older, and what is revealed is subject to chance-steered circumstance. Our character does not cause us to do anything but it does shape how we do things as it is what we are. It is neither unchanging nor unchangeable.

This, in summary, is the perspective with which, in the remaining chapters, I hope to illuminate chance's role in contemporary society, starting with the topic of education.

Notes

1. Terrell Carver notes that Engels was far keener than Marx to label their theory scientific. Engels had written two books intended to merge Marxism with evolutionism and, in Carver's judgment, he was responsible for weaving Marx's "guiding thread" of analysis into a pseudo-scientific hawser. See T. Carver, 1981, *Engels* (Past Masters). Oxford: Oxford University Press, pp. 40, 50.
2. F. Engels, "Speech at the Graveside of Karl Marx." In: Marx and Engels, 1977, *Selected Works.* London: Lawrence & Wishart, p. 429.
3. For the excruciating detail of Stalin's and the Politburo's reign, see Simon Montefiore's impressive study 2004, *Stalin: The Court of the Red Tsar,* London: Phoenix. Commenting upon the rise of ideological obsession, immune from the counter-evidence of famine, in Stalin's Politburo, Montefiori writes (p.88): "Stalin's 'order of sword-bearers' resembled the Knight Templars, or even the theocracy of Iranian Ayatollahs, more than any traditional secular movement. They would die and kill for their faith in the inevitable progress towards human betterment, making sacrifices of their own families with a fervour only seen in the religious slaughters and martyrdoms of the Middle Ages—and the Middle East."
4. L. Colletti, 1975, "Introduction," *Marx: Early Writings.* Harmondsworth: Pelican, p. 8.
5. These chronological details of the *Grundrisse*'s publication are taken from Martin Nicolaus's foreword to Karl Marx, 1973 [1857], *Grundrisse.* New York: Random House.
6. The *Grundrisse* notebooks also introduce the distinction between labor and labor-power, a distinction that Marx and Engels thought of as a theoretical breakthrough. This distinction allowed Marx to explain how a commodity could realize profit, it was through the capitalist's expropriation of the labor-power of the workers.
7. K. Marx and F. Engels, 1963 [1846], *The German Ideology.* New York: International Publishers, p. 7.
8. For the technical argument in favor of this reading of Marx's mature work, see S. Clarke, "The Labour Debate." In: M. Neary A. Dinerstein (eds.), 2002, *The Labour Debate: An Investigation into the Theory and Reality of Capitalist Work.* Aldershot: Ashgate.
9. This is not to suggest that if Marx's and Engel's earlier writings had been known to the Russian leaders then they would necessarily have acted any differently; as

I shall be arguing, it is the character of the reader, not the simply the characters in the text, which is a key to behavior.

10. Quoted in K. Thompson, 1982, *Emile Durkheim*. London: Tavistock Publications, p. 14.

11. For the new-born baby's social aptitudes (for instance, they can recognize their mother's odor as well as her voice and are born able to distinguish human faces from other objects), and their individuality (their distinct emotional expressions, sleep patterns, how much they cry and when, etc.), see L. Murray and L. Andrews, 2000, *The Social Baby: Understanding Babies' Communications from Birth*. London: CP Publishing.

12. Social theorists routinely focus upon Wittgenstein's accounts of "rule-following": this focus reflects the influence of Peter Winch's interpretation of Wittgenstein's mature work. In contrast, I am instead emphasising the philosopher's answer to the issue of essentialism, an issue which Wittgenstein tells us (Remark 65) is of the greatest import. Similarly, Karl Popper too believed that his alternative approach to this issue was what distinguished him from most other philosophers (and see note 14 below).

13. L. Wittgenstein, 1983 [1953], *Philosophical Investigations*. Oxford: Basil Blackwell, pp. 31-32 [Remarks 66 and 67, italics in the original, the latter Remark incompletely quoted].

14. There are in fact very few competitors. The other major twentieth-century alternative, also an attack upon essentialism, came from Karl Popper. To my mind, Popper's nominalistic approach is inadequate for it is geared toward representational language, e.g., names and propositions, and in itself cannot explain why some particulars rather than others become grouped in their specific categories. Wittgenstein's approach, by illuminating the socially constitutive nature of language, surpasses Popper's –an easy way to understand this point is to consider the phrase "Tony Blair"; this appears to be the name of somebody, a label by which we called the former British prime minister, but now consider the many, many other *uses* to which this phrase can be put (here, for example, it serves as an illustration of a contrast in twentieth-century philosophy). For Popper's argument, see K. Popper, 1972, *The Poverty of Historicism*. London: Routledge & Kegan Paul, ch. 1, part 10.

15. For a discussion of how linguistic principles facilitate future usages, see W. Sharrock and G. Button, 1999, "Do the Right Thing! Rule Finitism, Rule Scepticism and Rule Following." *Human Studies,* vol. 22, pp. 193-210.

16. A clear example of how Wittgenstein's arguments can be misrepresented is to be found in Thomas Kuhn's much-discussed study of how science changes over time. Kuhn argued that science is characterized by incommensurable scientific "paradigms," accepted models that determine the sorts of research and practices of scientific communities, and that the history of science is the history of wholly incommensurable paradigm revolutions. His argument is informed by a misunderstanding of Wittgenstein: it is not the case that words, or "paradigms," are or could be incommensurable—they are instead accumulations of past innovations, a process evident in the history of evolutionary science sketched in earlier chapters. (See T. Kuhn, 1970, *The Structure of Scientific Revolutions* [2nd edition]. Chicago: University of Chicago Press.)

17. N. Etcoff, 1999, *Survival of the Prettiest: The Science of Beauty*. London: Little Brown & Co.

18. Paul Ekman recounts the change of direction taken by his research, the opposition he met from culturally obsessed social scientists, and his own studies of facial

expressions, in his afterword to his newly definitive edition of C. Darwin, 1999 [1872], *The Expression of the Emotions in Man and the Animals.* London: Harper Collins.

19. Ekman. In: Darwin, 1999, *The Expression of the Emotions in Man and the Animals*, p. 379. In fact, the South Foreans did not replicate the identification of facial expressions made by literate subjects but "The only exception was that they failed to differentiate between the fear and surprise faces, although both were distinguished from anger, happy, sad, and disgust expressions."
20. For instance: D. Singh, 1993, "Adaptive significance of female physical attractiveness: Role of waist-hip ratio." *Journal of Personality and Social Psychology,* vol. 65, pp. 293-307; D. Singh, 1995, "Female judgement of male attractiveness and desirability for relationships: Role of waist-hip ratio and financial success." *Journal of Personality and Social Psychology,* vol. 69, pp. 1089-1101.
21. D. Singh, 2004, "Mating strategies of young women: role of physical attractiveness." *Journal of Sex Research* Vol.41, pp43-55. In this article (p47), Singh cites supporting studies suggesting that if digitally-altered photographs are substituted for the silhouettes then similar preferences are still made.
22. Singh, 2004, "Mating Strategies of Young Women," p. 44.
23. S. Chu and K. Geary, 2005, "Physical stature influences character perception in women," *Personality and Individual Differences,* vol. 38, pp. 1927-1934. I am grateful to Simon Chu for supplying me with a copy of this paper prior to its publication.
24. For a light examination of the influence of height, see R. Keyes, 1980, *The Height of Your Life.* Toronto: Little Brown & Co.
25. J. S. Gillis and W. E. Arvis 1980 "The Male-Taller Norm in Mate Selection." *Personality and Social Psychology Bulletin,* vol. 6, pp. 396-401.
26. W.E. Hensley and R. Cooper 1987 "Height and Occupational Success: A Review and Critique." *Psychological Reports,* vol. 60, pp. 843-849.
27. N. Persico, A. Postlewaite, and D. Silverman 2001 "The Effect of Adolescent Experience on Labor Market Outcomes: The Case of Height," *Journal of Political Economy,* vol.112, pp. 1019-1053.
28. "Past and Present, Taller People Tend to Live Longer," 2001, *Scientific American* (News In Brief), June 14.
29. R. Floud, K. Wachter, A. Gregory, 1990, *Height, Health and History: Nutritional Status in the United Kingdom, 1750-1980.* Cambridge: Cambridge University Press, p. 16.
30. Figures are from the National Centre for Health Statistics in collaboration with the National Centre for Chronic Disease Prevention and Health Promotion (2000). The comparable figures for American men are 50th percentile: 69 inches, 3rd percentile: 64.5 inches, 97th percentile: 75 inches: www.babysdoc.com/GIRLSHEIGHT-2TO20htm and www.babysdoc.com/BOYSHEIGHT2TO20.htm
31. "Napoleon's revenge: In the U.S., Height Hits its head on the Genetic Ceiling," 2001 *Scientific American* [News Scan] November 10.
32. C. Darwin, 1999, *The Expression of the Emotions in Man and the Animals*, p. 212.
33. Ibid., p. 83.
34. E. Prynn, 1981, *A Boy in Hob-nailed Boots.* Oxford: ISS Publishing in association with Tabb House Publishers, pp. 37-38 (italics in original).
35. A. Ralston, 2004, *Between a Rock and a Hard Place.* London: Atria Books.
36. M. Baker, 1982, *Nam:The Vietnam War in the Words of the Men and Women Who Fought There.* London: Abacus, p. 58.

37. This key influence upon Wittgenstein, upon both his early and later philosophies, had been noted by biographers such as von Wright and Ascombe, highlighted by writers such as Janik and Morris Engel, and then explored in Bryan Magee's study of Schopenhauer (1983).

38. A. Schopenhauer (trs. R.J. Hollingdale), 1970, *Essays and Aphorisms*. London: Penguin, pp. 168-169.

39. E. Goffman, 1980 [1959], *The Presentation of Self in Everyday Life*. Harmondsworth: Pelican, p. 59.

40. Quoted in C. Janaway, 1994, *Schopenhauer* (Past Masters). Oxford: Oxford University Press, p. 56.

41. C. Darwin, 1882 [1872], *The Descent of Man and Selection in Relation to Sex*. London: John Murray, p. 135.

42. Ibid.

43. Carver, 1981. *Engels*, pp. 27-28.

44. McLellan, *Karl Marx*, pp. 382-383.

45. A mistake made not just from the Left; the erstwhile Marxist-turned-postmodernist Michael Foucault, who was in a position to know better, also championed the Iranian revolution welcoming what he saw as a liberating movement of the oppressed: see J. Miller 1993 *The Passion of Michael Foucault* London, Harper Collins, ch. 9. On his return to France from Iran where he had witnessed for himself the delights of the revolution, Foucault advised his students not to learn lessons from the heroes of the Iranian revolution, but rather, and rather tellingly, from heroes of the New Right such as Hayek.

46. K. Marx, 1933 [1875], *Critique of the Gotha Programme*. London: Martin Lawrence, pp. 30-31.

47. K. Marx, *Economic and Philosophical Manuscripts*, p. 377.

48. Quoted in M. Chanan, 1995, *Repeated Takes: A Short History of Recording and its Effects on Music*. London: Verso, p. 26. My thanks to my friend Dr. Richard Smith for this reference.

6

Education for a Chancy World

Curiously, students will always sit in the same seats, week after week, (an obliging habit for those of us unable to remember people's names). I take the register; they all seem to be here, from Alison Arbutton, to Cathy Brighouse through to Kalam Patel,[1] along with those ever-present expressions of chance—contingency, coincidence, and character—whose names never appear on any register. The first time she came, Alison arrived a little later than the others and so she got the last available seat, the unpopular chair to my left. She's likely to keep this sinister seat for the duration of this course, for the next twenty or so weeks which, as I'm left-handed, and as I read groups like English books from left to right, means that she'll be asked more than her share of questions. Fielding more than her share of questions may or may not be an advantage, a discomfort, a trial, a bore or whatever but it will form part of her undergraduate experience, one small chance influence on Alison, one of many that together find their place onto the curriculum.

In this seminar group, the students' surnames all start with the letters A to P, from Arbutton to Patel. Alison and Kalam along with the other eleven students have been allocated to this seminar long before they arrived at university by my department's secretaries on the basis of their surnames, available rooms, the other courses they're taking, etc., an administrative necessity that guarantees chance a place round their seminar table for, as any lecturer not programmed to speak in mission statements will tell you, seminars are like parties: some work, some don't. Sometimes seminars flicker in to life, only to die down again the next week, sometimes after many frustrating weeks they suddenly burst into flame, some are roaring right from the start. What makes parties and seminars catch light or stay cold is of course chiefly the characters of those who've come to party, come to be educated. This lot has been thrown together by administrative fiat, they're coincidentally lucky, their seminar works well, I quite look forward to Fridays, 10-11 o'clock. Just as moribund parties are hell for their hosts, so too seminars that won't ignite are the dread of tutors who need to compensate by filling in the awkward silences left by their students. Naturally,

121

tutors accumulate an armory of techniques they can use to try to get a seminar group up and running, everything from threats to humor, and we would all like to believe that we can inspire and enthuse by personal example, but experience teaches us that some seminar groups will exhaust our strategies and exhaust us as much as the students. At the end of the day, it's all down to the interplay of the students' and the tutor's characters; it's little to do with the subject being discussed, the dullest topic won't dampen a lively seminar group, nor the most interesting fire-up a dead one.

We all know that chance plays its hand when it comes to things like how well seminars, or lectures, or parties etc. run but nonetheless we seem reluctant to admit commonsense, preferring instead to seek explanations in mysterious alternative qualities such as intelligence. If Alison or Kalam don't do well on their undergraduate course they probably won't reserve some of the blame for chance, some for the absurdities of capitalism, they'll instead blame themselves. Alison and Kalam probably secretly harbor one or all three of the undergraduates' common anxieties: "will they discover I'm too stupid to do the course?"; "will I make friends?"; "will I find someone to sleep with/love?" It's the first of these fears that will blind them to the role of chance in education; doing well at university, like making friends or falling in love, is weighed by luck. In fact, intelligence usually plays a minor part for the vast majority of students are quite capable intellectually, and do not differ much in intellectual skills. Just like their stature, most students will be much of a muchness, with only a few being unusually short or tall, dim or very bright and of course those who do struggle may be sufficiently intelligent but have characters otherwise unsuited to academic study. Doing academic work is just one exercise of intelligence and not to the liking of every intelligent person, besides, a lot of what students wrongly presume to be a reflection of innate "intelligence" can in fact be learnt. Note taking, essay writing, these sorts of things are skills that improve dramatically with practice, easily demonstrable by asking Alison and Kalam to compare the essays they wrote in their first, with those they write in their final, years. Educational skills, like other skills, improve with practice as does thinking itself; writing essays, for instance, encourages you to clarify your thinking, reveals what you don't really understand, as does presenting papers to your seminar group. Innate intelligence is most often a red herring: until recently the poor exam performance of British girls at school and university could be explained away by women's supposedly inferior intellects but the rapid improvement in women's exam results (they now match or outperform men at university) has rendered such explanations as incredible as the idea that these exams measure intelligence.

Alison, Kalam, and the rest of the seminar group may well come to measure their own academic worth by the marks they receive for their essays, projects, dissertations, and finally by their overall degree classification, by the currency of academic comparison. This academic currency, like the currency of capitalist commodities (their monetary price), is delusory, confusing, and likely to add to their anxieties. Students are likely to presume that the marks they receive for their essays do not reflect simply upon the piece of work they have submitted but also indicate how their own intellectual abilities measure up to the overall student standard. A moment's thought reveals this to be a delusion. There is surprisingly little difference between individual tutors' assessments of student essays, most tutors blind double-marking undergraduate essays will agree within five marks or so. Similarly, when it comes to exercising their judgment upon final degree classifications, for instance when a student is borderline between two classes, then tutors routinely, if slowly, concur. The exceptions to this general pattern of agreement over assessment happen, as you would expect, at the extreme ends of the assessment range, when it comes to Fails and Firsts. Both are treated seriously: Fails because not only are they outside the normal range, and we don't like to fail anyone, but also because universities are currently under considerable pressure from our capitalistically minded government paymasters (we shall return to this evil later in this chapter); Firsts because the distinction between an Upper Second and a First is subtle, slight, uncommon and hence, especially for academics themselves, precious—a slight difference, a touch of originality, a rare characteristic comparable in effect to the extra quarter inch of height that makes a person outstanding. All of which, you may think, is heartening and as it should be in seats of higher learning. But this superficial agreement, built upon the tutors' lengthy common apprenticeships (and it may be worth remembering that most academics, like their monastic forefathers, have very, very little personal experience of anything outside their cloisters), camouflages the truth, it masks the real variety of student achievements and abilities. Suppose that Alison and Kalam both submit course essays written on the same topic. Alison's essay suggests it was written hurriedly, it's based largely upon a couple of introductory texts she's skimmed through plus one or two articles she's downloaded from the Net, and her lecture notes. Her essay's structure is all over the place making her discussion incoherent. Her English, though serviceable, is dull, lacks adjectives, is peppered with ugly jargon, and her Americanisms betrays PC spell-checking. Kalam's English is better, except that like many British Asians he sometimes forgets to include grammatical articles, "a" and "the," a failing I put down to their absence in Gujarati, his parents' mother-tongue. His essay is better structured than Alison's but his conclusion is the usual drippy "on the one hand, on the other hand" and doesn't arrive at a firm answer to the set question. Nevertheless, judging by his bibliography, and his essay's discussion, he's read a lot of the set texts, he seems to understand the chief arguments, and he's obviously tried (the other meaning of "essay" when it functions as a verb). It looks as though Alison has not essayed, she's done little background reading but, unexpectedly, in her conclusion instead of drawing together the points she's made in her discussion, giving her own judgment on their respective strengths and weaknesses in the conventional way, she instead veers off into a page or two of her own thoughts on the essay's topic, several of which are not only striking, they're genuinely insightful. Both essays get a low Upper Second mark of 63 percent, but for different reasons, in Alison's case because, as I'll explain, to counter her vanity and boost her confidence. In the section for tutor's comments on their mark sheets I try to point out their essays' respective weaknesses and how they might improve in future submissions but I know that these comments, if they even read them, will count for less than that magical numerical mark, that 63 percent they both got, the common mark which I actually awarded for very different reasons which they will take as an indicator not simply of this particular essay performance but, and wrongly, as an indicator of their own comparative intelligences measured against a general, numerically measured, yardstick. The currency of academic comparison, essay marks, degree classifications, is delusory in the same way that the pricing of commodities in capitalism leads to intrinsically different products—for example a can of fancy shaving cream and a book of Blaise Pascal's best-known writings, the *Pensées*—both being sold for the same amount, in this example of the shaving cream and the *Pensées* both for £5.99p.

Alison, I discover as the term wears on, is intelligent, that is to say of above average intelligence, but intelligence by itself counts for naught, it won't motivate her, it won't get her a First, it is but one part of her overall character default. As I remarked at the end of the last chapter, our characteristics may not be in harmony, together they may play a discordant tune. So, although naturally intelligent Alison is also rather vain, she has both characteristics slightly more pronounced than the average. Her vanity and intelligence may on occasion lead her to play a bum note, like an organ whose pipes are irregular, out of true, the intelligent base notes drowned out by shrill vain trebles. This analogy with organ pipes I've wrenched out of its theological context from Pascal[2] who, grappling with the growing challenges to religion voiced by reason in seventeenth-century France, opted for faith over science because in his view: "The knowledge of outward things will not console me in times of affliction for the lack of moral rules, but knowledge of the laws of morality will always console me for lack of knowledge of the physical sciences."[3]

These laws of morality had been, in Pascal's view, composed by God and only the Christian God could retune the inconstant pipes of our character. Without God, believed Pascal, and as it says in Ecclesiastes, our lives are literally in vain ("Vanity of vanities, saith the Preacher, vanity of vanities; all is vanity"). Reason, says Pascal foreshadowing David Hume, is there just to show us the best strategy for achieving our aims and when it comes to the existence of God, his famous wager apparently shows that reason counsels us to bet on the existence of God because if we're wrong then it won't matter (not the sort of gamble, I feel, likely to impress an omnipotent being). Indeed, Pascal stands as a pioneer of our modern way of thinking and by using the balance of probabilities to weigh God's existence he helped usher in the modern age where both chance and certainty would meet a new rival sort of explanation, probability, whose prospects for explanatory success were odds on.

A divine tuner would certainly be of help to Alison, helping her to harmonize her vanity with her intelligence but, as I observed earlier on when discussing the example of Cat Steven's personal epiphany on Malibu Beach, a simple belief in chance coincidences can preempt the need to believe in, or bet on, a celestial lifeguard. It is the inclusion of chance variety in Darwinian evolutionism[4] which unsettles the religiously minded, just as much as the chance contingency of a purposeless world, the coincidental collisions that unexpectedly occur, the chance bequest of characteristics Alison received from her parents that combined intelligence with vanity. I reasoned toward the end of the last chapter, drawing upon Schopenhauer, that characteristics are *what* we are and that they were not motives causing us to carry out any sort of action or behavior: they flavor *how* we do things, but they are not causes or motives making us do anything. This line of reasoning sits comfortably when discussing intelligence because, I think, we wouldn't baulk if told that intelligence is not a motive but a quality of actions: Alison answers intelligently in seminars, writes the unexpected intelligent points in her essays, and the rest. Nonetheless, intelligence is an object of vanity so most of us, I guess, would only reluctantly follow Professor Gilbert Ryle: what we call "intelligence" is not, Ryle argued, some hidden quality the individual possesses, nor is it an act; intelligence is a skill which we admire, a point he nicely made using the example of an audience applauding "the cleverness of a clown":

> The spectators applaud his skill at seeming clumsy, but what they applaud is not some hidden performance executed "in his head." It is his visible performance that they admire, but they admire it not for being an effect of any hidden internal causes but for being an exercise of a skill. Now a skill is not an act. It is therefore not a witnessable nor an unwitnessable act. To recognise that a performance is an exercise of a skill is indeed to appreciate it in the light of a factor which could not be separately recorded by a camera. But the reason why the skill exercised in a performance cannot be separately recorded by a camera is not that it is an occult or ghostly happening, but that it is not a happening at all. It is a disposition, or complex of dispositions, and a disposition is a factor of the wrong logical type to be seen or unseen, recorded or unrecorded.[5]

Similarly with Alison's intelligent performances in seminars, when writing essays, sitting her exams: her intelligence is our judgment, our appreciation of *how* she performs, compared to her fellow students. Her intelligence, I am arguing, is a characteristic skill, a chance inheritance whose use is analogous to using a mental tool, a blade from her mental Swiss Army penknife, that she may exercise consistently, or sporadically as in her essay, which like all other chance genetic characteristics she may strengthen or let atrophy, one which is not necessarily exhibited in all that she does, and which may be flavoured, or confounded, by her other characteristics—in Alison's case, particularly by her vanity.

If you are reasonably comfortable with the view that Alison's "intelligence" is our evaluation of her dispositional skill, one of her characteristics, and not an act, not the effect of some hidden mental cause or other, you may, I suspect, still nonetheless remain sceptical when this line of thinking is then applied to her vanity. One good reason for your skepticism may be because unlike intelligence, vanity does appear to motivate actions—indeed, as Sir Bertrand Russell had warned in his acceptance speech for the Nobel Prize in literature (1950) vanity, along with acquisitiveness, rivalry, and love of power, is one of the unquenchable desires that distinguishes us humans from other animals. Russell believed that "All human activity is prompted by desires" and that the insatiable desire of vanity was of "immense potency," a point of view he supported with this observation:

> Anyone who has much to do with children knows how they are constantly performing some antic, and saying "Look at me." "Look at me" is one of the most fundamental desires of the human heart.[6]

Loath and nervous though I am to criticize Russell, a philosopher who proved that it wasn't necessary to write badly in order to think well, this example of the attention-seeking child just won't pass muster, for a number of reasons. First, "anyone who has much to do with children" knows that they do not all "constantly" say "Look at me." Second, different children are given to different levels of attention seeking. Third, children will seek attention in different ways, in different circumstances, from different people. In other words, children have their own characteristic ways of seeking attention. Why a particular child seeks attention is not because they have been prompted to do so by some insatiable, homogenous human desire, but for an infinite variety of reasons: for instance they feel they are being neglected by their parents; they seek reassurance that they can do a new activity properly; they are jealous of the attention being given to another child; they are bored; they have eaten too much junk food; etc., etc. Rather more importantly, seeking attention, saying "Look at me," is neither the same thing as vanity nor necessarily an expression of vanity. Vanity is a failing, an undue concern with other people's opinions. A vain person could just as well not seek to draw attention to themselves, fearful that others will judge them unworthy (another not uncommon reason why some students do not try their hardest).

Alison's vanity has been awoken for the best of reasons, and by chance. Like many another student she came to my course presuming she wouldn't like "theory," but against her expectations she's discovered she has a taste for the sort of ideas we're discussing. This characteristic taste has been sharpened because, by administrative fiat, she happens to be in a seminar with one or two other students who, for a variety of reasons, also are taking ideas seriously. Her intellectual taste has sensitised her to the course material and will prompt her to read, think, and contribute to seminar discussions. She has not chosen to like theory, nor will she choose which ideas she agrees with: instead, she will *select*, not choose, from amongst the ideas that week after week we consider. It is highly unlikely that Alison will, by a process of reasoning, change her mind significantly. Here, Alison is in good, or at least overwhelmingly common, company. It is very difficult to find an example of any philosopher or social theorist of note who admits they have changed their minds: Marx died a Marxist, Darwin a Darwinian. Go to a university library, go through the thousands of theory books on their shelves, and you will be hard pressed to find any book or article in which the author has written that they were wrong in the past and now think in a different way. This may seem obvious, but it is worth recalling that, the Gods apart, it is only by accepting past mistakes that we can improve upon our ideas. One of the very few exceptions[7] to this disquieting trend known to me is Wittgenstein who explicitly rejected his earlier ideas and then, in his later phase, set out on an iconoclastic campaign to destroy academic philosophy. Clearly, the reasons why professional theorists don't admit to past mistakes share much in common with the reasons most of the rest of us prefer to continue believing we're right even when, as for example in the recent case of Blair and the non-existence of "weapons of mass destruction" in Iraq, the falsifying evidence is unquestionable. In the short term, falsifying evidence often hardens our convictions, a peculiarity examined in a study undertaken by social psychologists of a 1950s American eschatological religious community who, when their prophecy that the world would end failed to be met, became more, not less committed to their faith.[8] Paradoxically, we seem to value thinkers who do not change their minds, who stick to their guns until their last. This is a twist on Ryle's notion of "category mistakes," the mistaken explanation of something resulting from us treating it as though it were a member of a category to which it does not actually belong, as in his example quoted above of treating intelligence skills as though they were an act or the work of some hidden mental entity. Rather than "category mistakes," the misappreciation of thinkers who do not ever change their minds and refuse to recognise their past errors is what we might call a "character mistake": because we value consistency as a sign of honesty, suspecting the integrity of those who keep changing their minds, we wrongly extend this evaluative criterion to other fields of behavior where it does not properly apply. An example of this sort of mistake is evident in pop music where "authenticity" is equated with the artists' unchanging views, dress, musical style and opinions. Partly for this reason, ageing rock stars become locked in a time warp where, regardless of their age, they cannot mature and must act, play, dress and speak in the same ways they did when they first became famous if they are to retain their "credibility."

I won't be able to change Alison's mind any more than she, as an act of will, will be able to herself. With luck, and so far luck has been with her, she will learn of some theory or other to which she is naturally drawn, she will adopt that point of view and that will be that. We do not change our characters, rather, circumstances change, we learn more about ourselves, we learn the extent of our character, our characteristic tastes, dispositions, lessons taught by chance coincidence, chance contingency. Later in her life Alison may look back and wonder why she was so taken with these ideas, why they meant so much to her, and ruefully explain it to herself as youthful naivety: she won't have changed her mind, she will have lost her youthful intellectual taste along with her taste for lurid lipstick. For the moment, young Alison is drinking up theory, really savoring each new idea as it becomes comprehensible. I'm delighted for there is nothing better for tutors than watching the responses of a student like Alison. Today, we're discussing Marx's analytical position on private property, I can actually see Marx's point about private property being a social relationship between people, not a relationship between individuals to things, click with her. It's like watching my elder son play for the first time a new piece on the piano all the way through. What Alison, but as yet few of the other students in her group, understands is the principle of Marx's argument; she understands how this point can be carried on to analyze capitalism in the same way that Wittgenstein argued we learn languages by learning the principles by which words may be used in new and unfamiliar circumstances. The principle is the meaning. Ironically, though, this comprehension, this relish, her blossoming intellectual skills, do not give Alison any more confidence in herself, rather the reverse. It is her heightened sensitivity to ideas, the seriousness with which she takes them that make her wish to do her best. Now, and as we saw in the previous chapter, we can only learn about our own characteristics comparatively, by comparing ourselves with others, there is no other way for Alison to discover that she is intelligent but she lacks the natural arrogance, the characteristic megalomania of academic theorists, she looks instead to others for her validity, to me, to her fellow students to confirm the value of what she says and writes. She does not trust herself. Regrettably, educational institutions can promote such feelings, they are institutions of insecurity, and most undergraduates will leave university feeling that they could or should have done better. Lecturers rarely sit and watch each other lecture or teach and have little idea how well they compare. Small wonder then, in this environment that Alison is feeling insecure, cannot trust herself. Here, vanity is true to its etymology, to its Latin root *vanus*, meaning "empty" (the further extension to include "conceited" was not made until the seventeenth century):[9] Alison suffers from a slightly exaggerated lack of confidence in herself, in her own character. This characteristic failing could be expressed in many ways dependent upon circumstance and a person's other characteristics: by conceit as when a woman constantly seeks confirmation she is beautiful; or in aggression as when an academic brooks no criticism, always tries to enforce her point of view on others; or as in Alison's case when her vanity prevents her from developing her own ideas without first seeking the agreement of Kalam who happens to be sitting opposite her, or from Cathy or me. This is the out-of-tune pipe in her character, the failing of vanity that may prevent her from realising her own intellectual potential. Just as she is unusually sensitive to theoretical ideas, so too she is overly sensitive to other people's opinions. So, what should I do to help combat this debilitating vanity? I've tried the run of mundane measures at my disposal, encouraging her when she contributes to discussions, being gentle in criticism, that sort of thing, but they're not working. I'll have to break a rule, the wretched modern rule of student anonymity. In the past, students wrote their names on essays, on exam scripts; nowadays, they type their Candidate Number and we can no longer match essays to students. This seems like a good idea, it seems as though anonymity would foster impartiality, lessen tutor bias, be fairer. Not so. Anonymity is supposed to reduce personal prejudice—a silly worry for if we are not trusted to mark impartially, why then should we be trusted to teach without bias?—but students actually want and need us to exercise our personal judgement on them as individuals, that's what we are here for. Reliance on personal judgements is an inevitable feature of all hierarchical organizations, not just universities: the higher you travel up the hierarchy of a company, organisation, government, or whatever, the fewer and fewer the people making decisions or judgements, holding power, hence the growing importance of individual characters. Fair judgment depends upon dons judging properly the student as well as their essay. So in my written comments I suggest to Alison she makes an appointment to discuss that essay she's submitted. Now, in truth, I already know that it was written by her; I suspected as much when I first read it, there are only thirteen students in her seminar group, it was her second submission, and I've a pretty good idea who wrote which essay because candidate numbers and equally anonymous word-processing aside, each of them has a distinctive, characteristic style of writing (Kalam's missing grammatical articles, Cathy's colloquialisms, George's wordy, overly long essays, that sort of distinctiveness, it's not rocket science). So, I'll invite Alison to make an appointment to discuss that essay, cautioning her that by discussing her essay with me she'll forfeit anonymity. I'm inviting her to confide in me, to share fidelity, to be trusting, the only road to self-confidence. If she's agreeable, then I'll be able to spend half an hour or so praising her essay's originality, explaining to her that what she wrote as her conclusion should rightly have been the essay's beginning, trying to convince her that at university, unlike in nearly all the other institutions in British capitalist society, she is not in competition with her fellow students (for if they all do brilliantly they will all get Firsts). And, if she doesn't agree to forfeit anonymity, or if she doesn't turn up, well, there's always that encouraging mark of 63 percent.

I'm lucky to teach Alison, she's engaged with the course. Many of the other students in her seminar group treat the theories we examine like wallpaper swatches, peeled off week by week for their entertainment. Crucially, they do not engage with the course because they do not commit themselves personally to any of the ideas or theories, they remain unmoved, disinterested. Some disinterest is to be expected because they have not chosen to take this course, its core to their degree programme, not optional. Not everyone will like theory, anymore than everyone likes statistics, aubergines or jazz. It's not to everyone's taste. Additionally, like Alison, many of the students are prejudice against theory believing it to be dull, dry, difficult. Some students like Alison will jump these perennial pedagogical obstacles but, in the last few years, a new hurdle has been erected by the self-styled "New Labour" government (like the "New Right" a double misnomer, being neither "new" nor "Labour"). Having himself benefited from a "public school" education (yet another misnomer), having spent his grant when he was at university, the Prime Minister has forced upon the less privileged a series of educational policies that are poisoning the state sector, both schools and universities. In the university sector, higher education grants have been scrapped to be replaced by rising fees, by a new tax on learning, and higher education has been explicitly linked to capitalism. The introduction of student fees was justified in economic terms, in terms of the higher wages undergraduates could expect to earn, and ideologically presented as an egalitarian measure "widening participation," supposedly encouraging more, and more children from poorer families, to apply for a place at university. As with most other policies introduced by Blair's administration a target, a target for "widening participation" was set; there is to be 50 percent of the age cohort at university by 2010, although why 50 percent, rather than say 35 or 72 percent was not explained. These educational policies were not included in New Labour's election manifesto, in fact the manifesto promised fees would not be introduced, and their introduction was opposed by among others students' and lecturers' unions. Owing, however, to the disproportionate Parliamentary majority held by Blair's administration, this informed opposition was ignored and the manifesto promise was broken. Opponents of the increase in student numbers were liable to charges of elitism but this is a New Labour calumny for opponents were and are not claiming that 50 percent of working class children were not intelligent enough to go on to university but that they may not wish to, that academic study may not be to their taste and as with other so-called New Labour policies, so-called "goals" were really diktats.

Profound changes to university funding and to the ethos of higher education are not subjects which academics should treat dispassionately. Some lecturers have lost their jobs, many more feel unable to speak out because of changes to British dons' employment contracts made by Thatcher's government in 1987, contractual changes that ended academic tenure and thus threatened the freedom of dons to voice or publish their opinions without fear of sanction. Their silence helps to keep hidden the insidious damage that these policies are causing, damage masked by the ugly, vacuous language of university bureaucrats (for instance, all British universities now publish meaningless "mission statements," I defy anyone to produce any evidence that these statements have in any way improved student education, a challenge that could be made to countless other university public relations gimmicks). These policies increasingly fund and treat higher education as a capitalist market; education, degrees, courses, departments, publications, students etc. are now viewed as commodities, and universities have become business corporations. Quite simply, because the present New Labour administration is not prepared to raise taxes, the funding of British universities is insecure and has been insufficient to fund this enormous expansion in student numbers, the quality of education has declined, morale among lecturers is at an all-time low, (a survey of lecturers conducted in 2006 found that 47 percent of the respondents had suffered ill-health because of their job and, most depressingly, that 55 percent would not recommend a career in higher education to their children[10]). Much of the damage is invisible to the public, not on display at Open Days. Students attending these Open Days arrive ill-prepared to ask the right sorts of questions, for example whether they will be taught by full-time lecturers, or by inexperienced temporary tutors on short-term contracts, they do not know that lecturers are now not rewarded for the teaching they do but for the quantity of publications they must churn out to conform to government edicts, they do not ask about the size or frequency of lectures and seminars, whether their exams will be properly blind double-marked, how available staff will really be if they have problems, the likelihood that the course or department will be axed. And lecturers are too cowed to tell them the truth, corrupted by capitalistic funding.

Pedagogic questions of this kind need, for students, to be weighed alongside other concerns. Rather obviously, if 50 percent of young people have a first degree then they will not all get "good jobs." Those who do not have a degree will form a new disadvantaged sub-class, thus widening, not narrowing social inequality (most of the expansion in student numbers has come from middle class entrants). More and more employers will demand employees are graduates, where before their jobs were quite adequately done by those who had not stayed on in education. On leaving school, commonsense and Pascal's wager suggests that going to university is the best bet, even if it saddles you with thousands of pounds of debt, and it has never been easier to go to university. And there are other factors to weigh the decision. University holds the promise of a three year reprieve from the world of work, three years of unparalleled social, sexual, and chemical opportunities. Unsurprisingly, then, numbers keep rising.

In my experience, students do on the whole still value and enjoy student life, but increasingly they do not value their studies. Surely, it is blatantly clear that education is not a commodity and students are not consumers. They do not consume anything (books are read, not consumed), they do not know what university study will be like and so they cannot make informed decisions: you may be able to judge the comparative monetary value of your favorite confectionery, the price of a Cavity Crunch compared to the cost of a bar of Chocorot, but you cannot make this assessment of degree programs. Most young people will only study once at university, they have nothing to compare, and they cannot know in advance how much they will appreciate or regret their time at college, nor can they gauge how going on to further study will affect them in later life. This inability to form any just estimation of university is partly because they cannot know in advance how chance will play its hand, who will be in their seminars, what their tutors will be like, how they will find sitting in the library hour after hour. The majority of freshers are too young to know their own characters, and cannot predict the chance events or influences that will reveal them. At best, they must act hopefully, at worst, go through the motions to get a graduate job-ticket. In these circumstances, students cannot be thought of as knowledgeable agents making informed choices, not as comparable to the sovereign consumers beloved of New Right thinkers, the fiction adopted by New Labour. How, then, should we organize university admissions, degree programs, the funding of higher education, in a chancy world?

An Immodest Proposal?

If you were a drinker trying for the first time absinthe, or a smoker trying a new strain of Dutch skunk, you'd be wise to have a small taster, not gulp down the whole glass, not smoke the entire spliff all in one go. The majority of the young people thinking of applying to university are in a comparable position to our fictional drinkers and stoners, having been through several schools, having, at least in Britain, experienced some thirteen years as a school pupil. For most of these years they were children, then teenagers. They went to school, like it or not, and were taught a prescribed syllabus oriented increasingly to passing exams. As they were growing up in the chancy world of classrooms and playgrounds they may have found they liked some subjects more than others, sometimes emphatically, sometimes marginally. At eighteen, upon leaving school, a few will be determined to study some subject or other, many more less certain, some will be persuaded by their parents to continue, others influenced by friends in the ways argued for by Judith Harris, or by older siblings who have already graduated, a proportion will be set upon a particular career for which they need a specific degree, etc. What these teenagers need is the chance to sample university life, sample different subjects, sample university level study, before irrevocably committing themselves to an intensive three-year degree program. So, I propose that there should be an intermediate stage between school and university, a year in which they can attend lectures and seminars on a wide range of subjects so that they may get a flavor of what will be involved. The same disciplines are taught very differently at university than they are at school and very differently in each university: unlike in schools, there is no set national curriculum. Universities are there, or at least used to be there, to help people learn, not to simply teach; learning for yourself is not the same as being taught. Having completed this introductory, intermediate year young people would be in a much better position to gauge whether or not they should commit themselves to three years of study at that particular institution. Like all the other measures I shall be sketching, this is not a perfect solution to the question of how we should organize admissions, but it is, I suggest, an improvement on the present practice. Perhaps this additional year would become a routine option for school pupils. It would cost money, a lot of money if done properly, but far less than the cost of putting half of all young people through three-year undergraduate programs. This funding must be secure, predictable, and be raised through taxation, not through fees, as a national insurance policy paid by tax payers who cannot know in advance whether they or their children would wish to study at university and so, as with other insurance schemes, they must make provision for the possibility, for the chance that they or their children will want to go on to university. In Britain, the mechanism and means for deducting this national insurance tax are already well established.

Having completed their introductory intermediate year, young people would be in a better position to judge whether they should continue, and university staff would also have a far better idea whether or not they would be suitable students. As an inducement, having successfully completed their intermediate courses, students would receive a certificate. Whereas entry onto the intermediate year would be open to all those pupils who had stayed on at school until they were aged eighteen, progressing onto the subsequent three-year degree program would not, and could not be open to all. There will always be limited places, some places will be more or less competitive. Selection, selection informed by their performance both at school and on the intermediate courses, would be made by universities whose staff are in the best position, and now having met and taught the applicants on their intermediate year courses, an improved position, to judge their suitability. On the basis of over twenty years teaching at university I firmly believe that—given the option presently denied to them by a system which means by the time they discover university is not for them it is really too late, they will get no reward for the time and money they have already spent at college if they leave—many students would not choose to continue, especially as in my proposal if they did choose to continue with an undergraduate program they would no longer be awarded degrees.

As a further disincentive to those who may be tempted to continue not because they find studying rewarding but because they expect to gain a job ticket, or a status enhancer, and as a measure intended to help break the pernicious link to the needs of capitalism and preserve the intrinsic value of higher education, we should stop trading in delusive academic currency: I propose that we no longer award undergraduate degrees. This is not the wildly radical step it may first appear. Up until quite recently many of the students attending British universities often did not concern themselves with getting a good class of degree, some didn't even bother graduating, usually only poorer students prized degree certificates. Gentlemen, and until very recently it was only the sons from wealthy Christian families, did not need a vocational qualification.

With the growth of the state, with the expansion of bureaucracies in the nine-teenth century, along with challenges to entrenched privilege, this all changed, a change first effected in the colonies, in India, when it became necessary to impose some restraint upon East India Company employees, to train up a cadre of civil servants, and to test the abilities and discriminate amongst native ap-plicants for posts or professions such as lawyers that could no longer be filled by just the sons of Imperial rulers. (In a nice ironical twist, many of the leading lights of the Indian Congress were lawyers, including of course Gujarat's most famous son, Mahatma Gandhi). As the East India Company transformed, in the second half of the eighteenth century, from a private trading business to the conquerors then national rulers of India the pressures to regulate the Company grew along with the nabobs' spoils, and it became necessary to administer the collection of taxes for paying the infrastructure of British suzerainty. As the Company became regulated by the government, as its role changed, so too did its ethos. General Cornwallis, appointed to oversee the reform of the Company's administration, 1785-1793, "introduced a professional ethos into the Company's bureaucracy," replacing patronage with "appointments based on merit with fixed, attractive salary scales."[11] In 1809 a new college for the training of young men wishing to enter the Company's service was opened, Haileybury College in Hertfordshire. The directors of the Company "...believed that what these students needed above all was moral training in British and Christian values,"[12] plus "...obligatory courses in Asian languages, laws and customs along with a smattering of political economy and accounting."[13]

In principle at least, after 1809 no new employee could sail for India before successfully completing the two-year College curriculum; Haileybury College existed to train prospective civil servants, its sister college at Addiscombe trained military cadets. How far Haileybury lived up to its founders' aspirations is questionable. John Beames, who went on to become a Company district officer, entered Haileybury in 1856 and recalled in his *Memoirs* that in those days:

> Haileybury was a happy place, though rather a farce as far as learning was concerned. In fact you might learn as little or as much as you liked, but while the facilities for not learning were considerable, those for learning were, in practice, somewhat scanty. The Professors gave certain lectures and one or two of them would allow us to consult them at their houses, but for the most part we had to rely upon reading in our own rooms. The men, few in number, who really "ground" or "mugged" or "sweated" (euphemisms by which the use of the word "worked" or "studied" was avoided) were looked upon by the majority as amiable but misguided enthusiasts and as fit objects for the more boisterous kinds of practical joking.[14]

Lectures were noisy, erratic, idiosyncratic, often badly attended. "Though the Directors of the Honourable East India Company promulgated very strict rules for the discipline of the College, no one seemed to take pains to enforce them."[15] Despite his disrespectful if affectionate attitude to Haileybury, John Beames did manage to complete the curriculum, he did join the Indian Civil

Service by the only route now open to applicants, regardless of their family's standing. Haileybury College closed in 1858 in the wake of the Indian Mutiny/ Uprising; four years later, in 1862, it reopened as a public school, today still educating, for a fee or a scholarship, young men now joined by young women. Nepotism, patronage, corruption, fortunes of birth, gradually, imperfectly gave way to supposedly impersonal meritocratic selection, universities became the purveyors of trusted qualifications, qualifications that were used for commercial as well as for government and professional jobs. Meritocracy certified by qualifications also came to oust fortunes of birth in the army: when in 1871 the tradition of purchasing commissions was ended, public schools fell over each other in their rush to put on courses preparing young men for the army training academies at Sandhurst and Woolwich, a competition won by the United Services College at Westward Ho!, the college attended by Rudyard Kipling whose own admission into the College illustrated the lingering influence of family connections.[16] Degrees remained the prerogative of the few, held by a tiny minority from socially privileged backgrounds, until after the Second World War when educational egalitarianism to secondary level was politically promoted by the Labour government headed by that Old Haileyberian, Clement Attlee,[17] and then demographically promoted by the "baby boom." Soon, having a degree will be a commonplace, for women as well as for men. Many British universities have quietly scrapped the lowest classification, the formerly respectable "Pass" degree, a new cult of the Upper Second is rampant, it has never been easier to be awarded a First. (Needless to say, your chances of getting a First varies enormously by university).[18] The saddest aspect to all this, as I have argued in this chapter, is that these classifications are delusory, they trade in an academic currency which is as absurd as the capitalistic pricing of commodities. Just as the same mark of 63 percent for Alison's and Kalam's essays were for different reasons, so too their overall marks upon which their final degree classification will be calculated are given for different, truly incomparable reasons. These overall totals are no more comparable than that fancy shaving cream is to Pascal's *Pensées.* A degree from my department is not comparable to a degree from another institution; the courses, resources, tutors are not the same.[19] This incomparability holds true for most subjects taught at universities, but there are exceptions. The exceptions come from degree programs which involve training students, for instance medical training, veterinary science, psychiatry, these sort of courses where a certificate of competence is desirable (I don't want Mssr. Maurice, our pet tortoise, far less my sons, to be treated by uncertified practitioners). In the case of these apprenticeships which lead to a certificate of competency in a particular profession, national comparability is needed and it should be the professions themselves which administer the same, uniform tests upon which their degrees are awarded. These professional exceptions and classificatory criteria of professional competence fall outside the remit of government or university bureaucrats.

If we are no longer to give marks to essays, nor award degrees, then how would students and third parties such as prospective employers find out what undergraduates are like, how well students had performed? Again, the answer lies in the past. In the past, people wrote character references, now increasingly they write about "personalities," employees are subject to "personality tests," job advertisements chillingly specify particular personality traits. By sampling situations vacant advertisements published in a British newspaper, the *Yorkshire Post* over a 130-year period, Roger Cremin[20] confirmed his impression that more and more such advertisements are requesting applicants possess particular "personality" traits; an advertising strategy now commonplace, found in 70.58 percent of sampled advertisements across all types of employment of the 2001 sample, below 20 percent in 1982, and none at all in 1870. A finding of this kind naturally stimulates sociological speculation and Cremin outlines some interesting hypotheses over the significance of this phenomenon and its effects upon the individual, concluding that personality, is becoming artificial and commodified:

> A personality culture in employment focuses attention on one's identity, manipulation and presentation of it. The mind is conscious of the need to stand out from the crowd and accentuate aspects of its personality that best reflects the wishes of the employer.[21]

Not only, according to Cremin, are we encouraged to "focus attention" on our personality, our personality traits also become revalued by the same processes that govern other commodities: "The free-market sets the price for these commodities, turning self-confidence, communication skills, pro-activity, and so on, into a rich seam for each of us to tap in to."[22]

Dr. Cremin in this article was "purposively disengaged with what personality [actually] is": it has been the argument of this book that personality is an expression of our inherited character default that, when expressed as commodified personality, may cast a shadow on ourselves. Unlike Peter Pan, in some circumstances we want to loose our shadow and when we write about students, we should write in terms of their character: character references. In practice, to some extent we often do this anyway when writing student references, but we do it as an adjunct to their overall degree classification. So, for example, I might write that "although Alison achieved a Lower Second, this was a disappointing performance and her written work suggested a greater academic potential," something along these lines. The weakness of this current format of student reference writing is that it does not challenge the veracity of the classification system per se, rather, the classifications are used as a starting point to which further observations, codicils, commendations, reservations and the like are then added. A proper character reference for students would not be predicated upon the delusion of degree classification, but upon a description of each student and upon their three year performance, deliberately specific, specific to the student's idiosyncratic character. Employees would in this way gain a far better picture of what their applicant was truly like. As I write this, another preposterous Blairite initiative is coming on stream, the demand for students to maintain a "personal profile" folder that they can present to prospective employees. Academics are supposed to assist students with this exercise in self-promotion. We are told that this exercise will encourage students to be self-reflective. In practise, it will encourage students to inflate or invent their strengths, it will lead them to rephrase themselves in the light of current labour-market demands, it will help lead to Cremin's commodification of personality. Writing that "I am not sure I will be able to do the job, but I will do my best," "I do not know whether or not I could have done better at college," or as in Alison's case "I do not think I am especially intelligent" may be honest, if as in Alison's case wrong, but they are not the sort of statements likely to land you an interview. Worse, writing that "I was just unlucky when at university" simply won't do, even if it is utterly true. And what precisely would you write if, like the student who sat opposite Alison, Kalam Patel, you have been saddled by chance with an "ethnic identity"? Even more puzzlingly, should Kalam, who also left with a disappointing Lower Second, tell prospective employers that his final year at university was hopelessly disrupted when, by chance, he fell in love, with Alison?

Notes

1. These names are, of course, made up. Alison, Cathy, and Kalam are fictional—and fiction has become the refuge of characters—but they are loosely based upon a composite of real undergraduate students I have taught.
2. B. Pascal, 1995 [1670], *Pensées.* Oxford: Oxford University Press, p. 22.
3. Ibid., p. 14.
4. For a characteristically quirky examination of variety and variance in Darwinian evolutionism, see S. J. Gould, 1996, *Life's Grandeur.* London: Jonathan Cape.
5. G. Ryle, 1978, *The Concept of Mind.* Harmondsworth: Penguin, p. 33. Professor Ryle examines our conceptualization of intelligence as part of his campaign against "category mistakes" in chapter 2.
6. Sir Bertrand Russell, 1950, *Nobel Lecture.* www.nobelprize.org Sir Bertrand, in this speech, argues that of the insatiable desires, the love of power is paramount and that intelligence is the "main thing needed to make the world happy."
7. Joining Wittgenstein in the Valhalla of theorists who have admitted mistakes is E. O. Wilson, 2005, "Kin Selection as the Key to Altruism: Its Rise and Fall." *Social Research,* vol. 72, pp. 159-166.
8. L. Feistenger, H. Riechter, S. Schachter, 1956, *When Prophecy Fails: A Social and Psychological Study of a Modern Group that Predicted the Destruction of the World.* New York: Harper & Row.
9. J. Ayto, 1991, *Bloomsbury Dictionary of Word Origins.* London: Bloomsbury. A good etymological dictionary, or an etymological companion of this kind, is I think a handy resource for Wittgensteinian theorists.
10. YouGov, *University Lecturers*, survey conducted 9-16 August 2006 on behalf of the University and College Union (UCU).
11. P. Lawson, 1993, *The East India Company.* London: Longman, p. 129.

12. M.II. Fisher, 2001/02, "Persian Professor in Britain: Mirza Muhammad Ibrahim at the East India Company's College, 1826-44." *Comparative Studies of South Asia, Africa and the Middle East,* vol. XXI, pp. 24-32, [p. 25].

13. P. Lawson, *The East India Company*, p. 129.

14. J. Beames, 1984 [1896], *Memoirs of a Bengal Civilian.* London: Eland Books, p. 63.

15. Ibid., p. 67.

16. Rudyard's mother, Alice Kipling, played upon her brother Harry's student friendship with the headmaster of the United Services College, Cormell Price, when she sought a place for her son. Andrew Lycett discusses Rudyard Kipling's time at Westward Ho! in the third chapter of his 1999 biography *Rudyard Kipling* London: Weidenfield & Nicholson.

17. In his autobiography Clement Attlee recalls his time at Haileybury when, in the 1890s, "The influence of Rudyard Kipling was very strong, especially as the School had a great tradition of service in the Army and the Indian Civil Service." Rt. Hon. Clement Attlee, 1954, *As It Happened.* London: William Heinemann, p. 11.

18. For illustration, in 2004 25 percent of finalists were awarded a First by Imperial College, only 11 percent by the University of Birmingham. Grade inflation is virulent. See M. Woolf, 2005, "Students at Oxbridge have Twice the Chance of Getting a First." *Independent on Sunday,* 4 December, p. 15.

19. In 1992, the British Sociological Association surveyed the national provision of the teaching of sociology. At the concluding session to this exercise, which I attended, it became abundantly clear—from the evidence of course outlines and from the discussions on how best to teach theory in future—that there was little consensus of any substance on how or what was taught. Aside from a general respect for the "Founding Fathers," theory was taught entirely differently, different theorists studied, the curricula were wildly disparate. I found this encouraging.

20. C.S. Cremin, 2003, "Self-Starters, Can-Doers and Mobile Phoneys." *Sociological Review,* vol. 51, pp. 109-128.

21. Ibid., p. 125.

22. Ibid., p. 126.

7

"Ethnic" Chance
(in which Alison remembers to say "please")

By mid-morning Kalam's mum, Mrs. Rupal Patel, has almost finished her preparations for the special meal she will serve to welcome home her son, now that he has finally finished at university. She has already made the *undyu*,[1] a Gujarati vegetarian speciality, the *tavnee* dal, the lentil soup, and *gulab jambu*, alarmingly sweet dumplings basking in sugar syrup. The remaining food for the welcome home meal—the rice, *bhat,* and the chapattis, called by Gujaratis *rotlee*, along with *chas*, a drink of spiced buttermilk, the assortments of pickles and carrot *raitu*, cooling yoghurt mixed with grated carrot that has been first sautéed with butter and mustard seeds—these will all have to be prepared at the last moment and so Mrs. Patel now has a little time in hand before she needs to set off for the station to meet Kalam. As today is special, she offered special prayers to Krishna whose small brass idol, his *murti*, has pride of place in her crowded *mandir*, the domestic temple at which she worships every day after her early morning shower. Lord Krishna shares the crowded family mandir (a present from her elder brother back in Dongeenagar, her father's village in central Gujarat), with an idol of Ganesh the elephant-headed god, with little stainless steel dishes containing rice and red powder, with some betel nuts, alongside several gaudy religious pictures taken from magazines and advertisements, a lamp made from a wick of cotton wool resting in ghee, a few strewn flower petals, some incense sticks, and a postcard showing a seated, meditative image of Pramukh Swami, the leader of a break-away faction of the Swaminarayan religious sect favoured by Patels. Large photographs of her late husband are displayed near the mandir, photographs whose frames are decked with garlands of dried flowers. Because she has time on her hands, Mrs. Patel leaves the kitchen and spends a little time sitting by the mandir reading once again her favourite verses from the *Bhagvad Gita*, the Song of the Lord, the verses in the *Gita*'s twelfth chapter where Lord Krishna prescribes the rightful disposition for a Hindu: "The man who has a good will for all, who is friendly and has compassion; who has no thoughts of 'I' or 'mine,' whose peace is the same in pleasures and sorrows, and who is forgiving..." Inwardly she considers her own feelings on this exciting day in the light of Krishna's teachings and is able to reconcile her own aching desire to have Kalam at home again with the Lord's advocacy of pure selflessness by firmly prioritizing her duty as a mother to her children, by placing her feelings and desires at the service of her family. She closes the *Gita*, verses of which she recites to herself every morning in Sanskrit, which she now knows off by heart, and offers up a final silent prayer to Ganesh, the God of auspicious beginnings, that the return of her son to his family will be lasting, trouble free, blessed by the Gods. Just then, she is interrupted by her daughter, Kalam's older sister Smitta, who is ready to leave to meet her brother and, made wary through long experience, has come to make sure that her mum is also ready in time. Smitta is wearing the standard British young women's Western outfit, low-slung tight jeans with tummy-revealing short t-shirt, that her mum secretly hoped she would not wear today of all days, but what can you do with modern girls? Mrs. Patel's own outfit is a plain white sari, no jewellery, the traditional outfit of widowed Hindu women. Perhaps, thinks Mrs. Patel, if I were to tell Smitta how nice she looks when properly covered up, when she wears that lilac coloured Banares silk saree, then she might quickly change? But before she has time to try this idea out Smitta is pointing to the kitchen clock, impatiently beckoning her mother to hurry up, bundling her into the car for the short journey to the underground station in north London where Kalam is soon due to arrive.

They are only a few minutes late, although it takes them an age to find a parking space. To their surprise, when they meet Kalam he has a companion with him, a young woman, a *doreea*, a whitey. By the rucksack and carrier bags she has with her, Mrs. Patel guesses that she too is a student; nonetheless, her presence is unsettling, why is she here? Why hasn't she gone home to her own family now that college is over? Then to add to the confusion this strange girl introduces herself—did she say that her name was "Alizeen"?—and gives her a large rather damp bunch of flowers. Mrs. Patel nods, smiles, accepts awkwardly the proffered flowers, looks to her son for some sort of explanation. A disturbing intuition catches at her but Kalam says little except that they were studying together, that he thought it would be nice for her to meet his family, and then he leads the way back to the car park. Little is said on the journey home, Smitta seems lost in her own thoughts, Mrs. Patel is too shy to make small talk with the strange English girl. Once back at home, Mrs. Patel escapes to the sanctuary of her kitchen, there to finish the preparations for the welcome home meal. Rolling out, then cooking the rotlee on a griddle pan, her unease is overridden by her duty to feed all visitors, although she cannot help worrying whether or not the English girl will like their food, or find it too hot. Smitta appears in the kitchen to help her mum. The English girl, she tells her, is a vegetarian, has been for almost two years since meeting Kalam. While Mrs. Patel places great store by vegetarianism, this dietary information reawakens her unease leading her to singe a rotlee. She shoots her daughter a quizzical look but Smitta has busied herself with taking the food out to their front room.

The Patels have been living in North London since they arrived as refugees from Kampala, Uganda in the autumn of 1972. Both children, both Kalam and Smitta, were born at the large, local N.H.S. hospital. They often have people round for a meal, often unexpectedly, but in over thirty years they have only once before had a doreeo as a guest. Mrs. Patel is thus rather flustered when at last they sit down to eat. At least the girl is respectably dressed in a long, modest skirt, her hair neatly arranged, her make-up not outlandish. Rather annoyingly, Kalam takes it upon himself to serve her, a serving role that his mum thinks rightfully hers, or if not hers then Smitta's, certainly not fitting for a man. He describes to her the various dishes, jokes that she should be careful as they will be *tiku*, spicy hot, explains that the gulab jambu are to be eaten alongside the savories, not separately as a dessert in the English fashion. Also, explains Kalam, we don't eat in the Western way with knives and forks, we use our fingers, except of course for the dal for which we use a spoon. Alison seems thrown by this news, "Why" she asks "do you eat with your fingers?" "It's our culture" Kalam explains, an explanation that must satisfy Alison who, after a moment or two watching how exactly the others eat with their fingers, after some encouraging if incomprehensible urging from Mrs. Patel spoken in Gujarati, is soon tucking in with gusto, with evident enjoyment, if rather messily. At the beginning, Alison uses both hands for eating but Kalam gently corrects her, explaining that it is "their custom" only to use their right hands, never their left. In the usual way of things, eating together helps dissolve the earlier awkwardness, Mrs. Patel plucks up confidence to speak to Alison and learns that she studied economics, met Kalam on a shared second year theory course and that they've been friends ever since. By late afternoon they and Smitta are sitting on the sofa chatting comfortably away about Gujarati food, Mrs. Patel's part-time job in the electronics factory, how much warmer it would be if they were living in India, Alison's family, and a host of other topics. When, after glancing first at her watch, then at Kalam, Alison announces she really must be off, Mrs. Patel's urgings for her to stay a little longer, to visit again soon, are genuine. They arrange for Alison to visit again next week, to come as early as she can so that Mrs. Patel can show her how to make *bhajyiya*. That night, as she drifts off to sleep, Mrs. Patel admonishes herself for her unwarranted disquiet: she is a nice girl; it's good Kalam can bring his college friends home; it's Alison, not Alizeen.

When, the following week, Alison knocks on their door at about 10 o'clock her first thought is that she may be too early but Mrs. Patel laughs at her concerns; why, she's been up since five-thirty, had her shower, done her *puja* to Lord Krishna, recited a chapter from the *Gita*, had her breakfast, tidied the house, been shopping—phuh, 10 o'clock, the day's almost gone! They go into the kitchen where Mrs. Patel brews some tea in the Indian fashion, boiling tea leaves with water in a saucepan, then adding milk plus a pinch of *chai masala*, mixed spices specially blended for tea, boiling it a little while longer then straining through a sieve into mugs. Alison isn't sure whether or not she likes the taste, it's certainly different, if rather strong. Perhaps, suggests Mrs. Patel, she would like some sugar? Mrs. Patel has already ladled several spoons into her mug: "Try, try," she urges, "it's the Indian way to drink." Tea finished, Mrs. Patel clears the kitchen table ready for Alison's lesson in cooking bhajiya. The two women peel and thinly slice potatoes, clean, then top-and-tail green chillies: Alison, observes Mrs. Patel, is no stranger to cooking, the girl knows how to handle a knife; best of all, she's patient, doesn't hurry-hurry, takes her time, unlike her own daughter Smitta who seems to think cooking is some sort of an Olympic event. Kalam is not at home, he's had unexpectedly to travel up to Wolverhampton to meet a cousin who has come over from Gujarat and is staying there with Kalam's uncle Nittin and his family. Smitta is at work, in her central London office at the firm of accountants she recently joined. The house to themselves, the two women have plenty of time to chat as they cook. As Mrs. Patel mixes the batter, gram flour with water, seasoning, half a teaspoon of baking powder, a little pinch of turmeric and chilli powder, a drop of oil, the batter into which the prepared vegetables will be dipped before deep-frying, she asks Alison about her family and learns that Alison is an only child, that her father worked as an English teacher in a local secondary school before taking early retirement, her mother, also a teacher, still works part-time helping out with problem pupils. Alison too is planning to become a teacher; she's due to begin her postgraduate teacher training course at the end of September. By midday, they have made a fair-sized mountain of bhajiya, a mound of golden battered misshapes that smell delicious. Mrs. Patel fetches two jars of pickles from her well-stocked, highly ordered, larder and they sit down together to lunch on the bhajiya they've made. Alison polishes off a more than generous third helping, to Mrs. Patel's pleasure. After clearing away their lunch things, they sit together in the front room. It's a hot day, Mrs. Patel fights back a wave of tiredness, Alison smothers her yawns, soon both are fast asleep and do not stir until startled awake by the sound of Kalam opening the front door. He teases Alison— "What? Now you are with my mother you sleep all day too?"—settles down to a plate of bhajiya ("Alison made those"), before telling his mum the news from Gujarat he's learnt from his cousin. After eating, Kalam goes off with Alison for a walk, when they return she drinks a final cup of chai and leaves promising to return to teach Mrs. Patel how to make scones ("no, no eggs in the recipe").

This becomes their pattern over the next month, with Alison calling round three of four times a week, the two women sharing recipes, Alison learning that Mrs. Patel doesn't care for pasta, and learning about her life before she along with her husband fled Kampala. They started, she tells Alison, as "traders": her husband's people first went to Uganda in 1905 "when it was still all jungly," two young Patel brothers, they settled first in the north, in Masaka where they knew family friends who ran a general store, neighbours of theirs' back in their Gujarati village. "Very hard, very hard." No proper roads, only the Europeans' Railway cutting through the jungle, laying down new towns as well as sleepers along the track. The brothers opened a shop, "everything they sold, open 24/7." When they'd saved enough, they bought into a transport company started by another Patel they knew in Kampala, three elderly lorries bouncing along the dust roads overladen with sugar cane bound for export from the port of Mombassa to the U.K. Worked so hard, bought more trucks, carried everything apart from animal carcasses but sugar cane remained the chief cargo. The Company took to processing the cane themselves, had a factory built, made *jaggery* and other sugars, sold the sugars to the Europeans. Mrs. Patel's husband joined the Company in 1969, a replacement for one of the two pioneer brothers who had since died. One year later his family were canvassing for a bride to join him in Uganda: "he came from a good Patel family, from one of the better villages, my parents said yes, I was on the boat by the time the rains came, I was eighteen."

"Did you like Africa?" asks Alison.

"Some of it I liked, yes some. Our life was good, we had servants, many servants, ran a car, had picnics most weekends. A Sawmiji mandir. It was beautiful but so dirty, red dust everywhere, the Africans were angry with us, they said we cheated them, sent our money back home, didn't mix with them."

"Did you mix?"

"Well what is 'mix'? Yes, we had good African friends, gave jobs to Africans—without us there'd be no economy, they couldn't do the accounts—we worked hard, didn't cheat customers, built schools, hospitals, proper shops."

"Why did you leave?"

Mrs. Patel tells Alison how Idi Amin seized power from Milton Obote in a military coup, how he promised ordinary African Ugandans they'd be rich, how the Ugandan economy faltered then collapsed, how the Indians' business confidence was punctured by Amin's wild economic policies, the country drained by his extravagances. How he began to identify then expel scapegoats he could blame for his own failure to deliver on his political promises. First certain African tribes, but not Amin's, then the Israelites, the Asians, lastly the Europeans—all expelled as sacrifices to Amin's ogreish, demented rule. How the Indians hadn't wanted to leave, so many had been born there, saw it as their country, they loved Uganda. How the Indian government then the British government had betrayed them, wouldn't let them into their countries even though they held British passports. Then, when she'd given up hope, how her husband, Jaybhai, had burst into their bungalow one evening, told her they had to leave, had to be standing outside Nittin Cinema at ten o'clock where a bus would take the Asians to Entebbe Airport. She hadn't known then where they were flying to, she just knew from Jaybhai's voice that this was it, that they were leaving for good. The long drive in the night toward the airport, the African soldiers with guns, the sudden halt on the moonlit road when all the women had to unlock the suitcases they'd had packed for weeks in readiness, watching as the soldiers, many drunk or high on bhang, threw the carefully folded clothes onto the dusty road in their feverish search for gold jewellery to loot. The arrival at Stanstead Airport, the cold wind of change, the National Front with their placards, the teams of volunteers waiting with cups of lukewarm, weak British tea, waiting to process the refugees. "I was twenty ," Mrs. Patel tells Alison, "your age, like Kalam is. We came here with nothing, with only thin clothes."

Bhajiya, minestrone, tavnee dal, pasta with tomato sauce, cauliflower and pea *shak*, nut loaf, rotlees, vegetable lasagne, afternoon naps, Mrs. Patel's memories—a recipe for the two women to become friends, the first real English friend Mrs. Patel has made, the second Gujarati Alison has befriended. (But, does Kalam count, she thinks, as a real Gujarati? Or, is he rightly a "British Asian"? And does he count as just a "friend"?) Theirs is a friendship eased by their mutual liking for cooking, seasoned by their shared concern with dieting, with watching their weights, and a friendship lubricated by their coincidentally shared sense of humour, both spotting odd laughable absurdities among the humdrum. Mrs. Patel, Alison soon learns, never uses a recipe book, nor does she measure out ingredients. Rotlees aside, most of her Gujarati dishes are prepared in advance then reheated when it's time to eat. Most of the peculiarities of Mrs. Patel's cookery seem straightforwardly explicable to Alison, she can easily guess why they're done that way, why for example it isn't desirable to have food served scalding hot if you are going to eat it with your fingers, the absence of recipe books and measuring tools she puts down to their not being available in India when Mrs. Patel was growing up in Gujarat. There are, however, a few things that do puzzle Alison and as she gets to know Mrs. Patel better, she feels able to ask her: "Do you only eat Gujarati food?" "Yes, only Gujarati. We're pure vegetarians, *shud shakaharee*." "Yes, me too," says Alison, "well, I eat eggs and I know you don't. But why don't you eat other vegetarian food? English vegetarian, you know, other sorts, other countries' vegetarian food, why only Gujarati?" "Well," replies Mrs. Patel, "it's our custom. What our religion tells us." This, it is dawning on Alison, is the stock answer to all her questions about her new friend's culture, a pat answer that, unlike her new friend's meals, leaves Alison feeling dissatisfied. One Friday morning, four weeks later, as they drink their morning chai waiting for the pizza dough to rise, Alison asks about something that she'd noticed on her very first visit: "Mrs. Patel, can I ask you, do you not say 'please' and 'thank you' in Gujarati?" Alison's questioning throws Mrs. Patel for a moment, what does the girl mean by this question?: "We are at all times polite when speaking," she answers, a tad defensively, "in our language everyone we call by their polite name, uncles we call uncles, elder brothers differently from younger ones. Anyway, why do you English always say 'please' and 'thank you'? Why say it when it's only their duty they are doing? Why do you say this all the time?" It's a good question, not one to which Alison has a ready answer: "Well," she says hesitantly, "I suppose it's our culture." Inwardly, Alison registers the lameness of her reply.

It is not just the definite articles that are absent in Gujarati, making it different from English, those small grammatical differences that allowed me to spot in the previous chapter it was Kalam's anonymously submitted essay that I had been marking: in addition, unlike English, Gujarati does not include the verb "to have" nor, as Alison noted, "please" nor "thank you." Politeness, and also possession, are expressed differently, and the chief reason, as is well recognized, stems from the emphasis Gujaratis along with other Indians place upon the family. The individual is seen first and foremost in relation to their family, not just their immediate family, but to their "extended family," for British Gujaratis an international family network. One's place in the extended family is a consequence of age, gender, and birth order: in the family hierarchy of status and deference, elder men come out on top, followed by the other men in order of birth, with women too graded by age, and also by the individual's marital position (married folk rising above the unwed or the widowed). Morality is viewed through this familial lens, what counts as good behavior is referenced to the individual's family role; so, for example, a "good son," Kalam for instance, is one who performs what is expected of him for his family's well being, in other words, his family duty. Gujarati contains a far larger lexicon of family terms than English allowing each individual, no matter how distantly related, to be located on the family map (it is, for example, possible to identify *Bhanej-jamai* and *Bhanej-bahu*, a niece's husband and nephew's wife where the niece and nephew are one's sister's daughter and son, respectively).[2] The various duties performed in the family, duties which will change as the individual ages, bring respect—this familial respect is the compass for Gujarati politeness. So, when Mrs. Patel meets that cousin who has come over from Gujarat to Wolverhampton for a visit, when she asks him about his parents, she will add the respectful suffix *bhen*, "sister," when she inquires about his mother's health because his mother is the wife of Mrs. Patel's older brother, but when she speaks to Smitta, she will not add this suffix, it is inappropriate for a young unmarried daughter. When Smitta comes home from work and makes her mum a cup of chai, her mother will not thank her for performing her daughterly duties, it's just not necessary, thanks are reserved for exceptional acts of kindness. Similarly, there is no need to say "please" when all that is being asked of someone is for them to act dutifully, as they should behave.

Alison, in contrast, was brought up always to say "please," she now says it reflexively, automatically, never has she stopped to think why she does so. She can't help saying "please," she continues to say it every time she and Mrs. Patel sit down to eat their lunch together even though she's learnt Mrs. Patel doesn't bother to say it and doesn't expect Alison to. Conversely, Mrs. Patel has occasionally to remind herself that English people expect you to say it, even when all you are asking for is for them to tell you what the is the time by their watch, and like Alison she too has never stopped to question her own Gujarati politenesses. Saying "please," this ubiquitous English expression of politeness, mirrors the emphasis placed upon individuals, the basic unit of English culture. Unlike Gujaratis, the English can presume that the individual has a choice over how they should act, and so it becomes necessary to request them to do something they are not obliged to do and to thank them for having done it. This presumption of individuals as free agents is marbled into Western culture: promoted by capitalism its genealogy is far older, stretching back to Classical Greece, a cultural feature absorbed in Christianity, a religion of converts who, at least ideally, choose Christ. Similarly, when Alison became a vegetarian she did so of her own free will, she converted to vegetarianism. Hinduism, in contrast, is an ascribed religion, one you are born into, to which, strictly speaking, conversion is impossible.[3] Mrs. Patel was born a vegetarian, she did not choose to forsake eating meat.

Just like the rest of us, Alison has never before considered the reasons she always says "please," she just does it automatically, expects it of others, it's a mundane social mantra whose countless daily repetitions reinforce the individuality that sustains English culture—a repetition of the social principles that underpin the language. She has, of course, her own characteristic ways of being polite, for instance her winningly guileless way of saying "please" that disarms you when she asks if she may have an extension to her essay submission date. Similarly, by omitting to say "please" or "thank you" and by always referring to people in family-based terms, Mrs. Patel is unwittingly reinforcing the priority of the family over the individual. Like Alison, she too has her own characteristic ways of using Gujarati form of politeness, for instance her adding the honorific suffix *jee*, as in Gandhi*jee*, to the names of all the young boys in her family, an affectionate deference only strictly obligatory for women of Mrs. Patel's status when she is addressing older men.

Just as their emphasis placed upon the family is the hub holding the spokes of Gujarati forms of politeness, so too the family is the chief reference for their traditional notions of possession. In English the verb "to have" has spread like a virus to infect all sorts of possession, used nowadays to express not only the relationship between individuals and things, but also for the ways individuals think, "I had an idea," the way they are feeling, "I had an appalling hangover," and even, as the philosopher John Austin noted, to describe chance events, as in "I was late because I had an accident." This verbal expression of possession has come to colonize English, clearly promoted by today's individualistic capitalism. English speakers may, if they wish, use alternative expressions of possession, such as "mine," an alternative also open to Mrs. Patel but one which, along with 'thoughts of 'I,''' Lord Krishna, in the *Gita*, tells her she should renounce. Gujarati sentences nearly always end with a form of the verb "to be," most often as *che*, and the individual speaker is less an agent in the

English individualistic sense, more a participant in what is occurring. So, for example, when it comes to possessing money, whereas English speakers might say "I have some money," a literal transliteration of the Gujarati for this phrase could be "I met some money." Just as in English you can now "have" an accident, good fortune, or whatever, in Gujarati you can meet with them.[4] That possession can assume differing expressions illustrates Marx's point about the delusion of private property, the Proudhonian argument that private property is in reality a relationship between people, not between individuals and things, not a "natural," timeless expression of human nature as some classical political economists supposed. What differs are the social relationships between people that lead them to view themselves, other people and their relationship to the created artificial world in diverse ways. The inheritance of property becomes a corollary of the varying emphases given to individuals and families in the two cultures with the English inheriting property as individuals, an individual 'right' upheld by law, while Gujarati property is passed down through families whose members benefit depending upon their gender and standing in the family. One further, significant, distinction between Western individualized and Hindu family cultures is that in the West all individuals, at least in principle, are seen as of equal worth, all worthy of thanks and equal property rights, equal in the eyes of God, whereas in Hinduism individuals are reincarnated into an unequal hierarchical caste system, given unequal respect according to their family standing, not accorded equal property rights, and not all equally likely to achieve salvation.

This divide between cultures prioritizing either individuality or the family is one of the varieties of the artificial world, both varieties are open to varying chance influences and have come to accommodate chance in different ways. Why this division, these two differing emphases on the individual or the family, arose may also be for chance reasons. Which brings us up against the notion of caste, not a term Mrs. Patel herself would use, a foreigners' word which, like chillies and the printing press, first was exported to India by the Portuguese. Oceans of ink have been drained by social scientists attempting to pin down the concept of caste, to the point whereby this observation is itself becoming a cliché, but as caste informs Mrs. Patel's world so strongly we need briefly to give this concept some analytical airing.

Of the 559,000 or so Hindu citizens living in Britain recorded by the 2001 Census, some 70 percent are Gujaratis, two-thirds of them were born abroad, some two-thirds of British Gujarati families have an association with East Africa, and most British Gujarati Hindus belong to upper castes, mainly to the Lohana and Patidar trading castes from the third hierarchical tier.[5] The caste to which Kalam's mum belongs by dint of birth is the Lewa Kanbi Patidars, commonly sharing the surname Patel. This is the group whom, as we saw in an earlier chapter, in the turbulent mid-eighteenth century took control of fertile lands in central Gujarat allowing them to distinguish themselves from non-land-owning agricultural workers, to raise their caste up the hierarchical ladder, and finance migration to East Africa, a caste biography riddled with chance. As I mentioned, a further consequence of this caste progression had been intense inter-caste competition for alliances with prosperous land-owning families, alliances cemented through marriage, marital competition that in the nineteenth century resulted in female infanticide, a practice soon outlawed by the British rulers. From their settlement with the British rulers, there emerged a patterning of Patel villages arranged in marriage circles, *gols*, clusters of villages arranged in a hierarchy of status with at the top the *chagam*, the most prestigious cluster of six villages.[6] Members of this caste have migrated around the world, especially to East Africa, Canada, Britain, and North America, and they have been remarkably commercially successful, success reflected in their stereotyped association with the occupations they have taken (leading to national stereotypes, in America "Motel Patels," in Africa "Patel Railway," in the U.K. as corner-shopkeepers).

The Patels' biography provides a good case study for examining caste. In the case of Patels we know why it was that they emerged as a distinct caste, due to changing patterns of land ownership, but we don't know about the genesis of caste itself. There are many rival secular hypotheses about the origins of caste, most of which locate its genesis at the time of the Aryan tribes' invasions of northern India round about 1500 B.C. and which postulate a process of separation by the Aryans from the indigenous peoples of India whom the Aryans saw as inferior as well as ritually unclean. As social groups separated themselves into discrete caste communities they also patterned their relationship to the means of production; this pattern was written in religious and social doctrine, the social principles that acted as the tramlines of culture, and the pattern had constantly to be reproduced, generation by generation. This caste pattern was and is constantly changing, not some static template, as the biography of the Patel's caste illustrates. The Patels have been and are a changing social group, upwardly mobile as a caste, whose occupations have broadened markedly, and who first distinguished themselves when their relationship to the means of production, to the land, changed in the mid-eighteenth century. This change in relationship to the land was not of course the genesis of caste per se, but it does suggest that Marx's stubborn focus upon production, the production of what I am calling the artificial world, has analytical mileage, helping to explain not simply the origins of Patels, but also how they sustain their caste as it became an international phenomenon.

Societies whose biographies did not conform to his story of conflicting class formations, to the Western procession of classical plebeians/patricians, feudal serfs/landlords, proletariats/capitalists, sat awkwardly in Marx's scheme of things and became relegated outside of his progressive history. In the 1850s, living in exiled poverty, Marx wrote articles commenting on then contemporary Indian affairs, often for the politically sympathetic *New York Daily Tribune*, but he did not produce a substantial or convincing explanation for the special, non-Western features of "Asiatic" modes of production. The relationship between Western centers of capitalism and their colonial satellites raised far-reaching political issues, in Marx's phrasing a "difficult question," that neither Engels not Marx was able properly to answer.[7] In the *Grundrisse*, those long-lost notes he wrote at the end of the 1850s when working toward what would be published as the first volume of *Das Kapital* Marx, in the *Grundrisse*'s general introduction, in the context of his critique of the classical political economists' treatment of production and distribution, reasoned that:

> A conquering peoples divides the land among the conquerors, establishing thereby a certain division and form of landed property and determining the character of production; or it turns the conquered people into slaves and thus makes slave labour the basis of production. Or a nation, by revolution, breaks up large estates into small parcels of land and by this new distribution imparts to production a new character. Or legislation perpetuates land ownership in large families or distributes labour as hereditary privilege and thus fixes it in castes.[8]

This analytical approach sketched in the quoted passage had earlier been used by Marx to examine the role of the East India Company in forging the British Raj[9] and in this section of the *Grundrisse* Marx then goes on to argue that what is being distributed, here land by the conquerors, is in fact the means of production, the means by which the artificial world is made and sustained. As a general methodological principle Marx's remarks would appear applicable to both the genesis of caste and to the emergence of the Patels. Patidars, Patels, did indeed emerge because of changing patterns of land ownership, patterns that not only allowed Patidars to distinguish themselves as a separate caste grouping, but also patterns that determined the "character of production," distributed "labour as a hereditary privilege" for the less lucky landless laborers, patterns that became perpetuated if not by formal legislation, then by equally binding custom, by caste ascription. The Patels can be seen as a small, localised instance of Marx's "conquering peoples"; on a grander scale, more in tune with the common picture of conquerors, are the invading Aryan tribes, the invasion commonly accepted as the precursor to the genesis of caste and an invasion for which there is now some preliminary evidence from population genetics.[10] Marx's analysis sketches the social process by which conquering Aryans dominated the means of production when they invaded India and is in line with the common historical picture of indigenous Indian peoples being forced to live on less fertile, less productive lands; a displacement still evident in today's State of Gujarat where the Scheduled Castes and Tribes who comprise some 23 percent of the State's population are demographically concentrated in the poorest rural areas, particularly in the Districts of Valsad, the Dangs and the Panchmahals.[11] These displaced peoples were not only physically relocated, they were also socially ostracized, placed outside the caste system. On a grander scale, it may well have been the case that the aboriginal peoples of India migrated south en masse, a migration for which the obviously different physical and cultural traits of southern Indians seems to speak strongly (southern Indians being, in aggregate, comparatively darker, smaller, with their own forms of Hinduism including distinctive temple architecture and temple governance, and speaking in Dravidian that has no relationship to any other family of languages).

What Marx's broad, general methodological principle cannot explain, however, is the specific form taken by caste exclusivity, how it was and is actually practised. In his insistence upon prioritizing issues of production, Marx underplays the significance of the natural circumstances in which production took place. Natural means of production are shaped by natural, non-human factors that influence how production is achieved, in the case of early Gujarati cultivators what crops may be grown, what sort of pests, climatic conditions, etc. they face. These localized natural influences affect not simply crops and harvests, they also of course affect the people themselves, the landowners, the laboring peasants, the merchants, the princes; in some cases everyone is prone to natural influences such as monsoons failing, or flooding, temperatures reaching the high forties, crop blight. Such influences do not respect social divisions. Of these natural influences, one acute problem that conquerors and other newcomers would have encountered is disease, illness, the hidden natural dangers that all of India's conquerors had to guard against, dangers well known to the British who might be chatting to a friend in the morning only to attend his funeral that afternoon, a tribute to the virulence of viruses in hot countries and to unsanitary conditions. "The life of a Company servant on Bombay is three summers," as the old British adage cautioned. What was most terrifying about such natural perils was that they were not understood, they arrived and acted mysteriously, seemingly at random, felling one man while his brother was unaffected. For the Aryan conquerors, such hazards must have been alarming, horrifying random diseases that could wipe out whole villages, diseases for which there were no known cures or remedies. Worse still the Aryan tribes, a collection of disparate peoples from many countries sharing the Aryan language, would have enjoyed little natural immunity to the new diseases, nor to the new strains of familiar diseases, that threatened them. Similarly, the indigenous peoples would have been equally vulnerable to the disease the conquerors brought with them. And not just Aryan invaders, for Gujarat has long been settled by outsiders, most Gujarati Hindu communities do not consider their origins to be Gujarati and the Gujarati, in common with the wider Indian, labor market was and is marked by constant movements of itinerant workers, by armies of labor seeking seasonal work in the fields.[12] Faced with this pressing health problem the many, many groups settling, or sojourning, or travelling through the region would have needed both to account for these mysterious perils and to take practical steps to keep healthy. They accounted for the phenomena in a religious framework, explaining afflictions as the work of the Gods caused by the personal shortcomings of the afflicted individuals—the only available explanatory framework. Practical steps would, presumably, have been based upon lessons from experience, experience teaching that mixing with certain people, eating certain foods, drinking from some wells, and the like lessened or increased vulnerability. Why, for example, drinking from some wells rather than others made you sick couldn't be known and wasn't discovered until John Snow's pioneering cartography correlated cholera with particular wells in nineteenth-century London, but there were pragmatic practical measures that hard experience showed prudent, while causes could be thought divine. Hence, the prevention of disease promoted social patterning, at least as big an incentive as mastery of the means of production, and one which I think may have parented the caste system. A primary reason for caste exclusivity, for many other caste customs, was the need for conquering Aryans and other newcomers to protect themselves by regulating strictly their contact with local people. The higher up the social scale, the less the contact: a social system, a hierarchy, of quarantine. Once established, babies, as well as subsequent settlers or invaders such as the Gujaras after whom Gujarat may have been named, could be located within the quarantining system of discrete family networks, the castes, whose boundaries had constantly to be policed.[13]

This theory of quarantining needs to be married to Marx's analytical approach to the conquerors' seizure of the means of production and it is a theory that demands circumspection, partly because it is of necessity speculative. If the theory is correct, then it is, to my mind, a powerful example of how truly chance factors might promote social change and it is a theory which is tempting because it can be used to shed light upon many caste customs, customs that in India were as important as Western class cultural codes in their bearing upon the production of the artificial world, and because it may also help clarify Mrs. Rupal Patel's thinking and behavior. In particular, it may explain a cultural idiosyncrasy of caste, the ways in which caste is bound up with notions of purity and defilement. Like the older picture of climatic influences upon culture that Montesquieu pioneered, that had then long fallen from favor until recently revived by Jack Diamond, the idea that Indian and other "primitive" cultures had arisen partly as health strategies was a commonplace of nineteenth-century thinking, a point noted by Mary Douglas in her well-known study *Purity and Danger*, a book whose subtitle, *An Analysis of the Concepts of Purity and Taboo*, reveals her predilection for conceptual, that is, philosophical, over empirical analysis. Having discussed ways in which Hindus view status in term of purity and defilement, how purity and defilement is embedded in Hindu culture, and how it shuffles the caste system, she goes on to reason that we cannot explain Hindu notions of defilement in psychoanalytic terms, reasoning she supports with the observation that while any contact with excreta is reviled, as evidenced in the lowly status of latrine cleaners, individual Hindus have a "slack regard" about the "act of defecation," defecating in public with no apparent inner anxiety as they squat by the roadside. We should, she thought, expect individual Hindus to be "controlled and secretive about the act of defecation" if the taboos surrounding excreta were of psychoanalytic origin, instead they are open, public and unconcerned, implying that:

> Rather than oral or anal eroticism it is more convincing to argue that caste pollution represents only what it claims to be. It is a symbolic system, based on the image of the body, whose primary concern is the ordering of a social hierarchy.[14]

This latter sentence in the above quoted passage encapsulates Douglas's thesis over purity and taboo, they are symbolic means to keep society in order, an hypothesis she then continues in the next paragraph to argue for by drawing attention to how "Indians" assess the polluting potential of different bodily fluids by unequal symbolic measurements:

> It is worth using the Indian example to ask why saliva and genital excretions are more pollution-worthy than tears. If I can fervently drink his tears, wrote Jean Genet, why not the so limpid drop on the end of his nose? To this we can reply: first that nasal secretions are not so limpid as tears. When thick rheum oozes from the eye it is no more apt for poetry than nasal rheum. But admittedly clear, fast-running tears are the stuff of romantic poetry: they do not defile. This partly because tears are naturally pre-empted by the symbolism of washing.[15]

Moreover, observes Douglas, tears are not connected to: "…the bodily functions of digestion or procreation. Therefore their scope for symbolizing social relations and social processes is narrower."[16] In answer to Jean Genet's question, in contradistinction to Douglas and rather more prosaically than she explains it within her symbolic universe, the reason for the different evaluations over tears, saliva, and genital excretions is all too plain as millions of AIDS sufferers and those who today caught flu when the person next to them sneezed amply testifies. Similarly, scrupulously avoiding other people's excrement, and those who have to clear it up, while being relaxed about defecating, makes good biological sense. Hindu practices concerning purity and taboo may have accumulated symbolic significance but their efficacy, their ancient pedigree, does not derive from how much or how little symbolic weight they are subsequently given but instead from hard-won pragmatic lessons from the past.

How does the chance development of a quarantining system of social order play out in Mrs. Patel's life in present-day North London? Many of her everyday practices happily conform to my "quarantine theory" of Hindu culture. For instance, the custom of only using your right hand when eating, for touching food arose presumably not from the near universal cultural deprecation of left-handedness (the sinister side) but more from the need to not use the same hand for eating that was used for cleaning your bottom after going to the toilet. Not only how you eat, but also what you eat may for Hindus be governed by health measures. Gujarat has the longest coast line of any Indian state offering Gujaratis high protein harvests from the sea yet, despite the chronic shortage of food, despite periodic famines and starvation, Gujarati Hindus, the majority social group, are either strict vegetarians or aspire to be so with vegetarianism a mark of upper-caste status.[17] Why? Well, again presumably, because although fish, molluscs and the like are prime sources of protein they are also prime carriers of disease, especially in fiercely hot conditions where they are prone to quickly going "off." Hence fish, as well as equally nutritious but similarly hazardous meat from, harder to husband, animals was avoided, proscribed from the Hindu diet. Commonplace domestic habits also conform, for example removing one's shoes when entering a Hindu home or temple, always bathing before any important event or ritual, speak clearly to the need for hygiene to be respected. Where Mrs. Patel grew up in her father's village in central Gujarat, in the small dusty ribbon village of Dongeenagar, quarantining measures were all too evident. In her childhood Dongeenagar comprised clusters of village homes with outcaste families living in huts some distance from the village centre. Out-castes drank from a different well, their work involved pollution, cleaning up the mess left by caste villagers, as road sweepers, latrine cleaners, or as leather workers making shoes, disposing of dead cattle. Outcastes never ate with caste families; rigid rules of commensality were followed. They walked on the other side of the road, their children did not play with those from caste families; very austere upper-caste Hindus avoided even the shadow of an outcaste. Outcastes who neglected, maybe accidentally, to respect these conventions could be, and were, punished severely. All of these village practices betray, to my mind the quarantining pedigree of Hindu caste practices.

While conditions in the small, isolated Gujarati village of Dongeenagar remain largely unchanged, Mrs. Rupal Patel's own life has altered hugely in consequence of migrating first to Uganda, then to England. As Steven Vertovec has noted,[18] while under African skies:

> …a caste system could no longer govern social, economic, ritual or other relation-ships, [nevertheless] caste identities among Gujaratis have continued to be of con-siderable importance with regard to status, marriage, social networks and formal institutions.

Selective migration from Gujarat, very largely from a limited number of trading castes, plus the exigencies of their new African home, disrupted the caste system that could not be replicated on the new continent; nonetheless, just because the system could not be shipped intact to East Africa, this did not stop Gujarati Hindu migrants from identifying themselves in caste terms. When in late 1969 she arrived in Kampala to be with her new husband Jaybhai, Mrs. Patel found herself thrust into a world that was both alien yet familiar; a country of Africans with their own, as she saw it, uncivilized, unclean ways, a small community of aloof Europeans, strange foods, smells, houses, songs, stars, animals, jungle. Amidst this new, alien country she also found a comfortingly familiar inner world of prosperous Gujarati traders and businessmen living together, physically separate from the other races, attending impressive mandirs, with their own schools and hospitals.[19] The Patel's home on Tklokweng Road was half way down one of Kampala's hills; at the top of the hill lived the European in their large bungalows, while Africans lived out of the city, only present during the day and then only as servants or as customers in the Asian-owned shops. Jaybhai was away at work most of the day, often returning late in the evening, leaving Mrs. Patel to run the home, give the servants their orders, a role that daunted her at first but one which she was soon able to carry out competently thanks to the help she received from the neighboring women, one or two of whom she knew of as distant relations and to whom she could introduce herself as family. On a typical day, having seen Jaybhai off to work with his tiffin, Mrs. Patel would meet with the other Gujarati wives for chai, for gossiping, for news from Gujarat, for religious observances. Along with chai, she came to share their fearful, paranoiac outlook; she came quickly to learn that just beneath their veneer of stability and comfort, the Asians were increasingly alarmed by events in Amin's polity. Soldiers were roaming in gangs, ill-disciplined, looting, fighting. The police had lost authority, it was becoming unsafe to venture outdoors. Tense and afraid, the women naturally drew together, prisoners in their own homes, huddled together indoors. If they could afford to, children were sent overseas, usually to Britain, for schooling; the new topic of conversation became whether it would be right to pack up and leave. As Amin began identifying, scapegoating, expelling the victims of his own failure, the tension became acute, life intolerable:

> When evening came the Asians hesitated before plucking up the courage to go out-of-doors. Their houseboys were becoming arrogant and insolent. Tension was developing in the peaceful atmosphere of their own homes.... Cases had been known of assaults on the daughter or daughter-in-law of the house. There was no direct danger from the houseboy when no man was in the house, but the boy might steal an army uniform and give it to some relation or acquaintance. Then afterwards Mama might be threatened by someone in army uniform coming to the house. Money or ornaments would mysteriously disappear.
> Such incidents were gradually becoming more frequent. It had, furthermore, become dangerous to walk along the streets, even in daylight, especially for the women. Nobody ventured alone to the shops or to the "sakoni" (vegetable market).[20]

When, in August 1972, Idi Amin finally turned on the Asians, accusing them of not mixing with or marrying Africans, of corrupt business practices, of remitting their profits back to India, and ordered them to leave within ninety days (a cruel reference to the Asians' standard ninety-day credit period), Jaybhai Patel felt almost relieved, relieved that the horrible uncertainty was now at an end, that now something would have at last to be done.

Mrs. Patel tries not to remember that coach journey from Nittin Cinema to Entebbe Airport, her last memory of Uganda. At least when they landed at Stanstead Airport Jaybhai's brother Nittin was waiting to meet them, waiting with a thermos of hot chai, so much nicer than those cups of lukewarm insipid English tea the volunteer helpers gave the newly arrived refugees. Although it seemed at the time to take an age for them to be processed by the authorities she felt safe, Idi Amin left far behind, no more kerosene lamps with frightening shadows, now the light came from naked neon tubes in the temporary halls hastily erected to receive the refugees, white light on the white faces of kind women volunteers, on the hard faces of the men standing outside the airport holding up placards that she could not read. Their processing complete, clutching their new documents, she and her husband were driven by car to London by Jaybhai's brother Nittin to a part of the city she would discover was called Wembley, where Nittin lived in the flat above the corner-shop he'd bought with the money he'd made in Nairobi from the garage he'd run before, in 1967, the Asians had fled Kenya in fear of African rule and impending British immigration restrictions. With sleep, with food, safe now among family, Mrs. Patel thanked Krishnabhagvan for rescuing them, thanks she gave for many months, thanks that grew as she learnt how fortunate they'd been to have Nittin waiting for them at Stanstead, family help that had meant she and her husband did not languish for months in the ex-army camps commandeered by the Ugandan Resettlement Board to house refugees with no one to take them in.[21] As had happened in Kampala, so too in Wembley Mrs. Patel was supported by a network of Gujarati women who'd come over to England from Kenya or Tanzania four or five years earlier, who seemed to know their way around, who helped her with the endless government forms she needed to complete, could show her where to buy the best vegetables, how to use the buses and the underground trains, counselled Mrs. Patel about the English ways ("always say 'please' to them, it's their way"). There was so much to learn, so much that was new. Her husband, Jaybhai, spoke some English, he'd learnt it living in Uganda in the course of his job managing the sugar-cane ginnery: two months after first arriving in England he was working as a storeman for a local English-owned company that made children's toys. Mrs. Patel soon realised that she too would have to find a job, most of the Gujarati women she met in Wembley worked. It was to be her first job, women hadn't gone out to work in Uganda unless their families were either poor or "modern" and she was apprehensive but once again Nittin came to her rescue, gave her a job serving in his cornershop. Here she met and, for the first time, talked to English people. It was so difficult at first, the hours were so long, but she managed to get by with a small vocabulary of phrases when serving customers, not just Englishers, customers from parts of the world she'd never even heard of, some of whom were regulars who knew Nittin, joked with him, were friendly in their odd foreign ways. A year after leaving Entebbe Airport, she and Jaybhai moved out of Nittin's flat to go to live in a nearby small terraced house they'd found to rent. By scrimping, by denying themselves all but essentials, they managed to save enough to enter a partnership with Nittin on another shop. Jaybhai gave up his job as a storeman, gave up the nightshifts he'd worked every day for three years to run their new joint enterprise. Now they worked even harder, but now they were working for themselves. Business was good, nobody tried to haggle, they just paid what was asked, said "thank you" and left. By the mid-eighties, after many frustrating years of trying, Mrs. Patel could write to her relatives back in Dongeenagar that she had been blessed with a baby; it was only a girl, Smitta, but there was still just time for her to bear a son, with Krishna's blessing. Sure enough, two years later, their son Kalam was born. Their life was good, they'd bought their own home before property prices rocketed, they had a car, a nearly new Datsun, a color television, two beautiful children who were both doing well at school. When she remembered how they'd come to Wembley penniless, like many of the refugees forced to leave their possessions and money behind in Kampala, Mrs. Patel could count herself lucky, blessed by the Gods, grateful as always to her family for their support.

Rupal's and Jaybhai's material success since settling in Britain is far from exceptional: so-named "African Asians," the majority of whom are Gujarati, have been one of the U.K.'s outstanding "ethnic" success stories. *The Third PSI Survey*, undertaken in 1982, noted that: 'The position of the African Asians has changed: in 1974 they had the lowest earnings median, but they are now one of the highest-earning black groups.'[22] Twelve years later Tariq Madood, commenting upon findings from the next, the fourth of these surveys, commented that:

> Chinese people and African Asians have reached a position of broad parity with the white population—behind on some indicators perhaps, but ahead on others. It would not be appropriate to describe them as disadvantaged groups.[23]

This notably rapid success story, achieved in just three decades, was fuelled by what Valerie Marett has called their "striving toward self-determination," by the sheer hard work of the first generation, coupled with some friendly chance factors. Compared to other immigrant communities, Gujaratis who'd arrived in Britain from Africa carried with them cultural, if not always monetary, capital, whereas most migratory patterns begin with single men who then, if successful, are followed by their family, the classic linkage of "chain migration," the African Asians arrived in family units; they often had business and commercial experience; they came from castes or communities with entrepreneurial traditions and ethos; they were a select bunch given that only the successful were likely to have remained in Africa[24] ; by the time they arrived, some families already owned property, especially in London, which had been bought to house sons studying in Britain or for businessmen visiting the U.K.; they had tasted success in Africa and wished to restore their fortunes; they valued education and unlike

many British Muslims, did not confine women to the home; and they were better acculturated than other Asian immigrant groups. Although not necessarily
well-educated, they were overwhelmingly middle class, coming from the self-
employed stratum or from state employment as administrators, teachers, clerks,
etc.[25] By far their greatest strength lay in their tradition of community self-help:
one of the government's aims in their response to the Ugandan Asian Crisis,
a crisis partly of Britain's making,[26] had been to disperse the refugees across
the country, an attempt to prevent the refugees from settling in areas already
having demographic concentrations of immigrants so, it was claimed, as to
lessen potential social conflict, a dispersal measure attempted with one eye by
politicians on public opinion, opinion which when voiced by newspapers such
as the *Leicester Mercury* was deeply hostile. This dispersal policy failed, the
refugees naturally went to areas where they already knew friends and family;
like Mrs. Patel going to stay with Nittin, 75 percent of the refugees did not need
much help with finding accommodation, either going immediately to stay with
acquaintances of after a short stay in the URB's camps.[27] Natural demographic
concentrations occurred in North London and in the Midlands. With astonishing
rapidity, the African Asians established themselves, "marching," as Vaughan
Robinson put it, "into the middle class."[28] By the time the 1982 PSI Survey
was conducted, 23 percent were in self-employment, a higher proportion than
any other British ethnic community, with 73 percent owning their own homes
compared to 59 percent for white Britishers.[29] In Leicester, an English Midlands
city that now has the highest "ethnic" proportion, including some 41,000 Hindus,
mostly Gujarati, there has been an inner-city regeneration thanks to the effort
of the African refugees and immigrants. Perhaps the most telling measure of
their success is given in a study published by Michael Lyon and Bernice West
in 1995 which revealed that British Asians then owned 70 percent of London's
newsagents and 50 percent of Britain's independent retail outlets, an astonishing
achievement in which the African Asians, especially the Patels, have played a
major part. This study also showed that, in 1986, the Patels they surveyed had
prospered in economic niches, two-thirds in Confectioner-Newsagent-Tobac-
conist shops, just under a quarter in Provisions and Food retailing, with only
12 percent in Professional Businesses.[30]

Twenty years on from Lyon's and West's study, the Patels in company with
other British Gujaratis have moved out from the narrow niches that the first
generation exploited so profitably, out of those small corner-shops, with the
younger generation, many of whom like Smitta and Kalam born in the U.K.,
using their impressive educational qualifications to enter the professions, particularly the "D.E.A.D." professions of Doctors, Engineers, Accountants and
Dentists. From out of what Professor Mamdami classified as their confining
African "commercial bourgeois" niche, then from their British retailing slot,
British Gujarati Hindus have diversified successfully not only in business and
commerce, but in the arts, in politics, and academia. By the early 1990s there

were at least 100 Gujarati millionaires living in Britain,[31] by 2005 some 10 percent of those featuring in the annually compiled "British Asian Rich List" had an African background. Unsurprisingly, along with wealth,[32] have come changes to customs and attitudes: when questioned over the importance they placed upon nationality, religion, jobs, the country their family came from, education, and skin color, "African Asians" sampled in the *4ᵗʰ PSI Survey* held attitudes virtually indistinguishable from the majority of Britishers in the Survey's samples.[33] Changes in attitudes, changes to customs, are what we should expect when Hindu castes have in short time migrated across two continents, twice established themselves often unwillingly in new, alien cultures. Only the old, outdated approach to analysing caste wherein caste was seen as essentially unchanging would be troubled by such cultural developments: this is an accumulative process of cultural change with new attitudes, new pattern of employment etc. added to expand their cultural repertoire. One indice of cultural change is the position of women; in the case of British Gujarati women their entry into paid employment was also joined on occasion by political activism, for instance in the industrial disputes of the seventies at Leicester factories, most publicly in the Grunwick photo-processing plant when Mrs. Jaybhen Desai became the spokeswoman for the predominantly East African Asian female workforce in their fight against the Company's exploitative work practices,[34] political action which as Avtar Brah remarked in 1987, hardly sat comfortably with the stereotyped picture of house-bound, submissive Asian womanhood.[35]

The progress of Gujaratis in Britain has in many respects repeated their African performance and bears out the truth of the old Gujarati saying, "Wherever there lives one Gujarati, there is Gujarat." And for Gujarati Hindus, this implies the rebuilding of their religious life, initially in their homes where the families' mandirs gave the murtees, the idols brought over in the refugees' suitcases, a new British home, and then the literal building of public mandirs. In the last three decades, over 150 mandirs have been built in Britain, many of the earliest housed with brutal symbolism in abandoned former churches. Just as they proved spectacularly successful in the material world of employment and wealth, so too they rapidly introduced the physical manifestation of Hinduism. The form of Hinduism introduced into Britain is not simply Gujarati, it is that which has grown along with the biographies of the overwhelmingly upper-caste Gujarati Hindu families settled in the U.K since the mid-1960s. Before then, the British Gujarati community was numerically insignificant, reckoned at just 8,000 in 1963,[36] and only inflated in consequence of migration or flight from Africa, since when along with the children born to those already living here, the consolidation of families, and marriage, that has brought Gujaratis over from the subcontinent and elsewhere, all going to achieve the current total of some 400,000. There were public mandirs in the U.K. before the arrivals from Africa, but few, with the oldest, to my knowledge, *sanatandharma*, "ecumenical," mandir inaugurated in 1968. In Africa, owing to the inauthentic caste composition of the Asian settlers, there was a shortage of brahmins to officiate at ceremonies, to oversee religious practice and so religious authorities were invited over from India, holy men often representing heteredoxical, guru-led *sampradaya* Hindu sects (of which the Swaminarayan sect is an example), that found favor with this wealthy overseas community. Different Hindu castes tend toward different expressions of Hinduism, follow specific sampradaya and for Patels it has been the puritanical, internally hierarchical, politically questionable Swaminarayans who have benefited. In Britain, this caste affiliation sponsored the Swaminarayan mandir in Neasden, north London, an improbable Disneyesque white marble confection puncturing drab suburbs, a temple opened in August 1995 with separate entrances for men and women, financed and built by a sect riven with factional disputes that has been linked to unsavoury Hinduvta[37] politics back in India,[38] and which is sometimes less than transparent in its campaigning activities.[39] What, then, we see in the unfolding of Gujarati Hindu settlement in Britain are two parallel trajectories: on the one hand, highly successful public roles adopted by Gujaratis, that is, capitalistic roles, individualistic, innovative—and on the other hand, after work is over, a return back to a private, traditional, Gujarati Hinduistic family world. The latter Hindu world crosses national boundaries as easily as e-mails and may be thought of as an international skein woven with extended Hindu families; a new international expression of caste that has accumulated, as I have sketched, partly because of chance opportunities that arose in the modern world as European colonial capitalists invented new African countries at the time when disease and famine struck Gujarat.

It might seem, at first blush, that these two trajectories would be incompatible with each other, their individualistic or familial bases in competition for the individual's loyalties, but for most of the time no such incompatibility arises. Just as Alison learnt to say "please" and "thank you" without first being taught the principles that inform these expressions, so too did Mrs. Patel when first she started working in Nittin's, her husband's brother's, north London cornershop. Both women learnt by simply copying what other people said and they imbibed the underlying principles unknowingly. Most of the time most of us do not question the foundations of the cultural habits we acquire, we unthinkingly accept them, use them as tools, in this case as tools for expressing politeness, courtesy and the like. The hidden principles on which our cultural habits are based are *social principles*, the principles that, as Wittgenstein reasoned, lend meaning to words and as Marx believed organize our relationship to the world we ourselves have made. By using language in culturally specific ways, we at the same time reproduce the social principles which support our culture and as we grow up we come to think of ourselves in terms of the meaning these hidden principles yield. Problems only occur when for some reason or other an incompatibility of social principles prevents the routine reproduction of our culture, and hence ourselves. And when it comes to cultural reproduction, the chief social mechanism, the mechanism permitting both genes and property to be passed on, is marriage. The quarantining system that the Portuguese were to call caste, just like the Western class system, needed to be able to reproduce itself with each new generation, but when two cultures try to wed their underlying social principles may come into conflict, a hazard laying in wait for Mrs. Patel and Alison as they search through recipe books for a cake recipe that doesn't include eggs.

Recipe books, pornography for those who are trying to diet, are still something of a novelty for Mrs. Patel though she first started browsing them fifteen years ago in the empty days after Jaybhai passed away. She herself learnt cooking from a young age by helping and watching her own mother and aunts. The recipes they followed were never written down, instead passed on by example through the generations, modified to suit family tastes and preferences. Ingredients were weighed by hand and experience. She hadn't realised just how guiltily pleasurable it could be to sit down and look at glossy photographs of tempting dishes, at pictures of sticky flapjacks dripping golden syrup, moist banana and date loaf, the jammy stratum of a Victoria Sponge cake. "No," Alison regretfully tells her, "we can't make that, it's got eggs in it." "Can we not make it without eggs?" asks Mrs. Patel, only to learn from Alison that as with most English cakes, eggs are essential, ersatz substitutes like baking powder just won't rise to the occasion. It's no big deal, Mrs. Patel has quite a number of mental recipes for medically hazardous Indian sweets she can teach Alison and the local library holds a few more European vegetarian recipe books, including recipes for treacle tart, baklava and Sussex Pond Pudding (using vegetarian suet). Similarly, Alison learns to measure rice by the handful, how to use an Indian rolling-pin with its swollen circumference at its centre tapering away on either side that facilitates rolling circles, ideal for rolling round rotlees. Mrs. Patel learns to handle the heavier, parallel-edged British pin. Both pins are interchangeable, to a degree, both better at rolling one particular shape, circles or squares. Both women easily accumulate more culinary skills, the humdrum accumulation of the mundane skills that go to make up cultural repertoires. This is not an evolutionary process, neither woman has lost anything, therefore no process equivalent to natural selection has occurred: instead, they have both gained by accumulating new techniques, new culinary knowledge.

Eggs, however, signal the end of easy cultural interchange; unlike rolling pins they're not to be accumulated. Mrs. Patel has never knowingly eaten one, the taboo against eating eggs is written for her as a religious edict, it's part of what she holds most dear, the religious principles of Hinduism, principles that, I am suggesting, have their origins in ancient quarantining and hygiene practices enforced by the invaders of India.[40] This ancient pedigree may account for the depth of feeling that such taboos evoke in Hindus for such taboos would have been continually accumulated by successive generations along with all the other lesser, more flexible customs that, unlike the vital need for dietary prohibitions and social exclusivity as a means for avoiding disease, could be altered to suit changing circumstances. In their passage from Gujarat to Africa, then to Britain, many Gujarati Hindu customs have indeed been altered, changed, neglected, abandoned: in the company of other Asians settled in Africa some Gujarati Hindus, as well as learning Swahili and English at the expense of Gujarati,[41] as well as joining heteredoxical sampradaya sects, started smoking, drinking, eating meat, and other unorthodox practices. For the Gujarati Hindus in Africa, such changes were patterned by local circumstances in the varying African countries, by family peculiarities, by caste (synonymous with the extended family), and by the characters of the migrants themselves. Unsurprisingly, the move from Africa to Britain has impacted upon the relationship British Gujaratis now have with their family back in Gujarat and with those living in other parts of the international Hindu family network. For British Patels, according to a study conducted in the late 1980s questioning Patels in London and in Gujarat,[42] the attitude of the emigrants changed markedly when they left for Britain. Whereas when they had lived in Africa the migrants were keen to maintain close familial links with those they had left behind in the villages, following their move to Britain: "…they have started to act as if India has become their wife's village (*sasru*) where they demand to be pampered and treated with extraordinary respect, and without reciprocity…"[43] Ironically, echoing Amin's accusation, the emigrants now face complaints over their unwillingness to invest in Gujarat-based enterprises or village improvement schemes and they may be viewed with suspicion by those villagers who imagine the emigrants have been corrupted by their exposure to Western culture. The authors of this study, Dr. Mario Rutten and Professor Pravin Patel, conclude that:

> …the first-generation of Patidar [i.e., Patel] migrants in Britain seems to have an ambivalent attitude towards their home region and their relatives back in the native village. They are very much attached to Indian culture and depend emotionally on their social linkages with their relatives and friends in Gujarat.[44]

For British Patels, the strongest link in the binding chains of "social," family, linkages back to Gujarat is marriage. Whereas Gujarati Hindus from the other main caste represented in Africa and now Britain, the Lohanas, stopped marrying spouses chosen only from their native Gujarati villages, Patels for their part maintained this village preference, with marriage to an "Africawallah" family by "*lagna* [marriage] permit," a key means for Patels to migrate overseas. Registers recording marriages are assiduously maintained by Patels throughout their international caste, including by Patels settled in Britain. Like the taboo on eating eggs, the issue of marriage can mark the closed frontiers of cultural accumulation—as Alison is just about to learn.

Back in Mrs. Patel's kitchen in North London, Alison is sifting the self-raising flour they will use to bake sultana scones. "When did you," she asks Mrs. Patel "last go back to India?" This will prove to be an unfortunate line of inquiry.

"Oh, last year, last spring, I was in Gujarat for two months" answers Mrs. Patel. "I took Smitta over to meet the family. I was thinking of her wedding. We went to Varodara [aka Baroda]. A big Patel *pasandgi mela*, we all went." "What's that?" "Like you'd say in English a 'fair,' a marriage fair." "Oh," Alison asks with a note of alarm in her voice that does not escape Mrs. Patel's attention, "you took Smitta off to fix her up with an Indian man?" "Fix her up" jars with Mrs. Patel just as much as Alison's evident alarm; it's not the sort of expression she'd use to describe what is perhaps a Hindu mother's most important, sacred duty. The marriage fairs, the pasandgi melas, literally "selection fairs," are just one of many innovations made in Gujarat, Britain and elsewhere by Patels to preserve their marriage customs in the face of fast-changing developments in their international caste network. At this annual marriage mart the parents of potential brides and grooms complete forms disclosing detailed information on their families, their backgrounds, providing references, "…and of course an important column, which all families concentrate on; whether the boy or the girl is settled abroad or whether there are chances of them going abroad."[45] This particular marriage mart is strictly limited to *Chagamna* Patels, to Patels from the most prestigious circle of six villages, so Kalam's mum who hales from the far-less prestigious village of Dongeenagar, and whose late husband hailed from the middling village of Koynathee, was chancing her arm but then, as she told her family, "*Chalo* [let's go]. Why not try? We live in London," an address that might just be enough to snare a Chagamna groom for Smitta. Youngsters who, like Kalam and his sister Smitta, were born abroad, in Kampala or North London, who were educated, grew up in, spoke the languages of those countries their parents had settled in naturally accumulated views, habits, opinions, attitudes, beliefs that differed from their parents'. In Britain, these new views included that underpinning principle of Western culture, the sovereignty of the individual, a sovereign served by free choice, a cultural ruler affronted by the traditional practice of parentally "arranged marriages." This issue of arranged marriages first caught the attention of British social scientists in the mid-1970s as part of a wider concern with the progress of the upcoming generation of young British Asians, a concern captured in the notion of "between two cultures," a notion that still stands in the foreground of discussions of arranged marriage. Studies carried out at this time were overwhelmingly of young women and were not longitudinal: there were, and are, very few studies of young Hindu men's, or older British Asians' experiences of marriage. This patchy research record is unfortunate because asking young people what they intend to do may well yield unreliable data, especially when the questioning is on a cultural practice often perceived as embarrassingly old-fashioned. Almost as soon as this between-two-cultures agenda came to be written it was sharply contested,[46] but thirty years on, the issue of marriage is still very much alive; even if it has now been swept under the social scientists' carpet; now regarded as analytically pejorative, old hat, it nonetheless continues to resonate with young British Asians for whom wedding bells announce cultural crunch time: it's time to decide which culture to say "I do" to, for the rest of your life.

Marriage and the treatment of nubile Hindu women are, along with the sanctity of the family, a familiar theme in Hindu religious texts and epics, heard loud in the two epics the *Ramayana* and the *Mahabharata*, which both revolve around stories of marital misadventures, played in the tales of Lord Krishna's early life, his *leela* (his "green time"), as recounted in the *Srimad Bhagavata Purana*. As you would expect marriage for Hindus is a family affair, it is families, not simply as in Christian ceremonies, individuals, who are solemnly joined, a family fusion made symbolically at the denouement of the Hindu wedding ceremony when the bride moves over to the groom's family's side of the *mandap*, the raised platform on which the ceremony is conducted. Studies promoted initially by the between-two-cultures agenda addressed the possible problems that the second generation faced, problems of reconciling parental expectations with the principle of individual free choice over spouses. Because by tradition sons remain living with their parents, whom they are expected to support in old age, while daughters leave to live with their new husband's family, the two genders have differing stakes in the marriage game, with British Hindu girls risking greater restrictions on their personal freedoms. Along with the understandable focus on how youngsters were coping with this system, researchers explicated rules of endogamy and exogamy, rules that differ from caste to caste, that have been modified in accommodation to the differing social milieu which the migrants have entered. Just as the Chagam villages have added another marriage bureau open to overseas members of their caste, the pasandgi mela that Mrs. Patel visited in 2004, so too Patels in Britain have innovated, for example by organising chaperoned meetings of eligible youngsters,[47] by using Web dating agencies. As with all marriage systems, Gujarati Hindu marriage rules tell you who you can and cannot marry: the key principles informing the Patels' marital traditions centre upon exogamy, you cannot marry someone from your own natal village, and endogamy, you must marry within your own circle of villages, within your gol. In her much-cited article, Maureen Michaelson described the workings of the Patel village system, a system that was continued in Africa, and then in the U.K.:

> The Patidars [Patels] within a single village are often members of a single patri-lineage, or otherwise related by more distant ties of descent. Within a village, all people, whether Patidars or not, are referred to by classificatory kinship terms, such as 'brother' or 'sister'. Like other North Indian castes, marriage with any known relative is strictly prohibited, and for Patidars marriage within the village is forbidden. They therefore have to look to other villages for suitable partners for their children. The various Patidar villages in Charotar [aka Kheda] are organised into a number of ranked 'marriage circles'. These are associations formed by a varying number of member villages, within which there are agreements to exchange children in marriage. These circles are supposed to be endogamous - that is, parents can be fined

or exposed to other punitive sanctions if they give a child in marriage to a village which is a member of a different circle.

      The Patidars are very concerned about relative status within the caste. Not only is each marriage circle assigned a particular status in relation to the others, but constituent villages within a circle are considered as being of higher or lower status. Since the status of any one particular family is measured by its affinal connexions, there is always a strong pressure on a father to marry his children, especially his daughter, into a higher status village or circle. Within the Patidar caste, therefore, an individual's very status and identity is tied up closely with his natal village. In East Africa, and in Britain, despite the fact that a child may have been born outside India, he or she still 'belongs' to the village of the father or paternal grandfather. This 'belonging' is not merely a matter of sentiment: it is intimately connected with the marriage patterns of the entire Patidar caste, whether in India, Africa, Britain, or elsewhere.[48]

The Patidars' village-based marital system, with its exogamous and endogamous principles serves, as do other caste systems, to transmit genes and property while maintaining a social exclusivity that, in my judgement, first arose as a quarantining precaution and then was preserved by pickling in religion. Women leave their parents' village to spread their genes, men remain in the village and inherit family property. Whether or not the trend for British Patels to marry within their caste is weakening is not, to my knowledge, properly known but anecdotes and researchers suggest that within this highly status conscious community, although "marrying out" may no longer be scandalous or rare, it is still nonetheless unorthodox. In Britain, South Asians are the least likely to marry someone from a different "ethnic" group among a total population of whom a mere 2 percent marry someone from a different "ethnic" background.[49]

      What may seem to be the pivotal issue—who is to make the decision, the family or the individual—has apparently declined in potency for British Gujaratis with the most recent *4th PSI Survey* reporting a marked falling off in parental choosing of spouses for younger generations of "African Asians," "Indians" and "Hindus."[50] That this Survey reported a decline in the rigid tradition of parents choosing and arranging marriage, that new hybrid arrangements giving children a greater say, or a veto, have been accumulated by British Hindus really should come as no surprise but these innovations are, at the end of the day, in the way of compromises: what matters is *not how or if* Hindu weddings are "arranged"—although questions of parental versus children's choice may be deeply distressing to individuals such as Kalam, Smitta, and Alison—*but rather who* is wedded, whether or not Hindus continue to marry members of their own religious communities, spouses selected from amongst their international family network, or individuals from other castes who can be absorbed into the network. Similarly, in Gujarat new caste lineages have formed over the years, partly owing to the differing demographies of castes, differing caste fortunes.[51] It is the continuance of the family-based marital preference, no matter how it is effected, which will sustain the caste in future, which will ensure that genes and property are passed on within the family network; for Patels, passed on within their village gols. Naturally, in the course of their migratory biography changes have and will be made to traditional caste customs, new variations will accumulate, but this does not spell the end of caste, merely changes to its composition, to its presentation. If British, American, Canadian, Norwegian, or other Patels marry Hindus from other castes then they will be accommodated within the international family network: similarly, if middle-class British girls marry working-class boys this does not spell the end of the British class system. If the entire cultural panoply of parentally arranging marriages fell in to disuse this would not lead to caste becoming extinct; arranging marriages is a means to an end, it has the aim of knitting together families, and there are plenty more knitting patterns to choose from.

Within the deeply patriarchal Hindu fold, property inheritance is traditionally a male prerogative, with women obliged to settle for dowries, jewellery, rather than a share in the family property that they left when they married, when they leave to broadcast their genes—a patriarchal distinction at odds with the British ideal of individuals holding equal legal rights, and a potential point of future cultural disruption, as in the headline-writers' dream case of the feud that beset the Pathak family in 2004 when two of the Pathak sisters claimed their fair shares in the *Patak* pickle empire, a claim contested by the Company's head Kirit who in the ensuing court case argued that his sister's claims for equality were "completely at odds with the Hindu culture and practices of the Pathak family."[52]

The troubles that rent the Pathak family when Hinduistic and Western principles of inheritance came in to conflict are of course not inevitable; the history of Gujarati Hindu migrants over the last century, in three continents, is a tribute to their caste system's resilience, to its exportability, to its inherent flexibility. More usually, as with national cuisines, British Hindus have simply adopted, adapted, accrued Western customs, Western ideas. Given that the British Hindu community is not that large and only became numerically significant, only began cultural establishment, thirty years or so ago it is really too soon to identify any lasting social trends or innovations. Compromises are more likely than cultural conflict except when, as in the example of eating eggs or selecting marriage partners, the issue strikes at the heart of current cultural practices (practices which, as in the example of vegetarianism may now be rapidly changing in India).[53] Whether or not conflict occurs or compromise is reached is open to chance, to chance coincidence, contingency, and individual character. Cultures rest on principles, they are not determined by inflexible rules: cultural principles are enacted by endlessly varied characters, not by cultural cyphers. One metaphorical approach to the question of how peoples or generations from different cultures rub along was proposed by Dr. Roger Ballard[54] as part of his challenge to the assumption that second generation British Asians would inevitably run up against a between-two-cultures crisis. Younger

British Asians were compared by Dr. Ballard with bilingualists, confident and comfortable with both cultural languages, able skilfully to negotiate their way around in both Asian and Western worlds without becoming tongue-tied or lost for words, happily switching from one cultural code to the other. In an extension to Ballard's simile I have suggested[55] that just as truly fluent bilingualists do not translate from one language to another, so too individuals negotiating between two cultures are inured from conflict because they do not routinely choose between two alternative cultural expressions, nor translate one into the other. Occasionally, of course, routine cultural negotiation is disrupted, much in the same way that a speaker of say German finds no equivalent in English for an idea or emotion that he wishes to express, say for the German concept of schadenfreude: in such exceptional cases it does become necessary to translate from one language to another. Just how well our illustrative German speaker accomplishes his translation depends upon his character and the circumstances (if he is speaking to a corporate audience he desperately wishes to impress, then his normal fluency in English may falter as he unexpectedly has to invent some clumsy phrase, something like "taking malicious pleasure in the misfortunes of others," clumsiness he characteristically tries to make light of). But when it comes to the incompatibility of cultural practices, translation is not possible: Alison has a pretty good, if weakly detailed, idea of what Mrs. Patel intends for her daughter Smitta; Mrs. Patel knows enough about what's involved with Western "love marriages," she's been living in London for over thirty years, for most of her life—the problem is that the underlying principles behind these two marital customs are incompatible, it's not a matter of translation, it's one of mutually exclusivity, either freely chosen or family selected spouses chosen from the caste pool. Both women believe passionately that their own cultural practice is not simply the better alternative, it is for both women the ideal alternative. A Patel, a Lewa Patidar, is for Mrs. Patel an aspiration,[56] an ideal to be realised by rightful conduct, an example from which her children can profit. Her Gujarati culture may not always work as it should, it's neither perfect nor consistent but then what culture is? When it does work then it can be wonderful. For example the cultural obligation of hospitality obliges Gujarati Hindus to welcome, feed, put themselves out for visitors regardless of what else was planned for the day, regardless of what you are doing when the doorbell rings. The unexpected ring on the door may well mean having to cook afresh for the visitors, giving over the day to gossip, postponing that planned trip to the cinema, foregoing that early night's sleep but in return may be given a day of spontaneity, spontaneous warm companionship—and company is, unsurprisingly, prized, solitude dreaded.

And so, when Alison describes Mrs. Patel's ambitious efforts to arrange her daughter Smitta's marriage at the pasandgi mela in Gujarat as "fixing her up with an Indian man" it is not just Alison's inept colloquialism, not just the unguarded alarm in her voice that jars with Mrs. Patel, it also reveals for her the depth of the cultural gap separating her from her new, her only, English friend who sits opposite. Both women have stopped what they were doing, half of the flour for the scones remains unsifted, the sultanas are still in their unopened packet. Alison notices for the first time that there is a clock in the kitchen. Her characteristic lack of confidence rises along with her heartbeat. But, she loves Kalam: it is not, as evolutionary psychologists, sociobiologists and cynics would have us believe that her love is nothing more than a mating strategy honed by millions of years of evolution to fool her into his bed; she's already slept with him, she lusts after him though not as frequently as he lusts after her, but she *also* loves him, the two feelings exist sometimes discrete, sometimes twinned, sometimes one, sometimes the other, but not in a permanently fixed relationship of master to slave with love merely the servant to reproduction as reductionists would have us think. It is not that love is an expression of sex, rather it is if we are lucky a companion to sex, and it is company chosen by chance for Alison and Kalam, company Alison wants to keep, even at the cost of overcoming her characteristic lack of confidence. She only has two more weeks before she has to leave to start her teaching course so although she hasn't talked it over with Kalam, she stands up, puts both her hands on the kitchen table, feels herself blushing furiously, and says to Mrs. Patel, "You do know Kalam and me want to get married, don't you?"

Mrs. Patel is thrown by Alison's question. She can't pretend to herself that she didn't suspect this was on the cards, it's not a surprise, instead, it is for her a novel predicament. (At this moment it suddenly dawns on her that Kalam's disappointing degree classification might be something to do with this). She hadn't ever expected to face a choice over her how her son should marry, the only choice she expected to make was from among suitable boys, from among eligible Patels. When it comes to the cultural intricacies of traditional Gujarati arranged marriages, the kind of marriage arranged by her parents for her with her late husband Jaybhai's family, she's well prepared, she knows what's expected, how to judge a family's worth, the pitfalls, the current dowry stakes, how to play the game of acceptance without being rushed into a hasty commitment, what her international family expect and hope for. Now she's all at sea with nobody to turn to, nobody to advise her, as far from cultural dry land as Alison's parents would find themselves if they had to arrange Alison's marriage to a traditional Gujarati family. Swirls of emotions, ideas, fears, concerns, envelop her. She wishes Jaybhai were still alive to help her, for without him, without any family help, she is thrown back on her own resources, her own character.

In times of trouble Mrs. Patel turns to religious authority for advice, to Lord Krishna's teachings: what would Shree Krishna counsel her to do? She knows full well he would remind her that: "The highest *dharma* [duty] of a woman is to serve her husband faithfully, to ensure the well-being of her relatives, and to nourish her children, that she should carry out her duties according to her own nature."[57] Ascribed religion brings with it ascribed character: in the case of

Hinduism, not a chance-inherited character that makes each of partly different and similar in our uniquely patterned ways, not the picture of character I have been trying to paint but, instead, ascribed caste character, a generalised ideal to identify with. Like Schopenhauer's[58] understanding of character, with which I am in some agreement, a person's character is for Hindus what they are but unlike Schopenhauer, Lord Krishna teaches that all individual characters are reducible to just four categories: "The four orders of men arose from me, in justice to their works." These four "orders of men," the four castes, have different jobs to do; the top two have their own special moral qualities:

> The works of Brahmins, Kshatriyas, Vaisyas and Sudras are different, in harmony with the three powers of their born nature.
> The works of a Brahmin are peace; self-harmony, austerity and purity; loving-forgiveness and righteousness; vision and wisdom and faith.
> These are the works of a Kshatriya: a heroic mind, inner fire, constancy, resourcefulness, courage in battle, generosity and noble leadership.
> Trade, agriculture and the rearing of cattle is the work of a Vaisya. And the work of the Sudra is service.[59]

The lesson Shree Krishna gives Arjun in the *Gita* is that he must live according to his 'born nature': as a warrior it is Arjun's duty, his dharma, to act as a warrior, to start the great battle, to give the signal he had initially shied from giving. He must renounce his own individual desires in favour of his ascribed caste duty. By renouncing his own desires the rightful Hindu extinguishes the source of his individuality, he extinguishes his unique character and merges with the natural order, an order stratified by caste categories. The apparent iniquity of caste ascription at birth is met by Lord Krishna in his lessons that it is possible, through working dutifully in accordance with your caste nature, to improve your eternal *atma*, your soul, in its next incarnation, a dutiful path to be followed by renouncing desire, those individual desires that inhibit the unwise Hindu from merging with the undivided eternal oneness. This picture of ascribed caste character, in addition to relegating hundreds of millions of Indians to lives of inescapable suffering, also has the effect of squeezing chance and variety right out of the frame. Chance, however, is not so easily thwarted.

For Mrs. Patel, as for other religiously-guided folk, nothing happens just by chance, everything happens for a set reason. The idea that people may fall in love by happy chance, and then may choose to marry on this chance basis is unacceptable to her; more than unacceptable, it's wickedly irresponsible, a selfish abdication of the responsibilities, of the duty, owed to one's family. Love is something she sees as a gift that may be given to couples as their marriage matures; it is certainly not the proper foundation of marriage. And so she says nothing, for she has nothing clear in her mind to say in answer to Alison's pleas. Alison takes her silence amiss, she presumes Mrs. Patel harbours reservations, or worse. "Oh, Mrs. Patel," and now her voice is trembling, "*please* let us get married. We love each other. Oh, *please.*"

Mrs. Patel looks away, Alison takes the opportunity to dab her eyes. She notices that Mrs. Patel's shoulders seem to be shaking, she sounds like she is sobbing and then Alison realises, she can't yet be quite sure, that actually Mrs. Patel is smothering giggles. "You said, you said," she can hardly get the words out, "you said *please.*" In her nervous state, Alison is even more susceptible to the infection of Mrs. Patel's laughter than usual, a chance mutual characteristic susceptibility to them both finding everyday absurdities irresistibly funny. They both rock with laughter, and fall into a clumsy hug. Later that afternoon, as they sit eating their sultana scones and drinking chai after their nap, Alison reflects that among a lot of other things she no longer has to worry much about, she no longer worries that she and Kalam are going to end up as just another sad between-two-cultures cliché (like 'stereotype', originally a printers' term).

Notes

1. As it is not possible faithfully to transliterate Gujarati into English, I have simply written what I hope will be a clear rendering of Gujarati words which are italicised on their first appearance.
2. My thanks to Mbhai and Ubhen for this information.
3. There are a few small avenues open for those who wish to become Hindus, for example by joining a modern unconventional sect such as the International Society for Krishna Consciousness, the colloquially called Hari Krishnas, but this sort of conversion in its turn raises the problem that in her past lives the convert was not a Hindu and so her actions could not have furthered or damaged her *karma*, the supposed lintel of her current existence.
4. The possession, of movable and immovable objects is, in Gujarati, denoted by two different forms of pronouns, *maree* and *mare*.
5. In Gujarat, unusually, trading and commercial castes from the third Vaishya tier of the caste hierarchy rival the second Kshatriya tier in terms of prestige and status; an unorthodox outcome probably reflecting the historically weakened position of warrior-governor Kashatriyas in a long-colonized region and the commercial prowess of Vaishya castes.
6. Exactly how many villages merit inclusion, their ranking in the hierarchy, and other such questions, is open to dispute but the primacy of the six *chagam* villages—Dharmaji, Bhadran, Sojitra, Vaso, Karamasad and Nadiad—is acknowledged by all.
7. For a selection of Marx's journalistic articles on India, written in the 1850s, see K. Marx 1973 *Surveys From Exile: Political Writings Vol.2* London, Penguin. David Fernbach's Editorial Introduction to this Volume summarises Marx's and Engel's analytical difficulties with India and China, pp. 24-28.
8. K. Marx 1971 [1857], "General Introduction." In: D. McLellan *Marx's Grundrisse* London, Macmillan, p. 29.
9. For example: K. Marx, 1853, "The Future Results of the British Rule in India." In: *Surveys from Exile.*
10. Two, at the time of writing, unreplicated genetic studies illustrate the caste dispersal of genes by women, rather than by men, and the degree to which castes share their genes with Western Eurasians, with the higher castes sharing more than the lower:

M. Bramshad et al 1998 'Female gene flow stratifies Hindu castes' *Nature.* vol. 395, p. 651; P. P. Majmuder et al. "Human-specific insertion/deletion polymorphisms in Indian populations and their possible evolutionary implications." *European Journal of Human Genetics,* vol. 7, pp. 435-446. While genetic evidence would seem the most promising way to clear up the controversy over the Aryan Invasion, these are relatively small, pioneering studies of localised caste groups.

11.   N. P. Das, 2000, "The Growth and Development of Scheduled Caste and Tribe Population in Gujarat and Future Prospects," paper given at the conference *Gujarat 2010: Challenges and Opportunities,* State Planning Commision, Government of Gujarat, Ghandinagar, p 3.

12.   On the movement of workers in and out of Gujarat, see J. Breman 1996 *Footloose Labour; Working in India's Informal Economy* Cambridge, Cambridge University Press, and for the migratory origins of Gujarat's communities see A. Yagnik & S. Sheth 2005 *The Shaping of Modern Gujarat* Penguin, New Delhi, Ch. 1.

13.   I first sketched this analysis of caste in "We are Family": The Changing British Gujarati Hindu community', pp. 13-16, a paper given at the Gujarat Studies Association Conference, S.O.A.S. London, 2006; forthcoming 2008. In: A. Mukadam & S. Mawani (Eds.), *Gujaratis in the West: Evolving Identities in Contemporary Society* Cambridge, Cambridge Scholars Press.

14.   M. Douglas, 1984 [1966], *Purity and Danger: An Analysis of the Concepts of Pollution and Taboo* London: Ark, p. 125.

15.   Ibid.

16.   Ibid.

17.   The history of Hindu vegetarianism has recently become controversial with Hindu hardliners successfully having Indian primary and middle school textbooks changed to remove references to the ancient practice of, especially upper-caste, Hindus eating beef, ritually slaughtering cows, offering up veal to Hindu deities. This rewriting of history was unsuccessfully opposed by the Indian National Council of Educational Research and Training. It is quite possible that the veneration of the cow and fundamentalist vegetarianism date only from the nineteenth century when some Hindus sought to redefine themselves in view of a perceived threat from British culture. See D. N. Jha, 2004, *The Myth of the Holy Cow,* London: Verso.

18.   S. Vertovec 2000 *The Hindu Diaspora, Comparative Patterns* London: Routledge, p. 92.

19.   For a revealing autobiographical account of the Asians' lives in Uganda (perhaps rather more revealing than the authoress intended), written by a Ugandan, now British, Muslim, see Y. Alibhai-Brown, 1999, *No Place Like Home* London: Virago.

20.   B. Naik, 1997, *Passage To Uganda.* Southall: Naik & Sons, p. 45. Balwant Naik's novel gives an Asian perspective on Amin's rule, an Asian flavouring also to be tasted in B. Kotecha's 1994 *On The Threshold of East Africa.* London: Jyotiben Foundation. Kotecha's autobiography is of interest partly because she was a daughter from one of Uganda's premier Gujarati families. Her book was translated from Gujarati into English by the estimable Englishwoman Lenore Reynell, who also gave "unstinted support and cooperation" to Balwant Naik in the preparation of his M/S, recorded talking books for blind Gujaratis and who, with great kindness and superwoman perseverance, tried to teach me Gujarati.

21.   For a bitter condemnation of life in one of the URB camps, see M. Mamdami 1973 *From Citizen to Refugee* London, Francis Pinter. Professor Mamdami later went on to write an economistic Marxian analysis of the Asians' class position in Uganda—1976 *Politics and Class Formation in Uganda* London, Heinemann—in which he argued that the Asians' restricted class position had been set by the

racialized politics of production. In this reductionist analysis there is, as with all reductionist analyses, no recognition nor room for chance. Professor Mamdami has recently reflected on the "... underlying causes of the anti-Asian actions" in Uganda: "The Asian Question Again: A Reflection," *Sunday Vision* June 4 2007 (www.sundayvision.co).

22. C. Brown, 1984, *Black and White Britain: The Third PSI Survey.* London: Heinemann, pp. 180-181.
23. T. Modood et al., 1997, *Ethnic Minorities in Britain: Diversity and Disadvantage.* London: P.S.I., p. 342.
24. G. Oonk, 2006, "South Asians in East Africa (1880-1920) with a Particular Focus on Zanzibar: Toward a Historical Explanation of Economic Success of a Middlemen Minority." *African and Asian Studies,* vol. 5, pp. 57-89.
25. Research published in 1975 showed that while only 47 percent of Ugandan Asian "heads of households" had been educated to "primary or less" standard, 85 percent were "middle class." Employment patterns varied between African countries with Asians in Uganda more concentrated in business and commerce, whilst those in Kenya had a higher proportion in local government work: see M. Bristow et al., 1975, "Ugandan Asians in Britain, Canada and India: Some Characteristics and Resources." *New Community,* vol. IV, pp. 155-166. For a contemporaneous survey-based discussion of the plight of the Kenyan Asians who in the late Sixties were having their trading licenses revoked by the Kenyan Government in its pursuit of economic "Africanisation," see P. Marris, 1968, "The Kenyan Asians in Kenya." *Venture* vol. 20, pp. 15-17.
26. The Crisis arose in part because four years earlier Wilson's Labour Government had rushed the 1968 Second Commonwealth Immigration Act through Parliament in response to the 'Kenyan Asian Crisis', an Act that deprived the African Asians of the right, printed on their passports, upheld in the 1962 first Commonwealth Immigrants Act, freely to enter and reside in the U.K. - a shameful Labour measure that with rueful hindsight Roy Hattersley now believes he should have resigned over (*New Statesman* 11th July 2005, p35). Consequently, when the Asians were ordered out of Uganda by Amin they had no country to flee to, India too having abdicated responsibility. For discussions of this shameful episode, see: J. Mattausch 1998 'From Subjects to Citizens: British East African Asians' *Journal of Ethnic and Migration Studies* Vol.24, pp121-141; M. Bristow *et al* 1977/78 'Ugandan Asians and the housing market in Britain' *New Community* Vol.V1, pp65-67; D. Humphrey & D. Ward 1974 *Passports and Politics* Penguin, Harmondsworth.
27. Community Relations Council 1974 *One Year On: A Report on the Resettlement of the Refugees from Uganda in Britain* London, C.R.C., p42.
28. V. Robinson 1993 'Marching into the Middle Classes? The Long-term Resettlement of East African Asians in the UK' *Journal of Refugee Studies* Vol.6, pp230-247.
29. C. Brown, *Black and White Britain*, p96.
30. M.H. Lyon & B.J.M. West 1995 'London Patels: caste and commerce' *New Community* Vol.21, pp399-419.
31. R. Dwyer 1994 'Caste, religion and sect in Gujarat: followers of Vallabhacharaya and Swaminarayan' IN: R. Ballard (Ed.) *Desh Pardesh: The South Asian Presence in Britain* London, Hurst & Co., p183.
32. It should not need stressing that there are also poor British Gujarati families, that wealth is unevenly, unequally held. In this chapter I am, most often, speaking of the whole community, not of individuals or particular families.
33. J. Mattausch 2000 'A Case of Mistaken Identity: Why British African Asians are not an "Ethnic" Community' *South Asia Research* Vol.20, pp171-181.

34. I summarise and examine these changing patterns in J. Mattausch 2006 *Out of Character—social science and British Gujarati Hindus*, paper given at the conference The South Asian Diaspora: The creation of unfinished identities in the modern world, Erasmus University, Rotterdam; forthcoming 2007 IN: G. Oonk (Ed.) *Global Indian Diasporas: Exploring Trajectories of Migration and Theory*.

35. A. Brah 1987 'Women of South Asian origin in Britain: Issues and Concerns' *South Asia Research* Vol.7, pp39-54.

36. R. H. Desai 1963 *Indian Immigrants in Britain* London, Oxford University Press, p19.

37. 'Hinduvta' translates roughly as 'Hinduistic principles', a political programme periodically launched in India that has the aim of purifying India of non-Hindu elements, i.e. non-Hindus.

38. R. Dwyer, 'Caste, religion and sect in Gujarat', p186. For an examination of the unsavoury political aspects to British Hinduism, see P. Mukta 2000 'The Public Face of Hindu Nationalism' *Ethnic and Racial Studies* Vol. 23, pp442-466. The masons brought over to work on the Neasden Swaminarayan mandir then returned to India to work on the murderously controversial mandir that some Hindus would like to see erected on the disputed Ayodhya site. The founder of the Swaminarayan movement, Sahajanand Swami, was himself born near Ayodhya. Just how dangerous Hinduvta fundamentalism, championed by parties such as the BJP (who currently hold power in the State of Gujarat), can prove was tragically illustrated in the 'communal', i.e. religious, civil war that in 2002 saw the barbaric slaughter of at least 2,000 Gujarati Muslims. It is difficult to overstate the barbarity of this genocidal episode in which children, the elderly, pregnant women and thousands of other innocent victims were not murdered with guns, but by hand with knives, farm implements and other tools. For a detailed consideration of the State's roles in this dreadful affair, including harrowing testimonies, see the Human Rights Watch report 2002 *"We Have No Orders To Save You": State Participation and Complicity in Communal Violence in Gujarat* Vol.14, No.3.

39. For example, the publicity for a screening of the Imax-format film *Mystic India* at the Science Museum in London in 2005 promised the audience would 'Discover a land of many mysteries and fascinations in this breathtaking giant screen film' - what the audience would not have discovered from this and further publicity was that this film had been made for the Swaminarayans and that it told a hagiographic tale of the sect's founder when he was a teenager known as Neelkanth.

40. If this quarantining pedigree is correct, then logically it was only one of many different alternative strategies that could have been taken to avoid ill-health: for instance, enthusiastic interbreeding would perhaps have led to children who inherited the local immunities that the Aryan invaders lacked. That quarantining was chosen could well have been just a hurried chance expediency, an expediency that also suited indigenous Indians vulnerable to newly-imported disease.

41. G. Oonk '"We lost our gift of expression": Loss of the mother tongue among Indians in East Africa, 1880-2000', paper given at the conference *The South Asian Diaspora: The creation of unfinished identities in the modern world* Erasmus University, July 2005, forthcoming in G. Oonk (Ed.), *Global Indian Diasporas*.

42. I am quoting from M. Rutten's & P. Patel's, at present, unpublished paper 'Contested Family Relations and Government Policy: Linkages between Patel migrants in Britain and India', p22, given at the conference on *The South Asian Diaspora: The creation of unfinished identities in the modern world* Erasmus University, July 2005, forthcoming in G. Oonk (Ed.), *Global Indian Diasporas*.

43. Ibid., p23.

44. Ibid., p24.

45. S. Mazumder-Bhan 2004 'Married to the Clan' *The Indian Express* March 7th, p17.

46. The term 'between two cultures' was used first in a 1976 study conducted by the *Commission for Racial Equality*, a study responding to worries over the second generation raised by community leaders. It was then used as the title for a well-known collection of essays edited by J. Watson 1976 *Between Two Cultures: Migrants and Minorities in Britain* London, Oxford University Press. Two years later Catherine Ballard challenged assumptions underlying the between-two-cultures agenda in her article, 1977/78, 'Arranged marriages in the British Context *New Community* Vol.V1, pp181-196.

47. The operation of one of these chaperoned caste marriage functions was captured in the documentary *A Suitable Girl, the reality of Asian arranged marriages* broadcast on C4 in August 1995. It would, I think, be fair to say that the filmed function lacked romance.

48. M. Michaelson 1979 'The relevance of caste among East African Gujaratis in Britain' *New Community* Vol.V11, pp351-360, [pp354-355]. I discuss the role of marriage in maintaining caste for Gujarati Hindus in J. Mattausch, *The Gujarati and the British*.

49. *National Statistics Online*, posted 1st April 2005

50. T. Modood *et al*, *Ethnic Minorities in Britain*, pp317-319.

51. For a study of changing caste lineages over time in a Gujarati village, Radhvanaj, not far from Mrs. Patel's native village Dongeenagar, see A.M. Shah 1977 'Lineage Structure and Change in a Gujarat Village' IN: P. Uberoi (Ed.) 1998 *Family, Kinship and Marriage in India* [Oxford Readings in Sociology and Anthropology] Oxford, Oxford University Press.

52. Kirit Pathak quoted in *The Salt Lake Tribune*, 5th March, 2004. This irresistible story was covered by the press world wide (e.g. *The Hindu*, 05/03/2004, *The Times* 24/02/2004) and ended with the two sisters victorious. Started by Laxmishanker Pathak in a North London kitchen, by a Gujarati who came to Britain from Kenya in the 1950s with just £5 in his pocket, who dropped the 'h' for the name of the Company brand, Patak's Foods, which now exports its products to 40 countries and has a reported turnover exceeding £50 million. In 1972 the Company benefited from a contract to supply the URB camps housing the Ugandan refugees.

53. Data from the authoritative Anthropological Survey of India, recently reported in the press, suggests that 'a historic dietary shift is taking hold in India' with the country's economic growth sponsoring a decline in strict vegetarianism as meat falls in price: Arvind Kala 2005 'The flesh-eaters of India' [Editorial] *The Times of India*, 2nd November.

54. R. Ballard (Ed.) 1994 *Desh Pardesh* London, Hurst & Co., pp30-33.

55. J. Mattausch 2006 *Out of Character?—social science and British Gujarati Hindus*, p16.

56. D.F. Pocock 1972 *Kanbi and Patidar* Oxford, Oxford University Press.

57. *Srimad Bhagvata Purana* 2003 London, Penguin, Book X, Chp.29, v24. For Krishna's teachings in this text over the individual's nature, karma and dharma, see for instance Chp.24.

58. Schopenhauer was familiar with an early translation of the Vedic *Upanishad*, a book he read with sympathy. His own solution to the problem he had identified of the evilness of the Will to Life is itself Hinduistic - renunciation.

59. *The Bhagavad Gita* (trns. Juan Mascaro) 1987 Harmondsworth, Penguin, Chp.18, Vs.41-44.

8

Poppy Seeds

The banns for Alison's and Kalam's marriage were first published in 1608 when the East India Company's ship the *Hector* had docked at Swally Hole, the natural harbor downriver from Surat in Gujarat, an event which acted as a wellspring for those historical currents which would some four centuries later bring Mrs. Patel to live in Wembley, via Kampala, where she would unexpectedly meet the girl with whom her elder son had equally unexpectedly fallen in love while they were both students and for whom chance had been their matchmaker. In addition to acting as a future matchmaker for Alison and Kalam, the arrival of the *Hector* in Gujarat signaled a new chapter in international trade, the point from whence we embarked at the start of the first chapter, as the cargoes from the European merchant-capitalists' ships, the indigo, opium, pepper, the strange animals, the news of sophisticated, different foreign cultures puzzled and challenged both natural scientists and social philosophers. Whether it was the tiny armies of exquisitely made insects or the cellular composition of cork observed by Hooke under his microscope, or the growing pantheon of gods or exotic social customs described by travelers and merchants, the diversity of the natural and artificial world needed cataloging then explaining. There was to be no entry for chance in the indexes of these new catalogues: the efforts of social theorists to explain societal and historical variety ostracized chance; contingency, coincidence and character were left out of pseudo-evolutionary supplantist pictures of societal change and outlawed in law-like explanations of the kind pioneered by Montesquieu.

Alison and Kalam were lucky, but not all the stories told by chance have nice happy endings. Not all potential mother-in-laws find they share a sense of humor with their son's lover, some cultural boundaries have armed guards, sometimes the profundity of chance events threatens more than just two families. The story of our artificial world, the world we have made for Alison, Mrs. Patel and ourselves to live in, our own history, has, like the history of natural evolution, been written with the font of variety, in a script of diversity. Rather than follow the orthodox strategy of trying to relegate chance to the third division of unimportant topics subservient to underlying regularities, the methodological goal not scored by sociologists, I have argued that variety is as intrinsic to societal as it is to natural history and that we are ourselves variations, an individual variety which is *the product of chance*—the chance shuffling of parental genes, chance genetic copying errors, chance gestatory influences on the fetus, producing individual characters distinguished by chance, characters living in a world of contingency where coincidences may occur. In the natural world, chance variety is the diet of natural selection that nurtures change; in the artificial world, change is a question of accumulating increasing variety, the manufacture of more and more things, that nowadays appear in the supermarkets as capitalist commodities, along with the accumulation of new customs, further knowledge, additional social patterns—not all of which are welcome. The direction of our history is toward variety, ever increasing variety achieved by accumulation. As variety grows, so too does the potential for chance to step in and influence events, thus the histories of accumulation and of chance go hand in hand. The pace of accumulation, the accumulation of variety, started to quicken at the start of the sixteenth century, in the last hundred years it reached an unprecedented velocity.

When confronted by the inherent variety of individual behavior, the second wave of social theory that clung to the coattails of neo-Darwinist science has been little more successful than the dismal record of Spencer, the Positivists, and the original nineteenth-century evolutionary sociologists. Variety has not been stripped away by evolutionary reductionism. Modern-day popularizers of reductionist evolutionary theory, who present their own explanatory poverty (just one Darwinian mechanism of natural selection) as a methodological virtue, find variety unsettling. There's just so many things we do, so many new varieties of human skills, our myriad accomplishments, that can't be cut to fit the Procrustean bed of reductionist explanation. As Professor Susan Blackmore observes:

> The problem is that these abilities seem surplus to requirements, going well beyond what we need to survive. As Steven Pinker of the Massachusetts Institute of Technology points out in How the Mind Works, "As far as biological cause and effect are concerned, music is useless." We might say the same of art, chess and pure mathematics.[1]

Now in fact Steven Pinker, in this quoted remark, simply underestimates the limitless greed of evolutionary reductionism; anything and everything is vulnerable to evolutionary reductionism, a point well made by Professor Steven Dawkins, yet another fine writer from the Darwinist stable, a stable in his case that's part of the Double D Ranch where Dawkins and Dennett are holed up with nothing apart from just one explanatory mechanism to sustain them. Art? Chess? Pure mathematics? Pah! These are no barrier to the man who explained "purpose" itself as an evolutionary development[2] and it is to Dawkins to whom

Professor Blackmore turns to explain why there's such an embarrassing variety of seemingly superfluous things cluttering up her nice neat Darwinian world:

> Few scientists would want to abandon Darwinian theory. But if it does not clarify why we humans have come to apportion so much of our resources to so many abilities that are superfluous to the central biological task of further propagating our genes, where else can we look?[3]

Why, in the eleventh chapter of Richard Dawkins' bestseller *The Selfish Gene*, the place where Dawkins first introduced the idea of a "meme," in Dawkins' original estimation a rather modest little conceptual beast that he had introduced "… to cut the gene down to size, rather than to sculpt a grand theory of human culture."[4] Since its modest entrance, the idea has outgrown the purposes of its creator having entered the Oxford English Dictionary, having given its name to a new science of Memetics, so modesty be hanged says Professor Blackmore, "… in fact his idea is dynamite," quite up to the task of reductively explaining a bit of pesky, superfluous variety:

> The answer, I suggest, lies in memes. Memes are stories, songs, habits, skills, inventions and ways of doing things that we copy from person to person by imitation. Human nature can be explained by evolutionary theory, but only when we consider evolving memes as well as evolving genes.
> It is tempting to consider memes as simply "ideas," but more properly memes are a form of information. (Genes, too, are information: instructions, written in DNA, for building proteins.) Thus, the meme for, say, the first eight notes of the Twilight Zone theme can be recorded not only in the neurons of a person (who will recognize the notes when she hears them) but also in magnetic patterns on a videocassette or in ink markings on a page of sheet music.[5]

In short, according to Dawkins it's not just genes that evolve, anything that can meet the criteria of what he called a "replicator" can too. The criteria that make for a replicator includes "variation" (the other two criteria are "replication" and "selection"). Memes meet the three criteria and so are evolving replicators, thus memes such as Pinker's puzzling music are open to Dawkinian reductionism and the burgeoning variety of the world is no longer an embarrassing conundrum for neo-Darwinist social theorists.

It may be worth spending a little time inspecting the examples of what Dawkins, Blackmore, and other memeticists would like to regard as evolving "memes." Their examples of memes all come from what I'm calling the artificial world, the environment in which our species increasingly lives, the world we make for ourselves, a world where, using Blackmore's examples of memes, there are "stories, songs, habits, skills, inventions," joined by items from Dawkins' list of examples, "tunes, ideas, catch-phrases, clothes fashions, ways of making pots or of building arches," all waiting as Blackmore tells us to be copied "from person to person by imitation." Successful memes are those that get copied the most, memes that have the largest number of offspring, that familiar evolutionary theme tune whose measurability for memetic transmission Dawkins illustrates with these examples:

> If it is a popular tune, it's spread through the meme pool may be gauged by the number of people heard whistling it in the streets. If it is a style of women's shoe, the population memeticist may use sales statistics from shoe shops. Some memes, like some genes, achieve brilliant short-term success in spreading rapidly, but do not last long in the meme pool. Popular songs and stiletto heels are examples. Others, such as the Jewish religious laws, may continue to propagate themselves for thousands of years, usually because of the great potential permanence of written records.[6]

If nothing else, the analogy between genes and "memes" signals the explanatory poverty of Darwinistic social theory, a poverty which fuels its adherents' reductionist tendencies. A quick reread of Blackmore's examples of "memes" ("stories, songs, habits, skills, inventions"), and Dawkins' examples ("tunes, ideas, catch-phrases, clothes fashions, ways of making pots or of building arches") reveals a certain bias: many of their chosen examples are of course a "form of information" communicated in codes, the symbolic coding of ideas, Jewish religious laws, inventions, stories, catch-phrases etc. all written in language, the medium for coding "memes" for most of our species history. But coded or not, in the real world, more rightly the real artificial world, tunes, ideas, stories, fashionable clothes, books of Jewish law, stiletto heels, inventions and even catch-phrases have now become commodities to be patented, copyrighted, bought, and sold, a grubby commercial reality not mentioned in the curiously apolitical world inhabited by memeticists. Professor Blackmore recognizes that these "memes" are recorded not only in people's minds, "but also in magnetic patterns on a videocassette or in ink markings on a page of sheet music," but she does not elaborate upon their artificial presence. In the real artificial world the production, ownership and movement of commodities is, as we have seen, steered by patterns of social relationships that in capitalism gave rise to individual private property, in traditional Gujarati society to family ownership, both with their own attendant patterns of inheritance. Perhaps Professor Dawkins needs to get out a little more, when did you last hear *anyone* whistling a tune in the street? In 1976, when the professor first published *The Selfish Gene*, you might occasionally have heard a whistler on the streets of Cambridge but these days the only tunes you're likely to hear are from your neighbour's overly loud MP3 Player—tunes, music of all varieties is a business, big business, nowadays you pay for tunes. As we turn more and more of our own creativity into commodities we come closer and closer to realizing the sad, silent dystopian nightmare that Rachel Carson warned of in her pioneering environmentalist book *Silent Spring*, but unlike the birds Carson foresaw killed off by our over-use of pesticides we are silencing ourselves by our use of the commodities that we ourselves have made. Whistling, along with humming and singing in public have not become extinct, but they are now lying dormant. The tunes that are recorded, played, broadcast, which are replicated are those that are profitable; for sure, popularity may lead to profitability, for example the popularity of mediocrity, the calculated appeal to the largest number of paying customers, but often the connection between popularity, profitability, and the survival of a "meme" is not so clear cut. For instance, most classical music survives whilst being deeply *unpopular*, medicines for the treatment of AIDS are just as popular with HIV-positive Americans as they are with fellow African victims yet they have spread far more widely within one continent compared to the other. These days, it's profitability not simple popularity that governs replication. What facilitates the reproduction of most "memes" in our world is not as Professor Blackmore thinks "that we copy from person to person by imitation," rather that they are made by machines as replica commodities to be bought, owned, inherited and sold. In fact, in the machine age "persons" really aren't that important when it comes to copying and machines care nothing for the popularity of the commodity they are busily replicating. Nor do machines themselves decide to produce anything; they're set by us to run for profit. And, as I've been keen to stress, today's music library is most unlikely to evolve for the simple reason that, as Arthur Sullivan had realized with prescient foreboding upon hearing the first phonograph, fewer and fewer tunes are now lost and without loss, there's no natural selection, no evolution and the parallel Dawkins tries to draw between genes and "memes" collapses. Further, it may be worth recalling the point I highlighted earlier, that no medium ever caused another to become extinct, the modern printing press hasn't replaced pen and paper, televisions did not silence the radio, the Internet has not led to the closure of libraries. Mobile phones, really just refined walkie-talkies, for example, don't "change for ever the way we communicate," they merely add another smallish variation to how we may speak to each other. New media are variations on old themes and being varieties they possess new advantages as well as disadvantages: as Michael Rosen, the British Children's Laureate, observed,[7] the much-vaunted speed of the Internet is, in some respects, a fault, a weakness, as slow reading permits time for things to sink in, for reflection on what is being read, virtues found in books, not on Web sites. Tunes, films, novels, inventions, catch-phrases, books of Jewish law, fashionable clothes, and all the rest are not simply being copied, they're now *accumulating*, silting up the wealthier cultures. Rather than Dawkins' memes acting as "replicators," the furniture of our artificial world—the things, ideas and social customs we've made—accumulates and so perhaps it would be better to speak of "accumulators" and an Age of Accumulation that began some five hundred years ago, an era in which variety has grown apace.

Over four centuries before Mrs. Patel's family first settled in Kenya, a hundred years before the *Hector* dropped anchor at Swally Hole, Gujaratis were already long-familiar visitors to the coastal towns of East Africa. When on 15

April 1498, having rounded the Cape, Vasco de Gama's fleet docked at the small Arab-ruled port of Malindi north of Mombassa they met Ram Singh Malam, an experienced Gujarati sailor who guided them on to India, a coincidental meeting not without irony considering the role the Portuguese came to play in Gujarat. Coincidence, joining the Portuguese quest for Christians and spices, helped to open up the world, it helped open up a new chapter of international accumulation, a chapter that only began once. Quite possibly de Gama might have met someone else who could have acted as a better pilot, or perhaps he might have pressed on unaided, hugging the East African coast line, then tacking eastwardly off Oman to land on the islands of Bombay, never visiting Goa. But he didn't, chance threw the die and it was only in 1962 that the Indian government was finally able to reclaim the anachronistic Portuguese colonies, one of which, the island of Diu off Gujarat's Saurashtrian southern tip, had to be strafed by Indian fighter planes in order to persuade the European colonists that their time was up.

Chance, rather than ideas or cultural capital, helped load the chief weapon in the armory of the Portuguese who followed de Gama's route as they built up their colonial empire along with their merchant economy. The pioneer European merchant-adventurers did not enjoy commercial advantages because of their commercial maturity:

> While European overseas trade later came to surpass that of Asia, at least during the period between 1700 and 1900, this was not the case at the time of the opening of the maritime route from the Atlantic. The initial advantage of the newcomers to the Indian Ocean lay in certain features of ships and guns rather than in the production and exchange of goods, for which they frequently had to provide precious metals in return, as the Romans had done before them, since they had relatively few manufactures or raw materials to offer.[8]

That the Europeans enjoyed comparative technological advantages in ships and ordinance was simply a chance contingency similar to the chance global distribution of spice plants and when it came to ordinance, one also enjoyed by the Mughal conquerors at a time when firearms were largely unknown in northern India. Babur, who would become the first of the "Great Mughals," was able to defeat his rivals, the Lodi Sultans based at Delhi, and so inaugurate the Mughal Empire, in part because he wielded a contingent advantage: his small invading army had firearms: "For what his forces lacked in numbers they compensated with a capacity, terrifying alike to man, horse and elephant, for deafening and increasingly lethal bombardments."[9] These contingent disparities became explosively influential when they coincided, when they were brought together by chance. The historical episodes in which they figured were not just ideas, they were events: nor were cannons made by ideas but by incremental craftsmanship accumulating past improvements, craftsmen with the right metals to hand that could be combined to make the brass alloy for siege cannons and field guns. Marx stressed the, as he saw it, unique human capacity to mentally picture products before they were made but he hadn't reckoned with the role played by accumulated templates, how for example "even the worst architect," Marx's own example, benefits not just from her own imagination but also, and probably more so, from existing examples of buildings and from accumulated architectural blueprints.[10]

Although Marx determinedly tried to map the pathways of historical development, he did to a limited extent recognize the periodic importance of chance-given disparities. These contingent variations led people living in different places to make different products, in differing ways, and Marx acknowledged that these variations led to differences in the way people lived, how they fostered different modes of production. He also thought that:

> It is these spontaneously developed differences which, when different communities come in contact, calls forth the mutual exchange of products, and the gradual conversion of those products into commodities.[11]

Nonetheless, the wrinkles of "spontaneous" differences gradually became ironed-out by the homogenizing powers of capitalism: in other words, while Marx was happy to accept that capitalism had origins in chance natural diversity that led men to exchange their differing goods when in the far distant past they encountered foreign tribes, he argued that chance was then neutered by the global growth of commodity production.

Marx too saw the sixteenth century as the opening of a new historical chapter; "The modern history of capital dates from the creation in the sixteenth century of a world-embracing commerce and a world-embracing market."[12] It was, he reasoned, the period when commerce began to accelerate, an acceleration which would lead to capitalism smothering all other forms of society, a growing trend now commonly known as "globalization," and a rare example of Marx prophesying accurately the future.[13] Fighting shy of predicting the shape of future communist society is one thing, being analytically incapable of anticipating two world wars quite another order of failure. With spectacular irony, Marx's grave was crowned by an imposing headstone in 1956, a headstone paid for from the voluntary subscriptions of his admirers: this was the year that saw the Soviet invasion of Hungary, the crushing of the Polish uprising, the year when news of Khrushchev's denunciation of Stalin at the Twentieth Congress of the USSR leaked out, the year of the Suez Crisis. The inscription on his headstone reads "The philosophers have only interpreted the world; the point, however, is to change it,"[14] but Marx's own theory was unable to guide the workers for it had little analytical purchase upon the reality of postwar life, the realities of the doomed Soviet attempt to live by his theory, the chilly realities of the Cold War, the ascendancy of the United Sates, the depletion of natural resources such as oil, the role played by individual characters such as Stalin and Mao, Bush and

Blair. Marx's identification of globalization, the increasing trend for capitalism to become internationalized at the expense of alternative forms of society, his characterization of capitalism as the exploitative production of commodities underpinned by the social relationships of private property, may all have stood the test of time but his stubborn insistence upon a reductionist analysis of our artificial world, insisting that production is the lodestone of theory, the key to societal dynamics, was misconceived. Circumstances, events, people, the stuff of history, the subjects of episodic chance experienced as contingency, coincidence and character, cannot be captured nor nullified by Marx's emphasis upon production, an emphasis that obscured the chance-infested trend to accumulation that is the true mechanism of societal change.

Marx insisted that concepts such as accumulation should only be analyzed by placing them in the period in which they occurred. Capitalist accumulation was of a specific kind and, reasoned Marx, necessarily led to competition. As we saw in chapter 4, in his early critique of political economy that Marx as editor published in the *Jahrbucher*, Engels had argued that private ownership led inevitably to mutual mistrust, antagonisms and competition between buyers and sellers as each was led to maximize their own advantage. In this way of reasoning, competition was an expression of capitalism, not as Adam Smith and now sociobiologists argue an expression of some innate self-interested motive that compels individuals to compete. In the first volume of *Capital*, Marx develops this approach arguing, in Ben Fine's summation, that:

> In a system of commodity production it is logically possible that the supply and demand for each product would exactly match, with each commodity exchanging at its individual value (the labour-time of production whether it be by the most or least efficient method). Capitalism, however, is dominated by commodity production, and the extension of the market ensures that prices for identical products do not diverge. Even if supply and demand match now, the only way that the owner of a commodity can ensure it sells at (or above) its individual value is by ensuring that this value is at (or below) the market evaluation. Competition is created between producers in the market.[15]

As capitalist production matures it creates a never-ending competition between producers, a ceaseless drive for profit, which in turn feeds the development of the two antagonistic social classes of capitalism. In Marx's words:

> As simple reproduction constantly reproduces the capital-relation itself, i.e. the relation of capitalists on the one hand, and wage-workers on the other, so reproduction on a progressive scale, i.e. accumulation, reproduces the capital-relation on a progressive scale, more capitalists or larger capitalists at this pole, more wage-workers at that.[16]

Capitalist production produces competition, competitiveness that grows with the maturation of capitalism, with its "boundless thirst" for profit. Just as natural "spontaneous" differences promoting commodity exchange become smoothed-out as commodity exchange gave way to capitalist commodity production, so too would different individual characteristics become obscured as the capitalist market commanded the production, the distribution then consumption of the commodities that furnish our artificial world.

The development of capitalism, thought Marx, was sponsored and accompanied by a growing division of labor—that near ubiquitous conceptual ingredient of early social theory—a division that led to individuals filling ever more specialized social roles which we've already examined in chapter 4. Crucially, just like his treatment of religion, Marx saw social roles as an expression of capitalist society, not as expressions of innate human drives. Some of these social roles—for example Mr. Perfidy, the estate agent who had been surprised to meet Mr. Mandela in an earlier chapter—can only exist when capitalism has turned things such as homes into houses that may be bought and sold as commodities. Marx had reasoned that the division of labor was first found in the family, its origins lay in our natural "differences of sex and age," whereas the division of labor in manufacture first arose after "different families, tribes, communities had come in contact," exchanged their "spontaneously" varied goods and then turned to production rather than simple exchange.[17] Scornful of Adam Smith's proposed solution to the harmful effects of the division of labor (his "homeopathic" doses of education for the masses), scornful of Smith's weak remedy for the ways in which increasing specialization in the factory led the workers to become "as stupid and ignorant as it is possible for a human creature to become," Marx nevertheless agreed with Smith that in its early years the division of labor was essential for capitalist manufacture to take root.[18] Unlike Smith however,[19] Marx recognized the lessening importance of the division of labor in comparison with the productive power of machinery, mischievously using Smith's own example of pin manufacture to illustrate the vastly greater productivity of powered production: whereas in Smith's example productivity rose from ten pins a day if each pin were made entirely by each worker, to 48,0000 if these same ten men instigated a division of labor, just one worker (a girl or woman in Marx's example) tending four machines could produce 600,000.[20] It was this astonishing rise in powered production that, freed from the competitive shackles of capitalism, would allow individuals to enjoy a far greater material standard of living and far greater leisure time to develop their own individuality once communism had been established. Missing, however, from Marx's analysis of capitalistic social roles was an explanation for individual variation, for *why* people had, as in the *Grundrisse*'s sketch, suppressed individuality awaiting communistic liberation, a question I am answering by chance-given innate character.

In *The German Ideology*, Marx had distinguished natural "constant" desires, such as hunger, from "relative" desires, desires relative to specific historical periods of societal development:

> In a communist society, the former ["constant" desires] would merely be changed and given the opportunity to develop normally, whereas the latter ["relative" desires] would be destroyed by being deprived of the conditions of their existence.[21]

Unwilling, as was his way, to prophecy or prescribe the precise manner in which natural constant desires would be changed, Marx rested his case upon his faith in the potential of communal creativity that was to be liberated from capitalism. Everyone was to be a worker, workers would no longer form a discrete social class as in capitalist society, this swollen labor force would benefit from mechanized, increasingly automated production; what was made, how it was distributed, and how much was made could be determined not by the relative desire for profit, not by competition but by a communal appreciation of the desirability of production. One major benefit of this move to communist production would be the lessening in the time we would spend working, our working lives would not be dictated by the limitless pursuit of profit, nor by insatiable relative desires, we would have, as Marx sketched in the *Grundrisse*, free time to develop our individuality. In a flowery, much-quoted passage from his earlier youthful *German Ideology*, Marx looked forward to the dissolution of fixed social roles:

> In communist society, where nobody has one exclusive sphere of activity but each can become accomplished in any branch he wishes, society regulates the general production and thus makes it possible for me to do one thing today and another tomorrow, to hunt in the morning, fish in the afternoon, rear cattle in the evening, criticize after dinner, just as I have a mind, without ever becoming a hunter, fisherman, shepherd or critic.[22]

A difficulty with all this, of course, is that while communism may liberate us to exercise our "constant" desires "normally," allowing us to shed the limiting "relative" desires and social roles promoted by capitalism, our new-found freedom would still be infected by chance, by chance differences of character that would presumably become transparent, by contingent disparities, by unpredictable coincidences—and so at best communism would allow us the freedom to cope with chance as best we are able.

Since his death, capitalism has in its way delivered the material wealth and leisure time that Marx presented as the foundation for future communist society. In a capitalist society social roles change, some roles star while others are resting, they are awarded fluctuating esteem and pay as patterns of competition alter, as technology develops, as political interventions take effect (for instance young boys in Britain no longer, mercifully, become chimney sweeps, no longer suffer cancer of the scrotum, which Marx identified as a hazard of their youthful sooty labor). Since the time Marx composed *Das Kapital*, working conditions in Britain have improved and the proportion of time spent at work has declined dramatically. In the U.K. in 1785, when the population stood at some 12,681,000, the "Hours worked per year per person" averaged 3,000, by 1913 the population had grown to 42,886,000 working on average 2,624 hours per year, two centuries later, in 1987, whereas the population had grown to 56,687,000 they were now getting by on just 1,511 working hours per year, half the number worked in 1785.[23] Now of course these working hours are just rough calculations disguising profound variations, the population figures are for the whole country rather than the work force, they do not include domestic work nor child-care nor other jobs not rewarded with wages, nor a host of other variables, but they nonetheless illustrate the uncontroversial point that more and more people living in Britain are spending less and less time at work. Further, in Britain, usually thanks to the struggles of trade unionists and progressive political activism, working conditions have improved, some fragile workplace rights have been won. That these improvements have been partial, that they have had to be fought for against the wishes of vested interests, that they are vulnerable and need constant vigilance if they are to be maintained, all this confirms Marx's telling observation, "What could possibly show better the character of the capitalist mode of production, than the necessity that exists for forcing upon it, by Acts of Parliament, the simplest appliances for maintaining cleanliness and health?"[24] But when it comes to showing the character of those of us living in contemporary British capitalism, later Acts of Parliament may also be revealing: one of my own favorite indices flashes up on gantries above British motorways; speeding motorists are reminded in big electronic letters "Do not use your phone when driving," a reminder of a legal offence and also a reminder that the character of individuals is not uniform, nor always consistent nor necessarily of the kind presumed by Marx in his picture of communist man liberated from his "relative," specialized social roles. Certainly, people have a natural desire to communicate (though this desire varies by degree), but the desire to own a mobile phone is relative to their invention and production as commodities—I had no aching desire for a mobile in the sixties, nor for that matter any desire for twenty-four hour communicability—but today not everyone owns a mobile phone nor do all those that do own one need reminding not to use them when driving. It's really this last point about individual variety that does not sit easily with Marx's revolutionary theory and which suggests that his picture of accumulation, his insistent reductionism, and his vision of relative human desires needed to be rethought.

Although Marx on the one hand believed that mechanized production could secure freedom from want in communism, on the other hand he did not think machinery had played a big historical role in first spawning commodity production:

> The Roman Empire had handed down the elementary form of all machinery in the water-wheel.
>   The handicraft period bequeathed to us the great inventions of the compass, of gunpowder, of type-printing, and of the automatic clock. But, on the whole, ma-

chinery played the subordinate part which Adam Smith assigns to it in comparison with division of labour.[25]

In this passage Marx is writing about the genesis of capitalism and as we've noted earlier, he was aware that that as capitalism matures the productive importance of the division of labor lessens with the growing adoption of engine-powered production. Marx recognized that chance physical features of the "temperate zone" had allowed it to become the "mother country," of capitalism but what, of course, Marx neglects to emphasize is the equally chancy nature of the accumulation of technology, for instance the Roman Empire's bequest of water-wheels, the motive force powering the early industrial revolution, the colonial bequest to that Empire's former European subjects not bequeathed to India, the technological step not taken in arid Gujarat for contingent reasons. Certainly, the division of labor was advanced in Gujarat as far or beyond the stage it had reached in Britain in the early seventeenth century when the first English-speaking "Hat Men" stepped ashore at Swally Hole and it continues to be finely advanced in present-day Gujarat. But, lagging behind in their adoption of what Marx called "type-printing," with no water-wheels, Gujarati production had been stymied by chance contingencies that restricted accumulation because accumulation was restricted by what could be passed down (skills, techniques, knowledge, and so on) from fathers to sons in a family-oriented oral culture dependent upon manual and animal labor. Without accumulated technologies a division of labor won't produce much and nor, contrary to Adam Smith, can an advanced division of labor produce homogenous machine-minding automatons. Machines can make replica commodities but it can't turn the machine's operatives into facsimiles. The mentally corrosive effects of an advanced division of labor cannot be used to explain why some individuals rather than others are made, in Smith's phrase, "as stupid and ignorant as it is possible for a human being to become," while their fellow workers doing the same equally repetitive task on the same production line go to evening classes, read avidly, watch Open University programs in the evening, study to become fluent in Finnish.

Modern capital's birth was attended by the opening-up of markets by men such as Vasco de Gama, and equally certainly, merchant capitalism then full-blown commodity production did set out to conquer the world. What, however, proved historically significant was not only the viral spread of capitalist social relations but also the growing accumulation of all manner of things, ideas, customs, social conventions and also people, that would distinguish the next five hundred years—an historical chapter without precedent. This unprecedented trend has of course not taken hold evenly across the globe—developmental trends are always uneven—and so whereas material things have accumulated in the developed world, people have accumulated in materially poor countries. Material accumulation is obvious, we've carpeted the globe with the things we've made, it's the less tangible accumulation of ideas, customs, social arrangements and the like that can lead to confusion, to the illusory belief in societal evolution which the lucky then may use to justify their own material privileges, to what I've called "supplantism" where societal history became pictured as a ladder of discrete steps rather than as I'm arguing a growing mound of sometimes chance-acquired technologies, customs, social patterns etc. whose accumulation is built upon earlier achievements (consider, for illustration, just how much needs to be known, how many technologies need to be accumulated, before reliable, practical telephones—let alone mobile phones—can be made, or alternatively, think of the tally of sociopolitical achievements underpinning even the crudest national democracy). As I've already remarked, those societies able to accommodate variety will develop while those that baulk at new varieties stay moribund. Further, those societies accepting of accumulated variety can gain in subtlety, from accumulated finer and finer distinctions, whereas societies that do not welcome variety have to settle for the grosser, stymied traditional discriminations.

Which is all very well, but not the sort of thinking likely to have impressed that redoubtable Victorian, champion of capitalism, misguided Lamarckian evolutionist and indefatigable theorist Herbert Spencer who, if exhumed, would be puzzled to find that despite our failure to discover any sociological laws, society and sociology still persisted. Nor, we can be sure, would Spencer's fellow Victorian, the equally redoubtable Marx be impressed by not only the failure of history to deliver his communist dream, but also our failure to pinpoint exactly why his communist dream now "weighs like a nightmare on the brain of the living." A philosophical answer to the two Victorian specters' puzzlement, I have suggested, may be deducible from Wittgenstein's mature writings, from his argument that we get along in life by using language as tools for accomplishing all manner of different tasks and that linguistic proficiency is achieved by us learning, albeit unconsciously, the principles that underpin the usage of words. Contrary to the reductionist enthusiasms of contemporary evolutionists, our minds have been equipped to allow us to learn and wield language, the medium of thought, in the same way that we use tools: our Swiss Army penknife of neurological circuits don't predetermine us to behave in set ways, instead they allow us to behave characteristically in future unfamiliar circumstances. We can happily agree with evolutionists that we retain a repertoire of behavioral strategies first exercised by our ancestors in response to problems or opportunities in hunter-gatherer societies, just as long as it is accepted that these are but one small part of a growing repertoire of subsequent strategies that has been accumulated over time, a repertoire that can not, and should not, be reduced to an essence of evolutionary presets. Selected adaptive neurological mechanisms may well have given us preferences but these preferences are still only at most preferred alternatives, not pre-set switches turning on predetermined actions: for illustration, most of us would prefer to have children of our own rather than initially to adopt other people's children, an obvious candidate for a reductionist "selfish gene" explanation, and in its way quite an acceptable explanation just as long as we remember that this genetically steered preference does not preclude us from *also* then fostering or adopting one of the 60,000 children currently in care in England.[26] Preferences are not diktats, preferences are just part of our behavioral repertoire that grows accumulatively. Similarly, our stock of principles underpinning what we do may be enlarged. For example, when Mrs. Patel first went to work in her brother-in-law's north London corner shop she unthinkingly absorbed pragmatically the principles underpinning the usages of English expressions of politeness, the when and how to say "thank you," and of course "please"—those new, unfamiliar phrases she *added* to her personal vocabulary, new principles and phrases she accumulated and then of course came to use in her own characteristic ways (the ways, for instance, she came to say "thank you" rather brusquely when serving shifty teenage customers). Because we operate with these flexible principles, rather than obey inflexible laws, and because we use them in our own individually characteristic ways, the future will never replicate the present and how it will change is open to chance factors. Indeed, thinking and behavior steered by principles is just what we should expect to find in a world routinely visited by chance; such principles allow us to cope with the unforeseen and allow us to adjust our behavior as we learn, perhaps because of some chance occurrence, more about our own individual characters.

All of this principle-steered, trend-patterned behavior depends upon the gross similarity of the species, a similarity that gives us theoretical license to speak of a common human, or if you like species, nature. Genetic science has revealed just how similar we are at the molecular level: of the three billion or so DNA "letters" that make up our genes, only 10,000 of them account for the differences between any two individuals, a genetic similarity that led Dr. Craig Ventner whose commercial company, Celera, was involved in the Human Genome Project to remark that "Really, we are just identical twins."[27] In order to appreciate the relative significance of our gross species similarity compared to our subtle individual differences, try this thought experiment: suppose that a hideous pandemic, for instance a viral "species-jumper" such as, potentially, the Asian Bird Flu currently on its jittery flight—alarming not least because whether or not it becomes a species-jumper is down to unpredictable chance—were to wipe out the entire human species leaving just one lucky couple alive; this lucky couple would be the last remaining breeding pair and with them would rest the hopes of saving our species from extinction, not just their wish to perpetuate their own genes, their own particular individual genetic variety. This overwhelming species similarity, just as much as any evolutionary pressure or selected neurological circuitry, is what has facilitated common, some universal, human behavior patterns, common expressions of the emotions, and the rest.

The current revival of interest in human nature by neo-Darwinists such as Pinker misses a crucial reason for the topic becoming sidelined by social theorists. It was not just the presumption of a "blank slated" mind, the presumption of empiricists that became adopted by key Enlightenment theorists which sent human nature to join chance in the outlands, it also fell off the intellectuals' agenda because of the concomitant picture of societal history that these theorists painted. The picture of societies developing in stages corresponding to the ways we organized material production, the picture first sketched by the Scottish School in the eighteenth century, a picture redrawn by Marx, a historical map of progressive sequential stages redrafted by premature evolutionist nineteenth-century theorists—this historical approach also dealt a fatal blow to the idea that we share a common human nature. For, if it were the case that what we know, how we behave, who we are and all the rest is the product of our social circumstances, and if these social circumstances change decisively in uniform historical transformations, then this will inhibit us from discerning the lasting features upon which a conception of human nature must rest. With their claim that we inherit a mind shaped by past adaptive pressures, evolutionary psychologists claim to identify species characteristics that transcend societal change but as we have seen, the critiques of Gould and others demonstrate that much of our past behavior was not necessarily adaptive and in any case the sum of our behavior is always marked by pesky variance so that even if at any one time everybody was behaving similarly, they would not be behaving identically. If, instead, we adopt the accumulated picture of societal change I am proposing then instead of incommensurable historical stages leading to incommensurable patterns of human behavior, we arrive at a picture of human nature that permits us to see ourselves as individuals partly similar and partly different from our fellows and from our ancestors with whom we share a common human nature. This human nature is shown in the range of grossly similar, subtly varied behavior expressed by our characters, it is the gross similarity that permits us to understand, perhaps sympathize with others, which permits us for example to appreciate how those living in cultures very different from our own may be feeling. When such cultural differences are acute, or individuals differ sharply, then we may misunderstand, we may not be able at first to sympathize, but thanks to our gross species similarity such differences are never alien to us, merely foreign. In the case of settlers like Mrs. Patel from family-oriented Gujarati Hindu culture, she may not have comprehended Alison's desire to marry her son out of love and individual choice, but she can immediately sympathize with Alison's distress, share a chance joke, and Kalam and his sister Smitta can add Valentine's Day to their calendar of annual events to be celebrated, a date on their calendar that also marks the traditional Hindu festival of *bhai-beech* which annually reaffirms the bond between brothers and sisters. Similarly, though for many Britishers the details of Mrs. Patel's culture may be unfamiliar, her wish to worship as she was brought up, stay with her own people, eat familiar foods, dress as she always has, marry her children within her own community, these would all have been readily appreciable by Victorian Englishmen living in India, or by any other ex-pat community. It is simply human nature, for which the settlement of Britishers overseas bears ample witness.[28] For us, the past might be a foreign country but it is not one we cannot visit: thanks to the accumulated history books, yet another fruit from the printing press, and our shared human nature, we can enter the past; if we cannot put ourselves into the shoes of historical characters then it is most probably because they had characteristics at the extreme edge of the human range: the problem with understanding Stalin is not one of ignorance about what he did, nor of ignorance about the circumstances in which he acted, but because of his incomprehensible character: how could he have done what he did? If Stalin were on trial today then it would be no easier for us to understand his character.

Returning to our two exhumed Victorians, whereas Spencer would be disappointed by the failure to discover any sociological laws, perhaps irritated to find he'd been wrong to champion acquired characteristics and progressive evolution, but not dismayed to find capitalism still continued, Marx on the other hand be deeply disappointed, but not confounded by the vigor of capitalism. For both men the world into which they had been raised from the dead would appear confusing, wonderful, unfamiliar but not wholly alien, for much of their world is still with us. Like the first economic migrants from the Soviet bloc arriving in the West, the goods in the shops would seem fabulous, but the queues to pay for them would not cause them puzzlement. Similarly, the corruption of modern-day politicians, religious fanaticism, patriotism, these would not call for an interpreter. But one feature of the twenty-first century, a feature our two Victorians would not at first notice as it is not so pronounced in Britain, one that would surely astonish both men, a feature not expected nor predicted by any of the social theorists mentioned in this book, has been the abrupt growth of the human population, a feature which may well surpass the two world wars, the collapse of communism, and all the past century's technological achievements put together in its lasting significance.

Unsurprisingly, analytically fixated with production, Marx considered population as a subsidiary subject, the rise and size of the population he considered in terms of its promotion of capitalism. Nevertheless, his analytical fixation with productivity notwithstanding, to Marx numbers mattered historically for only when "isolated independent labourers" were grouped together, he reasoned, could "the social productive power of labor that is developed by cooperation" be harnessed by capitalists whose investment in wages, factories etc. was responsible for bringing the workers together under one factory roof:

It is the first change experienced by the actual labour-process, when subjected to capital. This change takes place spontaneously. The simultaneous employment of a large number of wage labourers, in one and the same process, which is a necessary condition of this change, also forms the starting-point of capitalist production. This point coincides with the birth of capital itself.[29]

Capital, social productivity, the two classes of capitalism all then depended upon the "spontaneous" coming together of a sufficient number of workers; this grouping together would, as time went on, encourage the workers to realize for themselves their common class position and would help in their development of a revolutionary consciousness. Marx appreciated the unsurpassed material productivity of capitalist production and partly for this reason was scornful of Malthus's argument that the growth of population must exceed the growth in resources necessary to keep them alive. In the longest footnote to the first volume of *Capital*,[30] Marx dismisses Malthus's "Essay on Population" as a "schoolboyish, superficial plagiary" of earlier authors penned by a celibate Parson, an essay whose public success was due to the appeal of his "principle of population" for contemporary wealthy readers who welcomed a scientific justification for their own unwillingness to feed the starving. In a letter to Engels written in 1862, Marx expressed his "amusement" at Darwin's adoption of the Malthusian principle:

> It is remarkable how Darwin rediscovers, among the beasts and plants, the society of England with its division of labour, competition, opening up of new markets, "inventions" and Malthusian "struggle for existence."[31]

Marx's amused scorn would have been better directed toward Herbert Spencer and the Social Darwinists, rather than at Darwin himself. In his *Origin of Species*, Darwin had used the term "struggle for existence" in a "large and metaphorical sense," but nonetheless he believed that the "geometric increase" of the populations of "all organic beings" would, if left unchecked, be unsustainable in the same way Malthus had argued that human population growth would outrun the potential increase in the natural resources necessary to sustain it. You might have thought that as a celibate parson, Malthus should have been peculiarly well-placed to approve a prophylactic solution to this mathematical asymmetry noted earlier by the eighteenth-century French revolutionary theorist Condorcet, a personal hero of Malthus's own father, the champion of progressive laws of societal development admired by Auguste Comte[32] and, as Marx too had noted, the originator of the "principle of population." Bertrand Russell nicely sums up the difference between the pessimistic celibate English parson and the optimistic French revolutionary:

> He [Condorcet] was a believer in the equality of women. He was also the inventor of Malthus's theory of population, which, however, had not for him the gloomy consequences that it had for Malthus, because he coupled it with the necessity of birth control.[33]

Unlike other "organic beings," the human struggle for existence takes place in the artificial world, the world they have made and can modify. As it is modified, so too human behavior, including our sexual behavior and its consequences, will come to vary. Birth control techniques come to vary as new alternatives accumulate, reusable thick condoms, gossamer thin throwaway versions, the coil, the Pill, and other artificial aids accumulate to join the rhythm method and celibacy. Which of these contraceptives, if any, is used may well not be simply a matter of individual characteristic taste, or a couple's compromise, but a choice suggested by contraceptive technology, tradition, religion, moral beliefs, the fear of sexually transmitted disease, or societal pressures such as those currently encouraging French women to bear more children. Contraception is but one modifying influence on human populations, other artificial factors such as improved infant mortality rates, decent diets, more effective medicines, also play their part and as Malthus's own drastic personal measure of celibacy testified, just as we are not condemned to breed so too we are not faced with a fixed amount of resources to sustain us. Nowadays as Marx realized, food production, like all production is not a fixed quantity, it can increase, and its distribution can be changed so that, for instance, farmers in Africa can now grow food for obese Westerners that the farmers themselves cannot afford to eat.

In the last century, our species has grown six-fold. Population size and density matters, and not just as Marx considered it in terms of parenting capitalism. Marx's recognition that changes in quantity can lead to changes in quality (an Hegelian insight he followed in his historical account of the birth of the capitalist production process), may be extended so as to allow demographic change to become an independent variable that helps shape our twenty-first-century international artificial world.[34] We've seen how Marx recognized the historical role of chance, how it affected societal development at crucial junctures: "spontaneously developed differences," that is, chance contingent differences betwixt the environment and the natural features of early tribes had led "spontaneously" to the exchange of goods, equally contingent features of the "temperate zone" had led Europe to become the "mother country" of capitalism, modern capital emerged "spontaneously" when the productive power of labour was harnessed by harnessing workers together in the production process. Just as spontaneously our species population, confounding Malthusian wisdom, which had been growing in steady but unspectacular fashion alongside the growth of capitalism, abruptly rocketed in the last century: India alone now has a population larger than the total world population of 1900. The population of the world has more than doubled in my lifetime. This demographic explosion has, until recently, hardly registered in the rich West where demography has been comparatively stable for some time. In 1600, just before the *Hector* docked at Swally Hole, the population of (un-partitioned) India has been estimated as 140 million, the population of the U.K. at some 5 million.[35] In 1901, soon after Marx's death in 1883, the population of Britain had multiplied to over 41 million, India's had passed 238 million. When Mrs. Patel fled Uganda and arrived in London, the U.K.'s population was nearing 56 million and at the last Census in 2001 had grown to just over 59 million. In India, during the same period, the population was recorded at over 548 million in 1971, and well over a billion in 2001. If she had stayed living, had married and raised Kalam and Smitta in her natal village of Dongeenagar, Mrs. Patel's family would have contributed to a near doubling of the population of Gujarat in the past thirty years, from 26.7 million to 50.6 million, 1971-2001. Measuring between 1991 and 2001, the decadal growth for India stood at 21.34 percent, the State of Gujarat's at 22.48 percent. Now these are rough and ready figures[36] that skate over problems such as the difficulties of collecting accurate Census data in turn of the twentieth-century British India, the devastating earthquake in Gujarat that hampered the 2001 Census, and much more, but they serve I think to indicate the sheer scale of twentieth-century global population changes and the comparative swollen size of India's population when set aside that of the U.K. (Gujarat is likely soon to exceed Britain). Indeed, so vast is the population of modern India it may no longer be sensible to think in terms of a national population for many of India's federal states now exceed or rival the populations of other countries; Uttar Pradesh, the most populous, is currently larger than all but the five biggest countries in the world, and still growing. Further, the variation between and within the States of federal India, differences of religion, politics, caste and class composition, of size, literacy levels, gender imbalances, economic activity, culture etc. are as least as large as those between, for instance, those to be found in the much smaller European Union.

As globalization theorists are keen to point out, we can no longer use the dynamics of capitalist development within discrete capitalist societies, the dynamics of national class struggles, to explain what's going on. I think that this is partly because population growth has become an independent force for chancy change. The effects of this growth are all too readily apparent in those countries/continents such as India, Mrs. Patel would have seen previously peaceful towns in Gujarat grow rapidly to echo the crowded intensity of India's big cities as not only population size, but also population density grew. Whereas twenty years ago you could safely walk down the middle of the dusty streets in Dongenagar, Mrs. Patel's natal village, nowadays, at least if you're a trepidatious British visitor, you fear for your life when dodging the traffic that now has shiny new limousines vying for space with rickshaws, bullock carts, psychedelically-colored lorries, endless streams of pedestrians. In areas of Bombay (or, as her nationalistic rulers insisted, Mumbai), population density has reached scarcely credible figures. To illustrate this level of urban crowding the ex-pat Gujarati writer Suketu Mehta in his extraordinary, compelling portrayal of Bombay, his native city, draws these striking comparisons:

> India is not an overpopulated country. Its population density is lower than that of many other countries that are not thought of as overpopulated. In 1999, Belgium had a population density of 333 people per square kilometre, the Netherlands, 385; India under 304. It is the cities of India that are overpopulated. Singapore has a

density of 6,500 people re square kilometre; Berlin, the most crowded European city, has 2,900 people per square kilometre. The island city of Bombay in 1990 had a density of 45,000 people per square kilometre. Some parts of central Bombay have a population density of one million people per square mile. This is the highest number of individuals massed together at any one spot in the world. They are not equally dispersed across the island. Two-thirds of the city's residents are crowded into just five per cent of the total area, while the richer or rent-protected one-third monopolize ninety-five per cent.[37]

The suffering, violence, misery, enterprise, creativity, crime, politics, prostitution, gang culture, hope, and the myriad other social consequences that Bombay's population size and density have spawned beggars belief and has found in Suketu Mehta its own Zola.

Accumulation, the preservation and accessibility of knowledge and techniques, plus improvements to international communication, means that national barriers can no longer corral labour skills—especially helpful to countries like India that have developed an international service, rather than export-manufacturing, economy—especially unhelpful to countries such as Britain. Again, size matters: though some one-third of India's population remains illiterate, with only a small proportion gaining higher education or technological training, even a small proportion of India's labor force is still a massive cut-price competitor on the international labour market. Further up the coast from Bombay with its fabulously priced housing, its shiny new office buildings rising up from Hogarthian scenes at street level, back in Gujarat the availability of all-too-cheap labour has helped the local diamond cutting and polishing industry to thrive, an industry employing 20,000 children, paying £35 per month of twelve hour working days.[38] As the Antwerp Facets News Service (AFNS), which reports on the precious stones' market, noted in 2006 on their Web page:

SURAT, INDIA 24 January 2006—The Indian diamond polishing industry is spreading geographically through Gujarat state from the city of Surat.

While Surat processes 80 percent of the diamonds cut in India, the work is spreading, with some stones being polished at least in part in other cities, such as Ahmedabad, Bhavnagar, Amreli, Rajkot, Jamnagar, Mehsana and Banaskantha. It is thought that more than 1,000,000 people work in diamond polishing in Gujarat, including about 800,000 in Surat and more than 200,000 elsewhere.

Indian Diamond Institute Director K.K. Sharma said that Gujarat is responsible for 85 percent of India's 700 billion rupees ($15.84 billion) in diamond exports, of which Surat handles 65 percent and the other centres the remainder.

Chances are that the tiny diamond in Alison's engagement ring will have been polished in one of Gujarat's workshops. Population growth on this scale, with new density hot spots, guarantees that all bets on future global socioeconomic trends are now off. For instance over half of India's population, over half a billion people, is under the age of twenty-five; that's a lot of future old folk who are going to need an awful lot of special provisions, a biding problem potentially even worse in China where, unlike in India, because of cruel but effective family planning there won't be a commensurate number of young Chinese to pay for their ageing population's needs. Population growth may produce outcomes that are counter-intuitive; for instance in India as I write there is much pride taken by Indians in their country's "economic miracle," an indubitable economic surge, but one which seen in national terms is being felt by both a larger number of both rich and poor Indians, there has never been as many poor people in India as there are at present. It is not just that the global human population is growing, it is also growing at an unprecedented rate with millions moving from the countryside into the cities and towns: for the first time ever, in 2008 over half the world's population will be urban, in the twentieth century there was an increase from 220 million to 2.84 billion urbanites; we are living through a second "great transition," and unlike the first, this one is happening in poorer countries, countries ill-prepared for the demands of this demographic change.[39]

The "founding fathers" of European social theory would have been hard pressed to predict or prophecy this species population explosion and so it is only belatedly that social theorists are now peppering their articles with the totemic word "globalization." Regrettably the enthusiasts for globalization such as Professor Giddens have, as I remarked in an earlier chapter, the tendency to proclaim globalization as a wholly new social era with its own special logic, dynamics, and social character. This, then, is just one more example of fallacious supplantist history, globalization is of course an historical trend, a trend foreseen by Marx, not a wholly new era, simply the increasing tendency of capitalism to penetrate all other forms of economic activity and reshape them in its own image. But while he may have foreseen the trend toward international capitalism facilitated by improvements in communications, his commitment to class struggle as the motor of historical change blinkered him, as I've argued in this chapter, to the full effects of chance in the development of capitalism. Marx only gave chance an analytical role at the outset of societal changes, in the origins of commodity exchange between tribes, in the spontaneous birth of modern capital: once chance had set things on their way, Marx considered history would follow a predictable pattern in which class relationships were the engine of change. This analytical buffer stops us appreciating how the potential influence of chance has also grown in our over-crowded world where well over six billion individual chance-given characters live, work, produce, and exploit each other, a world already made quite chancy enough by capitalism. For capitalism is itself a producer not only of mobile phones and supermarket food, but also a guarantor of chance as one generation's wealth becomes inherited by their children who have no claim to have merited the advantages it may bring them, where commodities and people are both increasingly subject to absurd and non-rational comparisons, where profit dictates the shape of the artificial world.

This historical trajectory, this patterning of our history by accumulated variety in the natural and artificial world fuelled by chance expressed as character, coincidence and contingency is not necessarily a counsel of despair, but it can be, and too often is, a trajectory of tragedies. One example of the tragic stories written by chance, this time not a sweet story of the kind I made up about Alison and Kalam, is unfolding in Iraq where chance is embedded along with tame journalists.[40]

Amidst all the grand talk about a "clash of civilizations," the speculation over motives, overshadowed by petroleum politics, the role of chance in the West's latest attack upon Iraq has been neglected but chance has played an evil hand not only in Iraq but throughout the Middle East. Today, if chance is even recognized by students of international relations then it is granted only a minor role by academics as the search continues for those so elusive laws of political life, as they concentrate upon identifying common patterns of inter-state relations. Writing some two centuries ago, the military theoretician Clausewitz would have recognized this mind-set. In his opposition to the positivistic Prussian officers' obsession with a science of war, he was keen to remind his readers of the vital part played by chance, a topic to which he devoted a whole chapter in his masterwork *On War*, for as he knew, "Friction is the only conception which, in a fairly general way, corresponds to the distinction between real war and war on paper."[41] In this chapter, chapter VI, Clausewitz stresses the in-principle unpredictability of military conflicts; unlike Tony Blair, President Bush and many of the Prussian theorists who wrote about or directed war from the comfort of their armchairs, Clausewitz had considerable personal experience of fighting, he knew first-hand the importance of chance, not simply "the influence of innumerable trifling circumstances," little contingent chances, but also the importance of the individual's character, especially the character of the army's commander, and how the diet of fighting men must include a healthy portion of high morale. These chance influences went to make up the realities of battles, the environment of "friction" in which wars are actually fought. Contingency, coincidence, and character are as we have seen all expressions of chance and they have all had at least a walk-on part in the current phase of the West's campaign in Iraq.

Clausewitz's principal concern lay with the winning of wars, with the best, most effective strategy for using violence "to compel our opponent to fulfil our will." Strategies, plans, intentions, must however rub up against resistances in the messy, unpredictable arena of real warfare—the characteristic "friction" which distinguished "real war from war on paper." These frictions which populated the field of battle had as their "chief origin" chance, an argument Clausewitz illustrated with an example of unexpected changes in the weather as fog rolled over the battlefield preventing the "enemy from being discovered in time." However, although he claimed the frictions of battles had their origins in chance, Clausewitz did not also consider the possibility that the politics driving wars, or rather, the politics of which wars were simply an extension, could themselves be led by the bellwether of chance. Here, Clausewitz was if not in good, then at least in common company for despite their other, often profound, disagreements, analysts of the current attack upon Iraq also discount quite unthinkingly the possibility that simple chance may have helped kill so many, so many innocents.

The so-called "war" on Iraq is of course more rightly defined as an attack, for real wars require two sides to be in conflict with each other, and the West was not being attacked by Iraq and nor is there any evidence of this threat, despite the calculated lies told by Bush and Blair about "weapons of mass destruction." The Coalition's attack is an *event*, not an idea, not an action: certainly, the attack includes actions and ideas but restricting one's explanation to just these two elements will not capture properly the event, a methodological point Clausewitz well understood. We need to know, for starters, why it was that Iraq that loomed into the American's gunsights? Answering this question requires us to travel back in time before the First Gulf War, beyond the Balfour Agreement, long before the evolution of humans, to a time some 300 million years ago when chance threw the dice, to the time when tiny aquatic plants grew and animals swam in the seas and swamps of what would much later come to be a desert called Iraq. These little aquatic life-forms would perish, be crushed, heated and then over hundreds of millions of years come to form the second biggest proven oil field in the world. Although the first Iraqi oil well would not be sunk until 1927, crude oil rose to the surface of its own accord; the tenth-century Muslim historian al-Mas'udi recorded such natural oil springs in Iraq and throughout the Middle East. In Iraq oil has long been of importance, as a fuel for heating, refined as kerosene for lighting, as asphalt a road-building material.

That natural conditions led to oil being found in the Middle East rather than in Berkshire is simply owing to the chance global distribution of seas, plankton and diatoms, along with the equally chancy climatic and topographical changes that saw seas and swamps turn into deserts. These are examples of contingency (the way things are rather than how they must be), one of chance's costumes, and an oft-overlooked reason for divergences in the development of different human populations: for instance as I noted in an earlier chapter, quoting Brian Fagan, the lack of herdable animals on Australia put paid to Aborigines taking the step up from hunter-fishers to nomadic shepherds whereas on the eastwardly horn of the "Fertile Crescent" Iraqis were blessed by chance with sheep, goats, and boars along with the high-yielding einkorn strain of wheat, that happy natural mix which facilitated the first experiments with settled agriculture[42]; however, this eastwardly tip of the Fertile Crescent, the birthplace of human civiliza-tion, is currently a battlefield, a battle that, like the first farms, was started by coincidence, the coincidence of contingent factors.

That the Prophet Muhammad received the Koranic revelation in a mountain cave atop the world's largest oil reservoirs, that Islam became established in the Middle East, that Islam's holiest shrines are within the borders of a country whose princely rulers have been made fabulously rich by their control of black gold—all this is just down to simple coincidence. And when it comes to unearned, chance-given advantage the United States rivals in military wealth the oil riches of the House of Saud. For it was once again chance that helped to seat America at the head of the postwar international order, helped to give it a permanent seat and a decisive vote in the Security Council, an international supremacy secured by America's nuclear weaponry, a gift from Lady Luck. As European nuclear scientists fled National Socialists and other fascists who, in the thirties, had invaded laboratories and lecture theaters, they sought refuge in the only country able to meet the cost of what would be code-named the Manhattan Project, a safe country far from the theaters of war. It was largely Europeans, not Americans, who built the nuclear device exploded in the Trinity Test, the bombs carried to Hiroshima and Nagasaki, the decisive advantage which, after the war, only America enjoyed and which, as Truman told the world, she intended to hold in "sacred trust." Although America's fortuitous nuclear monopoly only lasted for four years her military supremacy endured and the number of nuclear-capable states grew slowly with just one Middle Eastern country, Israel, acquiring nuclear weaponry despite the new-found wealth of her Arab neighbors. Unable to purchase nukes, Saddam Hussein went shopping for the next best things available in the terror supermarket, for Russian-built SCUD missile systems, for the truly horrifying Tabun deadly liquid gas sold to Saddam by Western businessmen—weaponry bought with oil money banked by chance. It had been the fear of unleashing his Tabun gas that, on 9 January 1991, caused Secretary of State James Baker to tell his Iraqi counterpart Tariq Aziz in no uncertain terms that if Iraq breached international prohibitions on poisonous gases then America would nuke Baghdad; not an empty threat as, unknown to the Iraqis, the U.S. battleship *Wisconsin* stationed in the Gulf was armed with three nuclear-warheaded Tomahawk Cruise missiles.[43]

America's growing military-technological preeminence informed postwar international relations: only America, for example, could supply other favoured states with nuclear weapons systems, systems which, starting with the acquisition of the American Polaris submarine system in the early sixties British politicians, usually Labour politicians, had purchased at more than merely monetary cost. This historical pattern, a pattern placing Britain in a client relationship to the U.S., has continued with Tony Blair secretly negotiating for Trident's replacement as the attack on Iraq unfolded. America's military preeminence included conventional as well as nuclear technology, a military superiority demonstrated to devastating effect in the First Gulf War that, in the judgment of Erik Durschmied,[44] had been all but won by the Coalition forces in "the first hour of the attack" thanks to America's "blatant technological superiority": the first phase of Operation Desert Storm, the air attack on Baghdad launched in the early hours of the 17 June 1991, proved decisive as 2,340 planes, including ghostly F117A Stealth Bombers, systematically destroyed Saddam's military capacity. But, despite the American's boasts of "precision bombing" not every American missile hit its intended target, some hit cowering children, and Co-alition Forces did a poor job in locating and destroying Saddam's Scud mis-siles. Eighty-eight Scuds hit Allied territories, including one hitting Tel Aviv, a missile strike whose political repercussions threatened to upset the Coalition forces' unity and one for which the Americans were obliged to offer the Israeli government substantial compensation. Other political consequences of the American-led Coalition's strategy took longer to become apparent: stationing American troops in the land of the Prophet's birth must have seemed a quite desirable move for the Americans, placing their troops on top of the world's largest oil field, in the heart of the Middle East. Stationing troops, launching the Coalition air attacks from Riyadh, keeping American troops in the Prophet's country of birth after the First Gulf War had ended, did not, however, appear acceptable in the eyes of Bin Laden, nor in the view of fifteen of the nineteen terrorists who left to take flying lessons in America, lessons paid for from the oil boom economy of Saudi Arabia. These consequences were, however, in the future; at the time, a "kill ratio" of 100,000 Iraqi troops killed for the loss of 192 Coalition troops (only 158 of whom were killed by Iraqis, the rest by "friendly fire" and mishap) must have seemed an obvious lesson to draw, a lesson for the president's son and political heir, George W.

It is in these rather specific senses that I have sketched in chapter 5 that Tony Blair should be judged as vain, as having the characteristic of vanity, a common failing among politicians. His vanity was not the cause of his warmongering, nor indeed of any of his other political actions; rather, it disposed him, ren-dered him vulnerable to the playing the role he took alongside President Bush (analogous to tall American boys' susceptibility to playing basketball). An early manifestation of his disconcerting vanity appeared in 1997 when Blair, quite sincerely, interpreted the landslide 1997 Labour electoral victory as a vote for him personally, rather than as is more likely, a vote against the Conservatives, a vanity mocked by subsequent electoral verdicts. This early vanity pales when compared to the presumptions he, along with Bush and his compatriots, dis-played in attacking Iraq: not only did they presume that they could command vast armed forces and would win, they also, with a certainty that few social scientists would dare to venture, presumed that they could make democracies, bring capitalist democracy to Iraq, rebuild what they would render a bomb-site as a copy of their own polity. This is vanity on an awesome scale, there are few if any social scientists who would be willing to bet even one life, certainly not their own lives, on their being able to carry out this scale of social engineer-ing; this sort of ambition is usually only harbored by historical villains such as Stalin. But, as luck would have it, Blair happened to be prime minister, a man untroubled by self-doubt, basking in the applause of the American senators, lapping up their applause for their favorite collaborator. And then, a little later, refusing to admit that all the talk of "weapons of mass destruction" had been a deceit—for vain men are not inclined to admit that they could ever be wrong, about anything, regardless of the evidence, or lack of it.[45]

Our modern disinclination to acknowledge the part played by chance may be deep-seated, we want there to be some good *reason* for evil just as we would like to believe there is some purpose to our chance-given lives. Just as we invent philosophies and religions to hide the true banal purposelessness of our existence so too we would perhaps like there to be some further, hidden reason for the deaths of some one million Iraqis (from 1991 to the present, not just from the start of the current attack as far too many media commentators date it). However, as Hannah Arendt observed, evil is characterized by banality, as too are many of the roles played by chance. If there were no oil beneath Iraq, if Islam had not been founded in the Middle East, if John Smith had lived, if a whole host of other chance contingencies, coincidences, and characters had not been present then perhaps we would not have to listen to our politicians telling us lies, while in the same breath refusing even to tally the dead.

When and why wars begin, how they play out and the lurking effects of their festering legacies are all beyond what we can predict in advance, wars always catch us napping as the last century bears witness. At best, all we can do is point to the heightened risk, the increase in probability, that a war will occur but we can't point to the date on the calendar when the generals will be asking for our sons. And this, of course, is because wars often have chance leading the attack. Contingency and coincidence are expressions of chance that we cannot command. Some contingent features such as oil in the Middle East have ancient pedigrees and lie undiscovered, dormant awaiting coincidence to bring them to life; other potential contingencies, such as those we have accumulated in our artificial social world, are of our own making but once again may lay dormant for centuries until, like Frankenstein's monster, a bolt of lightning breathes life into them. For example, the "Kosovo Girl" proved a popular character in the epic retellings of Prince Lazar's last battle, reputedly nursing dying soldiers, and a popular subject for nineteenth- and twentieth-century Serbian artists. Whether or not she actually existed is unknown for there were no eyewitness accounts of what took place on the Field of Blackbirds in 1389,[46] but myth or not she did not perish, she just rested for six centuries, waiting in the wings until she once again awoke, ready to do her duty as a unifying symbol of heroic Serbian national identity. We cannot predict how societies will change in the future nor foresee how elements of our artificial world may make chance mischief in the future and our recent unprecedented, still vigorous population growth in our increasingly internationalized capitalist economy has magnified the scope for chance, as contingencies and coincidences, to operate.

As I am writing this yet another war has broken out, this time Lebanese children are paying the blood price for the chance distribution of oil and weaponry, for the chance variety of the politicians' characters, for our own insatiable greed. Once again, Blair deceived the public, having known well in advance that the attack on Lebanon was imminent.[47] Nobody can say how it will eventually turn out, anymore than we know what will occur in Afghanistan or Iraq, but we can, however, be confident that the hatred, mistrust, fear and disillusionment with the West that these attacks are provoking will accumulate, a poisonous legacy for our children, waiting like the poppy seeds of Flanders to be watered by some chance future event. The gods to whom the Israelis, Palestinians, Americans, British and Lebanese pray won't stop the wars, they won't save any more children in Beirut or Baghdad than they did in Auschwitz. It may be hard, unpalatable to accept the roles chance plays but perhaps this is the mark of true cultural maturity: the christener or sociology, that mentally infirm Frenchman Auguste Comte, predicted a peaceful future in which war and conflict would have withered away in the Positivist world he believed imminent, confidently predicting, in 1842, that "At last the time has come when serious and lasting war must disappear completely among the human elite."[48] In his Positivist dreams, Comte prophesized a society in which we would have reconciled ourselves to our natural limitations revealed through the new creed of Positivism. In the past men and women had tried to explain what happened in terms of divine or natural causes but when Positivism had supplanted its preceding form of society we would become content to temper our wishes and actions to the limitations of our gender and to the laws of social life. Comte's biological knowledge and especially his views on evolution were unsound, Positivism did not come to pass, no such positivist laws of society were ever found, an acceptance of science was simply added to earlier religious beliefs. What persisted was the prejudice of thinking that not only is there a cause for everything that happens, but also that there must be a reason, divine or scientific: chance, as I have tried to argue, may be a cause, but a cause without rhyme nor reason. This is part of what is meant by chance. What we may now need to do is reincorporate chance back into our thinking; this may be the next chapter in our accumulated intellectual history and the hallmark of true political sophistication. It is not, as Shakespeare has one of his characters say in *King Lear*, that we are killed for sport by the gods, but rather that we are swatted by chance. And for those who would still champion free will, as the means for choosing a god or whatever, I would wish to point out that the options of free versus unfree mirrors the false dichotomy of determined versus undetermined; false because, as I have argued, determinism and chance are not mutually exclusive. When we act, the distinction is not between slavery and freedom, but between determinism and chance; the latter is a test of character, not of free will. Little throws of chance's die we can live with, for example Alison and Kalam can put their coincidental meeting down to love finding a way, single rolls of the die of contingency whose effects are large but take centuries to become apparent, for instance the chance distribution of oil or printing presses, put down to mysterious religious, national, sociological or evolutionary forces. It may now be time to abandon these *noms de plume* and call chance by its own name.

Notes

1. S. Blackmore, 2000, "The Power of Memes," *Scientific American,* vol. 283, pp. 52-61, [p52].
2. Professor Dawkins reasoned that, while evolution itself was a truly purposeless process, purpose itself had evolved, been naturally selected for the reproductive advantage it conferred, in his television broadcast *The Big Question:"Why are we here?"* Ch. 5, 2004.
3. Blackmore, "The Power of Memes," p. 52.
4. R. Dawkins, 1989 [1976], *The Selfish Gene.* Oxford: Oxford University Press, ch. 11, fn. 1.
5. Blackmore, "The Power of Memes," p. 52.
6. Dawkins. *The Selfish Gene*, p. 114.
7. Speaking on *You and Yours*, BBC Radio 4, 12/04/05.
8. J. Goody, 1996, *The East in the West.* Cambridge: Cambridge University Press, p. 83.
9. J. Keay, 2000, *India: A History.* London, HarperCollins, p. 291.
10. K. Marx, 1977 [1887], *Das Kapital,* vol. 1. London: Lawrence Wishart, p.174.
11. Ibid., p. 333.
12. Ibid., p. 145.
13. Marx had earlier predicted globalization, and the role of communication in facilitating globalization, in the *Manifesto of the Communist Party*.
14. The inscription is taken from the, last, of Marx's *Theses on Feuerbach*, a synopsis of his critique of Idealist philosophy.
15. B. Fine, 1979, *Marx's Capital* (Macmillan Studies in Economics). London: Macmillan, p. 34.
16. Marx, *Das Kapital*, vol. 1, p. 575.
17. Ibid., p. 332. In a footnote, Engels tells us that after "very searching study," he concluded that it was actually the tribe which was the first form of human association, from which the family then emerged.
18. Ibid., p. 329.
19. In his *Wealth of Nations*, Smith did remark upon how the introduction of machinery would "abridge labour, and enable one man to do the work of many" (Heilbroner, *The Essential Adam Smith*, p. 14), but writing before the introduction of the steam engine, Smith did not foresee the quantum leap in productivity that engine-powered machinery would achieve.
20. Ibid., p. 432. Marx, or his translator, calls Smith's pins "needles"; I have kept to Smith's nomenclature.
21. McLellan, *The Thought of Karl Marx,* p. 215.
22. Ibid., p. 217.
23. M. Livi-Bacci, 1992, *A Concise History of World Population.* London: Blackwell, p. 137: the figures are from Livi-Bacci's adaptation of data in A. Maddison, 1982, *Phases of Capitalist Development.* Oxford: Oxford University Press.
24. Marx, *Das Kapital,* vol. 1, p. 452.
25. Ibid., p. 329.
26. These figures are from the British Association for Adoption & Fostering's Website: www.baaf.org.uk/info/stats/england.shtml. Of the 60,900 children in the care of English local authorities in 2005, 68 percent were living with foster carers, 5

percent were placed for adoption, 9 percent were living with their parents, leaving 16.6 percent in children's homes or other placements—in the round, a tribute to kindness and to the hard work of Social Services, rather than to the machinations of selfish genes.

27. Quoted in R. McKie, 2001, "Revealed: the secret of human behaviour." *Observer* (No. 10,992), 11 February, p. 1.
28. I discuss this point about the ubiquity of ex-pat settlement in Mattausch, "We Are Family."
29. Marx, *Das Kapital*, vol. 1, p. 317. Chapter XIII, "Cooperation," examines in some detail the economic effects wrought by grouping together workers, focusing them on the same production process.
30. Ibid., pp. 578-579, fn. 2. This lengthy footnote soon degenerates into a broader attack on parsons and religion in general.
31. Marx-Engels Correspondence 1862, London 18th of June 1862: www.marxists.org
32. As I have already noted, Condorcet was given the dubious privilege of a place in the very short list of thinkers Comte considered his worthy predecessors—an honor granted by Comte because of Condorcet's emphasis upon laws of progressive societal development.
33. B. Russell, 1948, *History of Western Philosophy.* London: Allen and Unwin, p. 750.
34. Marx was keen to challenge the idea that demography was the master of economics, a view that had first been proposed by the seventeenth-century founder of British population studies William Petty, now remembered if at all for his part in dividing the spoils of Ireland but a thinker admired by Marx who considered him as the "founder of Political Economy" who had identified the productive importance of the division of labor a century before Adam Smith. See A. Roncaglia, 1985, *Petty: The Origins of Political Economy.* Cardiff: University College Cardiff Press, especially pp. 65-67 & 91.
35. These population estimates are given in Keay's *India: A History*, p. 320.
36. These rough and ready figures were taken, for Britain, from the British Government's Web site www.statistics.gov.uk and for India and for the State of Gujarat from the Gujarat government's site www.gujaratindia.com/Useful-Info/Socio percentReview
37. S. Mehta, 2004, *Maximum City: Bombay Lost and Found.* London: Headline Review, pp. 17-18. The current "average population density in the UK is 224 people per square mile" (Economic and Social Research Council's *Population in the UK* fact sheet).
38. K. van Lohuizen, 2006, "Rocky Road." *Telegraph Magazine,* 27 May, pp. 32-33.
39. The figures for urbanite growth are from the UNFPA's 2007 *State of World Population: Unleashing the Potential of Urban Growth*, p. 7, accessible from their website at: www.unfpa.org/swp/2007/presskit/pdf/sowp2007.eng.pdf
40. This example of the role of chance in the attack upon Iraq is an abridged version of an article which was first published as J. Mattausch, 2006 "Friction in Iraq," in: G. Drewry & S. Haines (eds.) 2006, *Politics and Conflict: Domestic and International Implications of the Iraq War* Dept. of Politics and International Relations, Royal Holloway College.
41. K. von Clausewitz, 1965, *On War,* Chicago: Gateway, p. 132.
42. B. Fagan, 2004, *The Long Summer: How Climate Changed Civilization.* New York: Basic Books, pp. 93-94.
43. E. Durschmeid, 2002, *The Hinge Factor: How Chance and Stupidity have Changed History.* London: Hodder, p. 348.

44. Ibid.
45. As I write this, the closest Blair and Bush have come to an apology was in May 2006 when, nearing the American mid-term elections, the British prime minister "apologized" for underestimating the strength of the "insurgents" in Iraq—a characteristically bathetic deceit.
46. T. A. Emmert, 1990, *Serbian Golgotha: Kosovo, 1389* (East European Monographs). New York: Columbia University Press, p. 142.
47. J. Kampfner, 2006, "Blood on his hands." *New Statesman*, 7 August, p. 5.
48. Quoted by Raymond Aron in "War and Industrial Society," in: L. Bramson & G.W. Goethals, 1968, *War.* London/New York: Basic Books, p. 360.

Bibliography

Y. Alibhai-Brown. 1999. *No Place Like Home*. London: Virago.
Aristotle. 1992. *Physics, Books 1 & 11* (W. Charlton, tr.). Oxford: Oxford University Press.
——. 1974. *Ethics*. Harmondsworth: Penguin.
R. Aron. "War and Industrial Society." In: L. Bramson and G.W. Goethals. 1968. *War*. London/New York: Basic Books.
C. Attlee. 1954. *As It Happened*. London: William Heinemann.
J. Austin. 1961. "A Plea for Excuses." *Philosophical Papers*. Oxford: Clarendon Press.
A. J. Ayer. 1965. "Chance." *Scientific American*, vol. 213, pp. 44-54.
J. Ayto. 1991. *Bloomsbury Dictionary of Word Origins*. London: Bloomsbury.
C. Ballard. 1977/78. "Arranged Marriages in the British Context." *New Community*, vol. VI, pp. 181-196.
R. Ballard (ed.). 1994. *Desh Pardesh*. London: Hurst & Co.
M. Baker. 1982. *Nam: The Vietnam War in the Words of the Men and Women Who Fought There*. London: Abacus.
J. Beames. 1984 [1896]. *Memoirs Of A Bengal Civilian*. London: Eland Books.
Bhagavad Gita, The .(J. Mascaro, tr.). 1987. Harmondsworth: Penguin.
S. Blackmore. 2000. "The Power of Memes." *Scientific American*, vol. 283, pp. 52-61.
R. Boudon. 1986. *Theories of Social Change: A Critical Appraisal*. London: Polity Press.
A. Brah. 1987. "Women of South Asian Origin in Britain: Issues and Concerns." *South Asia Research*, vol.7, pp. 39-54.
M. Bramshad et al. 1998. "Female Gene Flow Stratifies Hindu Castes." *Nature*, vol. 395, p. 651.
J. Breman. 1996. *Footloose Labour: Working in India's Informal Economy*. Cambridge: Cambridge University Press.
M. Bristow et al. 1975. "Ugandan Asians in Britain, Canada and India: Some Characteristics and Resources." *New Community*, vol. IV, pp. 155-166.
——. 1977/78 "Ugandan Asians and the housing market in Britain." *New Community*, vol. VI, pp. 65-67.
British Association for Adoption & Fostering www.baaf.org.uk/info/stats/england.shtml
C. Brown. 1984. *Black and White Britain: The Third PSI Survey*. London: Heinemann.
I. Bruce-Watson. 1976. "The Establishment of English Commerce in North-western India in the Seventeenth Century." *Indian Economic and Social History Review*, vol. 13, pp. 375-391.
——.1978 "Between the Devil and the Deep Blue Sea: Commercial Alternatives in India, 1750-1760." *South Asia* [NS], vol. 1, pp. 55-64.

206   Chance, Character, and Change

T. Carver. 1981. *Engels* (Past Masters). Oxford: Oxford University Press.
R. Chalmers. 2003. "Back on the Peace Train." *Independent on Sunday,* 12 October, p. 12.
M. Chanan. 1995. *Repeated Takes: A Short History of Recording and its Effects on Music.* London: Verso.
S. Chu & K. Geary. 2005. "Physical Stature Influences Character Perception in Women." *Personality and Individual Differences,* vol. 38, pp. 1927-1934.
S. Clarke. 1982. *Marx, Marginalism and Modern Social Theory* Macmillan, London.
K. von Clausewitz. 1965. *On War.* Chicago: Gateway.
C. Cockburn. 1991. *Brothers: Male Dominance and Technological Change* (revised edition). London: Pluto Press.
M.S. Commissariat. 1957. *A History of Gujarat, Vol. 1 The Mughal Period from 1573 to 1758.* Bombay: Orient Longmans.
Community Relations Council. 1974. *One Year On: A Report on the Resettlement of the Refugees from Uganda in Britain.* London: C.R.C.
A. Comte. 1853 *The Positive Philosophy,* vol. 1. London, John Chapman.
L. Coser. 1977. *Masters of Sociological Thought,* 2nd edition. New York: Harcourt Brace Jovanovich.
L. Cosmides & J. Tooby. 1997. *Evolutionary Psychology: A Primer* www.psych.ucsb.edu/research/cep/primer.html.
C.S. Cremin. 2003. "Self-Starters, Can-Doers and Mobile Phoneys." *Sociological Review,* vol. 55, pp. 109-128.
C. Darwin. 1882 [1871]. *The Descent of Man and Selection in Relation to Sex.* London: John Murray: http://darwin-online.org.uk/content/frameset?itemID=F937.1&viewtype=text&pagesseq=1
——. 1979 [1859]. *On the Origin of Species by Means of Natural Selection, Or the preservation of Favoured Species in the Struggle for Life.* London: Faber & Faber.
——. 1999 [1872]. (With an Introduction, Afterword and Commentaries by P. Ekman) *The Expression of the Emotions in Man and the Animals.* London: HarperCollins.
N.P. Das. 2000. "The Growth and Development of Schedules Caste and Tribe Population in Gujarat and Future Prospects," paper given at the conference *Gujarat 2010: Challenges and Opportunities,* State Planning Commission, Government of Gujarat, Gandhinagar.
R. Dawkins. 1989 [1976]. *The Selfish Gene.* Oxford: Oxford University Press.
——. 2004 *The Big Question: "Why are we here?"* Broadcast on Ch.5, 7 January, 19.30-20.00.
R. H. Desai. 1963. *Indian Immigrants in Britain.* London: Oxford University Press.
J. Diamond. 1997. *Guns, Germs and Steel: A Short History of Everybody for the Last 13,000 Years.* London: Vintage.
M. Douglas. 1984 [1966]. *Purity and Danger: An Analysis of the Concepts of Pollution and Taboo.* London: Ark.
E. Durschmeid. 2002. *The Hinge Factor: How Chance and Stupidity have Changed History.* London: Hodder.
R. Dwyer. 1994. "Caste, Religion and Sect in Gujarat: Followers of Vallabhacharaya and Swaminarayan." In: R. Ballard (Ed.) *Desh Pardesh: The South Asian Presence in Britain.* London: Hurst & Co.
Economic and Social Research Council [E.S.R.C.]. *Population in the UK* fact sheet: www.esrcsocietytoday.ac.uk/ESRCInfoCentre/facts/.
E. Eisenstein. 1993. *The Printing Press in Early Modern Europe.* Cambridge: Cambridge University Press.

T. A. Emmert. 1990. *Serbian Golgotha: Kosovo, 1389,* East European Monographs. New York: Columbia University Press.

N. Etcoff. 1999. *Survival of the Prettiest: The Science of Beauty.* London: Little Brown & Co.

B. Fagan. 2004. *The Long Summer: How Climate Changed Civilization.* New York: Basic Books.

S. Faulkes. 1994. *Birdsong* London: Verso.

L. Feistenger, H. Riechter & S. Schachter. 1956. *When Prophecy Fails: A Social and Psychological Study of a Modern Group that Predicted the Destruction of the World.* New York: Harper & Row.

L.S. Feuer (Ed.). 1969. *Marx and Engels: Basic Writings on Politics and Philosophy.* London: Fontana.

B. Fine. 1979. *Marx's Capital,* Macmillan Studies in Economics. London: Macmillan.

G. Fine & J. Deegan. 1996. "Three Principles of Serendip: Insight, Chance, and Discovery in Qualitative Research." *Qualitative Studies in Education,* vol. 9, pp. 91-101.

M.H. Fisher. 2001-02. "Persian Professor in Britain: Mirza Muhammad Ibrahim at the East India Company's College, 1826-44." *Comparative Studies of South Asia, Africa and the Middle East.* vol. XXI, pp. 24-32.

A. Flew. 1986. *David Hume: Philosopher of Moral Science.* Oxford: Basil Blackwell.

R. Floud, K. Wachter & A. Gregory. 1990. *Height, Health and History: Nutritional Status in the United Kingdom, 1750-1980.* Cambridge: Cambridge University Press.

P. Gay. 1969. *The Enlightenment: An Interpretation, Vol. 2.* London: Weidenfeld & Nicholson.

A. Giddens. 1999. *Runaway World,* BBC Reith Lectures: Lecture One (published online at: http://news.bbc.co.uk/hi/english/static/events/reith_99/week1/week1.htm).

G. Gigerenzer et al. 1997. *The Empire of Chance.* Cambridge: Cambridge University Press.

J.S. Gillis & W.E. Arvis 1980. "The Male-Taller Norm in Mate Selection." *Personality and Social Psychology Bulletin,* vol. 6, pp. 396-401.

E. Goffman. 1980 [1959]. *The Presentation of Self in Everyday Life.* Harmondsworth: Pelican.

J. Goody. 1996. *The East in the West.* Cambridge: Cambridge University Press.

S.J. Gould. 1996. *Life's Grandeur.* London: Jonathan Cape.

——. 1999. "A Division of Worms (Jean-Baptiste Lamarck's contributions to evolutionary theory, Part 1)." *Natural History,* vol. 108, pp. 76-81.

——. 2000. *Wonderful Life: The Burgess Shale and the Nature of History.* London: Phoenix.

S.J. Gould & R.C. Lewontin. 1979. "The Spandrels of San Marco and the Panglossian Paradigm: A Critique of the Adaptationist Programme." *Proceedings of the Royal Society of London,* Series B, vol. 205, pp. 581-598.

J. Gray. 2003. "E. O. Wilson," Great Thinkers, *New Statesman,* 14 July, p. 22.

Gujarat: Official Portal of Gujarat Government www.gujaratindia.com/Useful-Info/Socio%Review.

D. Hamer & P. Copeland. 1998. *Living With Our Genes: Why They Matter More Than You Think.* New York: Doubleday.

J.R. Harris. 1995. "Where is the Child's Environment?: A Group Socialisation Theory of Development." *Psychological Review.* vol. 102, pp. 458-489.

——. 1998 *The Nurture Assumption: Why Children Turn Out the Way They Do.* London: Bloomsbury.

———. .2006. *No Two Alike: Human Nature and Human Individuality.* London: W.W. Norton.

R. Hattersley. 2005. "The Importance of Loyalty to an Idea is not Just a Matter of Personal Conscience." *New Statesman,* 11 July, p. 35.

G.W.F. Hegel. 1987 [1822/28]. *Lectures on the Philosophy of World History: Introduction.* Cambridge: Cambridge University Press.

R.L. Heilbroner (Ed.). 1986. *The Essential Adam Smith.* Oxford: Oxford University Press.

W.E. Hensley & R. Cooper. 1987. "Height and Occupational Success: A Review and Critique." *Psychological Reports,* vol. 60, pp. 843-849.

C. Hill. 1993. *The English Bible and the Seventeenth Century.* London: Allen Lane.

Human Rights Watch. 2002. *"We Have No Orders To Save You": State Participation and Complicity in Communal Violence in Gujarat,* vol. 14, no.3.

D. Humphrey & D. Ward. 1974. *Passports and Politics.* Penguin: Harmondsworth.

C. Janaway. 1994. *Schopenhauer,* Past Masters. Oxford: Oxford University Press.

D.N. Jha. 2004. *The Myth of the Holy Cow.* London: Verso.

Arvind Kala. 2005. "The flesh-eaters of India" (editorial). *Times of India,* 7 August: *www.timesofindia.indiatimes.com/articleshow/1273309.cms.*

M. Kamerkar. 1980. *British Paramountcy: British-Baroda Relations, 1818-1848.* Bombay: Popular Prakashan.

J. Kampfner. 2006. "Blood on His Hands." *New Statesman,* 7 August, p. 5.

I. Kant. 1934 [1781]. *Critique of Pure Reason.* London: Dent & Sons.

J. Keay. 2000. *India a History.* London: HarperCollins.

R. Keyes. 1980. *The Height of Your Life.* Toronto: Little Brown & Co.

B. Kotecha. 1994. *On The Threshold of East Africa.* London: Jyotiben Foundation.

T. Kuhn. 1970. *The Structure of Scientific Revolutions,* 2nd edition. Chicago: University of Chicago Press.

R. Kurzban, J, Tooby & L. Cosmides. 2001. "Can Race be Erased? Coalitional Computation and Social Categorization." *Proceedings of the National Academy of Sciences,* vol. 98, pp. 15387-15392.

P. Lawson. 1993. *The East India Company.* London: Longman.

W. Lepenies. 1988. *Between Literature and Science: The Rise of Sociology* (R. J. Hollingdale, tr.). Cambridge: Cambridge University Press.

M. Livi-Bacci. 1992. *A Concise History of World Population.* London: Blackwell.

K van Lohuizen. 2006. "Rocky Road." *Telegraph Magazine,* 27 May 2006, pp. 32-33.

S. Lukes. 1973. *Emile Durkheim.* London: Penguin.

A. Lycett. 1999. *Rudyard Kipling.* London: Weidenfeld & Nicholson.

D.T. Lykken. 2002. "How Relationships Begin and End." In: H.T. Reis, M.A. Fitzpatrick & A.L. Vangelsti (Eds.). *Stability and Change in Relationships Across the Lifespan.* New York: Cambridge University Press.

D.T. Lykken & A. Tellegen. 1993. "Is Human Mating Adventitious or the Result of Lawful Chance?: A Twin Study of Mate Selection." *Journal of Personality and Social Psychology,* vol. 6, pp. 56-68.

M.H. Lyon & B.J.M. West. 1995. "London Patels: Caste and Commerce." *New Community,* Vol. 21, pp. 399-419.

A. Maddison. 1982. *Phases of Capitalist Development.* Oxford: Oxford University Press.

P.P. Majmuder et al. 1999. "Human-Specific Insertion/Deletion Polymorphisms in Indian Populations and Their Possible Evolutionary Implications." *European Journal of Human Genetics,* vol. 7, pp. 435-446.

K. Malik. 2000. *Man, Beasts and Zombies.* London: Phoenix.

M. Mamdami. 1973. *From Citizen to Refugee.* London: Francis Pinter.

——. 1976. *Politics and Class Formation in Uganda.* London: Heinemann.

——. 2007. "The Asian Question Again: A Reflection." *Sunday Vision*: www.sundayvi-sion.co.ug/detail.php?mainNewsCategoryId=7&newsCategoryId.

J.G. Manis & B.N. Meltzer. 1994. "Chance in Human Affairs." *Sociological Theory,* vol. 12, pp. 45-56.

P. Marris. 1968. "The Kenyan Asians in Kenya." *Venture,* vol. 20, pp. 15-17.

J. L. Martin. 1995. "Chance and Causality: A Comment on Manis and Meltzer."
Sociological Theory. vol. 13, pp. 197-202.

K. Marx. 1933 [1875]. *Critique of the Gotha Programme.* London: Martin Lawrence.

——. 1973 [1857]. *Grundrisse.* New York: Random House.

——. 1973. *Surveys From Exile: Political Writings, Vol. 2.* London: Penguin.

——. 1975. *Marx Early Writings.* Harmondsworth: Penguin.

K. Marx & F. Engels. 1963 [1846]. *The German Ideology.* New York: International Publishers.

——. 1975. *Collected Works, Vol. 3.* London: Lawrence Wishart.

——. 1977. *Selected Works.* London: Lawrence & Wishart.

——. Marx-Engels Correspondence 1862, London 18 June 1862: www.marxists.org.

P. Mason. 1986. *A Matter of Honour: An Account of the Indian Army, its Officers and Men.* London: Macmillan.

J. Mattausch. 1993. *The Gujaratis and the British: A Social and Historical Survey with Special Reference to the Gujarati Tradition of 'Arranging' Marriages.* Centre for Ethnic Minority Studies, Royal Holloway College, Occasional Papers No.1.

——. 1996. "A Penury Of Bookes": The Printing Press and Social Change in an Indian Setting." *South Asia* [NS], vol. XIX, pp. 59-83.

——. 1998. "From Subjects to Citizens: British East African Asians." *Journal of Ethnic and Migration Studies,* vol. 24, pp. 121-141.

——. 2000. "A Case of Mistaken Identity: Why British African Asians are not an 'Ethnic' Community." *South Asia Research,* vol. 20, pp. 171-181.

——. 2001. "After Ethnicity: Migration, Identity and Political Economy." *Immigrants & Minorities,* vol. 20, pp. 59-74.

——. 2003. "Chance and Societal Change." *Sociological Review,* vol. 51, pp. 505-527.

——. 2005. *Out of Character – Social Science and British Gujarati Hindus,* paper given at the conference The South Asian Diaspora: The creation of unfinished identities in the modern world , Erasmus University, Rotterdam; forthcoming 2007. In: G. Oonk (Ed.). *Global Indian Diasporas.*

——. 2006. "'We are Family': The Changing British Gujarati Hindu community." Paper given at the Gujarat Studies Association Conference, S.O.A.S. London; forthcoming 2008. In: A. Mukadam & S. Mawani (Eds.) *Gujaratis in the West.*

——. 2006. "Friction in Iraq." In: G. Drewry & S. Haines (Eds.). 2006. *Politics and Conflict: Domestic and International Implications of the Iraq War.* Dept. of Politics and International Relations, Royal Holloway College.

S. Mazumder-Bhan. 2004. "Married to the Clan." *Indian Express,* March 7, p.17.

R. McKie. 2001. "Revealed: The Secret of Human Behaviour." *Observer* [No. 10,992], 11 February, p. 1.

D. McLellan. 1971. *Marx's Grundrisse.* London: Macmillan.

——. 1972. *Marx before Marxism.* Harmondsworth: Pelican.

——. 1972. *The Thought of Karl Marx.* London: Macmillan.

S. Mehta. 2004. *Maximum City: Bombay Lost and Found.* London: Review.

M. Michaelson. 1979. "The Relevance of Caste among East African Gujaratis in Britain." *New Community,* vol. VII, pp. 351-360.

J. Miller. 1993. *The Passion of Michael Foucault.* London: HarperCollins.

T. Modood et al. 1997. *Ethnic Minorities in Britain: Diversity and Disadvantage.* London: Policy Studies Institute.

S. Montefiore. 2004. *Stalin: The Court of the Red Tsar.* London: Phoenix.

C. de la S. Montesquieu. 1949 [1748]. *The Spirit of the Laws.* London: Collier Macmillan.

A. Mukadam & S. Mawani (Eds.). 2008. *Gujaratis in the West: Evolving Identities in Contemporary Society.* Cambridge: Cambridge Scholars Press.

P. Mukta. 2000. "The Public Face of Hindu Nationalism." *Ethnic and Racial Studies,* vol. 23, pp. 442-466.

L. Murray & L. Andrews. 2000. *The Social Baby: Understanding Babies' Communications from Birth.* London: CP Publishing.

B. Naik. 1997. *Passage To Uganda.* Southall: Naik & Sons.

National Statistics. www.statistics.gov.uk.

M. Neary & A. Dinerstein (Eds.). 2002. *The Labour Debate: An Investigation into the Theory and Reality of Capitalist Work.* Aldershot: Ashgate.

G. Oonk. 2005. "'We lost our gift of expression': Loss of the mother tongue among Indians in East Africa." Paper given at the conference The South Asian Diaspora: The Creation of Unfinished Identities in the Modern World. Erasmus University, Rotterdam, forthcoming 2007. In: G. Oonk (Ed.). *Global Indian Diasporas.*

——. 2006. "South Asians in East Africa (1880-1920) with a Particular Focus on Zanzibar: Toward a Historical Explanation of Economic Success of a Middlemen Minority." *African and Asian Studies,* vol. 5, pp. 57-89.

G. Oonk (Ed.). 2007. *Global Indian Diasporas: Exploring Trajectories of Migration and Theory.* Amsterdam: Amsterdam University Press.

B. Pascal. 1995 [1670]. *Pensées.* Oxford: Oxford University Press.

N. Persico, A. Postlewaite & D. Silverman. 2001. "The Effect of Adolescent Experience on Labor Market Outcomes: The Case of Height." *Journal of Political Economy,* vol. 112, pp. 1019-1053.

S. Pinker. 1998. *How The Mind Works.* London: Penguin.

——. 2002. *The Blank Slate: The Modern Denial of Human Nature.* London: Allen Lane.

D.F. Pocock. 1972. *Kanbi and Patidar.* Oxford: Oxford University Press.

K. Popper. 1945. *The Open Society and its Enemies.* London: Routledge & Kegan Paul.

——. 1972. *The Poverty of Historicism.* London: Routledge & Kegan Paul.

R. Porter. 2000. *Enlightenment: Britain and the Creation of the Modern World.* London: Penguin.

J-P. Proudhon 1994 [1840] *What Is Property? or, An Inquiry into the Principle of Right and of Government,* Cambridge Texts in the History of Political Thought. Cambridge: Cambridge University Press.

E. Prynn. 1981. *A Boy in Hob-nailed Boots.* Oxford: ISS Publishing in association with Tabb House Publishers.

A. Ralston. 2004. *Between a Rock and a Hard Place.* London: Atria Books.

N. Risch, E. Squires-Wheeler & B.J.B. Keats. 1993. "Male Sexual Orientation and Genetic Evidence" (letter). *Science,* vol. 262, pp. 2063-2065.

R.M. Roberts. 1989. *Serendipity: Accidental Discoveries in Science.* New York: John Wiley & Sons.

V. Robinson. 1993. "Marching into the Middle Classes? The Long-term Resettlement of East African Asians in the UK." *Journal of Refugee Studies,* vol. 6, pp. 230-247.

A. Roncaglia. 1985. *Petty: The Origins of Political Economy.* Cardiff: University College Cardiff Press.

M. Rosen. 2005. *You and Yours* (speaker), BBC Radio 4, 4 December 2005.

J-J. Rousseau. 1974 [1762]. *Émile.* London: Dent.

B. Russell. 1948. *History of Western Philosophy.* London: Allen and Unwin.

——. 1950. *Nobel Lecture.* www.nobelprize.org.

M. Rutten & P. Patel. "Contested Family Relations and Government Policy: Linkages between Patel Migrants in Britain and India," paper given at the conference The South Asian Diaspora: The creation of unfinished identities in the modern world , Erasmus University, Rotterdam; forthcoming 2007. In: G. Oonk (Ed.). *Global Indian Diasporas.*

G. Ryle. 1978. The *Concept of Mind.* Harmondsworth: Penguin.

A. Schopenhauer. 1970. *Essays and Aphorisms* (R. J. Hollingdale, tr.).London, Penguin

Scientific American. 2001. "Past and Present, Taller People Tend to Live Longer," News In Brief, 14 June.

——. 2001."Napoleon's Revenge: In the U.S., Height Hits Its Head on the Genetic Ceiling," News Scan, 10 November.

A.M. Shah. 1977. "Lineage Structure and Change in a Gujarat Village." In: P. Uberoi (Ed.). 1998. *Family, Kinship and Marriage in India,* Oxford Readings in Sociology and Anthropology. Oxford: Oxford University Press.

W. Sharrock & G. Button. 1999. "Do the Right Thing! Rule Finitism, Rule Scepticism and Rule Following." *Human Studies,* vol. 22, pp. 193-210.

R. Sibeon. 1999. "Agency, Structure and Social Chance as Cross-Disciplinary Concepts." *Politics* vol. 19, pp. 139-144.

——. 1999. "Anti-Reductionist Sociology." *Sociology,* vol. 33, pp. 317-334.

P.H. Silverman. 2004. "Rethinking Genetic Determinism." *Scientist,* vol. 18 (published online at www.the-scientist.com).

D. Singh 1993 "Adaptive significance of female physical attractiveness: Role of waist-hip ratio" *Journal of Personality and Social Psychology* Vol.65, pp293-307.

——. 1995. "Female Judgement of Male Attractiveness and Desirability for Relationships: Role of Waist-Hip Ratio and Financial Success." *Journal of Personality and Social Psychology,* vol. 69, pp. 1089-1101.

——. 2004. "Mating Strategies of Young Women: Role of Physical Attractiveness." *Journal of Sex Research,* vol. 41, pp. 43-55.

H. Spencer. 1876. *The Study of Sociology,* 5th edition, The International Scientific Series, vol. V. London: Henry S. King & Co.

Srimad Bhagvata Purana. 2003. London: Penguin.

S. Steinberg. 1955. *Five Hundred Years of Printing.* Harmondsworth: Pelican.

K. Sullivan. 1997. *Steam Trains.* London: Brockhampton Press.

E. Thompson. 1978. *The Making of the Indian Princes.* London: Curzon Press.

K. Thompson. 1982. *Emile Durkheim.* London: Tavistock Publications.

M. Torri. 1982. "In the Deep Blue Sea: Surat and Its Merchant Class during the Dyarchic Period." *Indian Economic and Social History Review* [NS], vol. 19, pp. 267-299.

W. Trevor. 2002. *The Story of Lucy Gault.* London: Penguin.

M.T. Tsuang, W.S. Stone & S.V. Faraone. 2001. "Genes, Environment and Schizophrenia." *British Journal of Psychiatry,* vol. 178, pp. 18-24.

E. Turkheimer. 2000. "Three Laws of Behaviour Genetics and What They Mean." *Current Directions in Psychological Science,* vol. 5, pp. 160-164.

J. Uglow. 2002. *The Lunar Men.* London: Faber & Faber.

UNFPA. 2007. *State of World Population: Unleashing the Potential of Urban Growth*: www.unfpa.org/swp/2007/presskit/pdf/sowp2007.eng.pdf.

S. Vertovec. 2000. *The Hindu Diaspora: Comparative Patterns.* London: Routledge.

R. Waterland & R. Jirtle. 2003. "Transposable Elements: Targets for Early Nutritional Effects on Epigenetic Gene Regulation." *Molecular and Cellular Biology,* vol. 23, pp. 5293-5300.

J. Watson (Ed.). 1976. *Between Two Cultures: Migrants and Minorities in Britain.* London: Oxford University Press.

J.D. Watson & F.H.C. Crick. 1953. "A Structure for Deoxyribose Nucliec Acid." *Nature,* vol. 171, p. 737: www.fossilmuseum.net/Biology/WatsonCrickNature.htm

F. Wheen. 2000. *Karl Marx.* London: Fourth Estate.

E.O. Wilson. 1978. *On Human Nature.* London: Penguin.

———. 2005. "Kin Selection as the Key to Altruism: its Rise and Fall." *Social Research,* vol. 72, pp. 159-166.

L. Wittgenstein. 1958. *Philosophical Investigations.* Oxford: Basil Blackwell.

M. Woolf. 2005. "Students at Oxbridge Have Twice the Chance of Getting a First." *Independent on Sunday,* 4 December, p. 15.

A. Yagnik & S. Sheth. 2005. *The Shaping of Modern Gujarat.* Penguin: New Delhi.

YouGov. 2006. *University Lecturers,* survey conducted 9-16 August 2006 on behalf of the University and College Union (UCU): www.ucu.org.uk/media/excel/i/7/yougov_ucupollresults2006.1.xls.

D. Young. 1992. *The Discovery of Evolution.* London: Cambridge University Press in association with Natural History Museum Publications.

Index

spontaneity, 181
Sutton, Walter, 24-25
Synthetic Theory, 25-27

tabula rasa, 6, 8, 72, 189
Thackeray, William Makepeace, 51
tradition, 144-147, 156, 161-165
Trevor, William, 58-59
Turkheimer's Laws, 33-34

twins, 32-34
Tyson, Edward, 2

vanity, 124-128, 199-200
Vertovec, Stephen, 153

Wallace, Alfred, 17-18, 19
Watson, Walter, 25
Wilson, E.O., 26-28, 37, 64-65
Wittgenstein, Ludwig, 96-99, 110